A Trip to Oz

A Memoir of Self-discovery thru Australian Adventures

by
Alice Parker

EXPLORA BOOKS
700 – 838 West Hastings St. Vancouver, BC V6C 0A6
www.explorabooks.com
Phone: (604) 330 6795

ISBN: 978-1-998394-17-3 (Paperback)

Table of Contents

Prologue ii

A Dreaming Land 5

The Weight of Potential.. 34

Chapter 2 - Truly, a Different World 35

Self-Limitations 54

Chapter 3 - Journey to 'The Rock' 55

New Transitions... 68

Chapter 4 - The Rocks 69

Almost Always Counts.. 104

Chapter 5 - To Climb the Rock 105

The Trapeze Flyer... 137

Chapter 6 - A King of a Canyon 138

Chapter 7 - Discovering Alice 180

Time Travel.. 218

Memories of Australia 252

Chapter 9 - Cairns & Kuranda - Memories................. 253

Female Knowledge 283

Chapter 10 - Self-discovery on The Reef..................... 284

THE END.. 317

Zen & Now... 318

Appendix:... 319
Rain On The Rock.. 321

Passed Present Future 335

Bibliography... 337

Acknowledgements... 341

DEDICATION

To All women, no matter your age, to find your true Self through your independence, with total confidence and acceptance of who all you want to be, to empower others.

Prologue

The middle of August - Australian Winter - 1992 - An American, just finished her second divorce, and has worked for four years in Japan as a Corporate Business Trainer. A Memoir of her true stories, and Self-discovery thru the Australian Adventure. Some with four other mid-forties women she meets, from four countries. Their physical-self-testing in the Red Centre, which brings them support, in growth and understanding of themselves.

My Australian friend Pat, introduced me to the delights of a Cappuccino. Since living in Japan, I stayed about one step or more, behind whatever was trendy in the Statues or elsewhere. We had closely taught together in Japan for three years, before she left to travel. I'd come to appreciate her lady-like decorum, sophistication and propriety. Perhaps, those particular traits came from the many years she'd lived in preferred England. I'd not qualify them to the typical, laid-back Aussies, nor did I feel I possessed them, being a mid-western American, from Chicago suburbs.

We had delectably indulged several times in Cappuccino, while visiting together in her adopted city of Brisbane. But unfortunately, the following attempts to treat myself, outside the city restaurants and cafes, had been somewhat disappointing. As the the case now, I sat in the rather sterile environment of the Brisbane domestic airport coffee shop, and the Cappuccino was barely more than a cup of expensive coffee. I'd been in, even stuck in, worse airports and certainly drank worse coffee. Still, was not easy to soothe my disappointed taste buds.

I'd begun glancing over my brochures of Alice Springs and Ayers Rock, starting to get excited about my approaching great adventure, when two young Japanese women sat down at the next table. Though I *basically* loved the Japanese people, the young, vacuous-ladies, were beyond annoying, and the ones I particularly enjoyed getting away from. Well aware of how popular Australia was to the Japanese, I knew they weren't 'following' me, but still. Not paranoid, but maybe jealous since their poor, hardworking 'Daddy' always paid for them. Yet, most of all, their constant *unawareness* of absolutely everything, then *stunned* at the most common of things happening around them.

Granted, paid well myself, to mainly support my globetrotting addiction, but… Wherever I saw them, they amazed me at their lack of *unpreparedness and ambivalence,* to what other tourist were *wearing or doing.* I admitted, I enjoyed the knowledge their many duty-free bags contained ridiculously-expensive items purchased at Japanese shops. These shops in turn, made payoffs to the Japanese tourist agencies, for shepherding the non-questioning souls, into their establishments. All done so they wouldn't have to deal with speaking English. In my four years in Japan, no one took more advantage of the Japanese than other Japanese. Of course, most Japanese traveled in their group tours, to not have to deal with the non-Japanese world.

With my corporate schedule, I traveled three times a years - three to six weeks per break. Part of the fun for me was researching, then immersing myself in as much of a local culture as I could. This was my fourth trip to Oz, so I'd developed several dear friendships with people, who opened up their lives and homes to me. With nothing better to distract me in the limited airport, I began observing the 'girls' with glances. As a *'gaigin'* - foreigner in Japan, *we* were all a sport to be stared at, and myself especially, being blonde and 'full breasts.'

Many gaijin could not handle the pointing and staring, so common, as well any snickers or other shock-noises, as to faux pas or accidents newbies made. One learned to apologize for any perceived mistake, then usually the Japanese apologized themselves, which never made sense to most of us, but it *was their culture*. Yes, living in a foreign country, one usually does learn it's cultural foibles, and perhaps even adapt to them to fit in. So, it was almost cruelly-amusing to watch the Japanese on foreign soil, broken-English, madly flagellating the cultural waters to keep afloat. They truly were lost, without their 'mother-figure' tour guide, telling them exactly what to do and where to go, as well what to eat and drink.

Having traveled to numerous countries over my four years, I'd struggled many times even with extensive reading. Depending on how much of an outsider I was, I'd celebrate the small triumphs and accomplishments of *doing* what I had wanted, or *getting* to where I chose. Some of these obstacles-challenges made good fodder, for my stories upon my return for friends, and specifically my management students, who would shortly be going overseas themselves for business. Sometimes, the whole situation of being a woman traveling alone, though I did make several trips with my former husband, and more recently with other female teachers. So, perhaps taking travel as an adventure, or even pushing the envelope, so to speak was more of a Western-Independence. I did feel a definite personal, self-esteem created through my travel experiences. Since I believed, we never miss what we've never had, most Japanese do not know how good surmounting the odds on one's own can be.

* * * * * *

A Dreaming Land

I come from a Dreaming Land,
that shines like sun on rock/with violent Seasons.

Surrounded by three oceans and a sea.
Even water evaporates. Even the brightest leave.

You cannot know this land, unless you Dream.
All dreams connect - some are older than time.
Boomerangs in the Pyramids. Song cycles. Tribes.

As large as the Un-united States.
Population of New York.

Leave the fertile hinterland -
move towards rock. Desert.
Uluru, a song more beneath than above.
Olga's - 32 monolithic stones.

Kimberleys, call in gorges with water hidden.
Arnhem
Land, indigenous hunting grounds.

It will take all your lives
to cover the tracks of Ancestors Stories.
Too many forgotten,
like rotting cities clinging to the coastline.

Fly in, but you must
move towards the Red Centre of our Heart Land.

And when your Dreaming returns,
you will learn-how, like a grain of sand we are.

How like one falling star.

Thom o Oz - Native Australia

Chapter 1 - A Real Trip to the Destination

The tinny-loudspeaker announcement brought me out of my pop- psychology analyzing, as I gathered up my shoulder, tote bag and headed for the gate. So, I left behind the Japanese, in more ways than one, as my thoughts returned to the upcoming week, with anticipated excitement for my senses and physical abilities. I settled into my aisle seat, while my brain began again to question exactly *why* I truly planned this portion of my trip. I'd never been one of those 'man against nature' people, or 'conquer it because it's there' types.

And yet, the nature of this barren-body land, with it famous outcropping, somehow was calling to me. *What AM I trying to prove? AND, to whom? Is this about my being on my own, after ten years a couple, not the answer?* I am neither young, nor athletic, and taking on challenges, or even 'dares,' is not something my somewhat, independent soul relishes. Still, adventure of an experiential nature had sort of *squeezed* its way into my heart. If there were 'things out there' which could give me a controlled, safe thrill, I would go for it.

No need for a reality check here. I knew this was a dichotomy, which could not logically allow the juxtaposition of two such beliefs, in the same soul/heart. But there it was. I may not ever consider bungee-jumping, yet I had gone flying in a stunt plane, and bamboo- rafting down a mountainous white-water river in Thailand, without a life-preserver. Some things, like flying in a hot-air balloon, just bellowed out to my spirit, and some did not even give a limp-whisper.

Still, not one to ignore someone's good advice. Perhaps, one of the reasons I'd taken the opportunity to speak to a well-known clairvoyant in Brisbane. A part of me did not want to acknowledge, what she'd said about my being in physical danger. Then rather shocked, after her statement, I proceeded to tell her I planned to climb Ayers Rock. I listened to her, as also to the guidance from my older Australian friends, who'd just 'done the climb' themselves. Generally speaking, I was neither a novice, nor foolish. *Yes, maybe foolish in choosing husbands, but let's not think about that right now.* Truly, part of this was an independence test - yet, my intuition still had not clarified the why and wherefores to me.

* * * * * *

There was a seat between me and the young woman next to the window, which made it more comfortable for this long flight. I relaxed to enjoy the take-off, while requesting Source to keep my 'Golden Light around protecting me, and my White Light guiding in front of me,' for this somewhat auspicious trip. We were barely on our way, when the Captain announced the winter headwinds - 'Westerlies,' which came straight from Antarctic - were blowing strong, so we would probably run about twenty minutes late, on our arrival to Alice Springs. I thought of the other long hauls, I usually made flying out of Japan, this four hours *should be* taken up quickly.

Even before we had a first drink, I'd escaped into the airline magazine. On one of the first pages, it mentioned the whale-watching season. Colorful, exciting photos showed a momentous, splash-filled breach, which brought back my own recent memories spent with my friends, Barb and Paul, on Oz's east coast. We'd gone up to Hervey Bay, just south of the Reef, to see the big guys - humpback whales - and they did not disappoint us. Truly overwhelmed by it all, I joined the "Adopt-a-Whale" program in my son David's name. I knew he'd be thrilled to have one these 'gentle giants' named after him, and to learn all about them. My trips having turned into a kind of 'Auntie Mame' character, he'd become familiar with me sending him strange and curious gifts from my trips around the world. His only comment later was to ask, "Gee, Mom, where to you think I can get a fish tank big enough?" I loved his cryptic sense of humor, as those times, I did not doubt he was a child of my womb and mind. Others, I questioned.

I glanced through more of the advertisements of the popular whale-day trips, one of our many good times together. I smiled broadly, as I closed my eyes, thinking back on what good, supportive friends they'd been. I retraced my memory-bank through our short, though pivotal history of friendship. I chuckled lightly as I recalled, our serendipitous-encounter on a fateful Saturday night in Hawaii.

* * * * * *

Travis - my now ex-husband - and I had stopped there for five days on our return to Japan, after visiting friends and relatives on the Mainland. Two years in Japan, it had been our first sojourn back to the States, with lots of stories and *omaige* - souvenirs for everyone. To our amazement, or rather shock, most relatives could not have cared less about what it was like living in Japan. Neither of us, rarely got to say more than the perfunctory sentence or two about the experience, which had already radically changed our lives. Most of relatives were actually more concerned about relating their mundane problems with car repairs, or how prices had risen, or even where we should shop.

I wanted to talk about the Palace in Bangkok, or the exciting shopping in Hong Kong, while they were ecstatic over the new Walmart. I thought, because I was the one with the different lifestyle, traveling to exotic countries, they'd hang on every word, as I reiterated it all. As usual, Travis was rather pissed off, to say the least, for here he had thought everyone would be clamoring to hear his stories. In our mutual opinion, most of the people we knew had a basic case of 'American-moribunditis.'

Like so many others, we had to leave the U.S. to become objective about it and what was happening to the people. Definitely, my first well-learned lesson - Americans deserve all the criticism they receive for being so insular, plebeian, unworldly and non-international, as well all other negatives. They truly deserved to be called 'couch- potatoes.' If it does not take place between their two shores, not worthy to learn or even discuss.

I wasn't quite licking my wounds, as Travis' ego was, as I was more determined to have a good time, no matter what. My well-earned and deserved vacation was mine to enjoy. I also didn't take things as personally, as Travis did. So, great site-seeing in Honolulu all week, and I didn't have a need to see Hawaii's Don Ho show, having seen it on TV many times. We decided to stay in, and do some laundry in the nice facilities provided, as we'd be leaving for Japan shortly. So, Voila'! There was Barb merrily doing hers. Upon seeing the two of us, some people would have thought immediately we were sisters. Physically, we both had a quick smile, bright eyes and laughed easily at the slightest thing. A little older than me, she looked really good and quite active, as myself. So, once I had my wash going, and she sat going through a magazine, I spoke up to ask where she was from.

"Australia … Queensland…" I detected some hesitation, and already knew most Aussies believed most Americans did not know much about Australia, and were usually correct.

"Oh, really. My husband and I were there a year ago last Christmas. We caught the tail end of the Bicentenary. We were in Brisbane some of the time … Where about in Queensland do you live?' The enthusiasm in my voice relaxed her, and she quickly smiled. "Mooloolaba. It's about 100 kilometers north of Brisbane, on the Sunshine Coast."

"Mooloolaba? Aboriginal name, huh?" Being from the outside, anything Aboriginal brought a certain fascination to me. "We're going to be traveling down the coast from Townsville to Brisbane this coming summer - your winter, I mean." Seeing the bright response on her face, I continued. "We'll fly into Brisbane to visit some friends there, then on to Darwin and the Kakadu National Park. Have you been there? I'm interested in the Aboriginal culture, and I've heard the park is really good with the rock paintings and such."

Again, a bit more hesitant, "Well … no, we haven't. Actually, it's cheaper to travel out of the country than in Australia. My husband likes Hawaii, so we've been here a few times." Easy to see she was rather proud of their international travel.

"Yes, I really learned from our last trip, Oz is as big as America, but with so few people, the flying around is considerably more expensive. The is our first trip to Hawaii. We just stopped for five days on our way back to our home in Japan. "

With her startled response, she rose from her chair to come towards me, as she showed both intrigue and amazement. "You live in Japan? But, aren't you American? … I mean, I thought from your accent … What do you do in Japan?" Now, both used to and proud of creating this kind of reaction, I smiled. The idea of really living in a foreign, non-English-speaking country still gave me a feeling of being interesting, and good about my accomplishments. All my life I dreamed of traveling the world, not being 'ordinary,' like my family.

I chuckled, not wanting to embarrass her. "Yes, we're from Texas. Well, I'm originally from Chicago, but I lived in Texas for ten years before going to Japan. I teach business management and my husband teaches technical English. He's a mechanical engineer." I then paused, to give a bit of drama to my next statement. "Actually, we'd both like to live and work in Australia. We really like it that much." I could see clearly, as I had experienced it previously, as this was a shock for most Aussies. They usually felt many Americans had it all, and would never leave America.

"But, what would you do in Oz?" She laughed, "We already speak English, no matter what the Brits might say?" We were now both laughing like schoolgirls, leaning on our respective washers, while they whirled away doing their chore.

"Yeah, I know what they mean. You guys are sometimes hard to understand, but not any worse than when I first moved to Texas. Probably the nicest thing I was called was a 'Yankee.'" At this point I kind of chortled, remembering all the bullshit and hassles I'd suffered through for years. "They're not only chauvinists, but prejudiced, too! I guess it's why my husband likes Oz so much … the people, especially Queensland, reminds him of his childhood in Texas in the '50s." Momentarily I thought I had stuck my foot, as usual, in my mouth, but then Barb was laughing almost hysterically.

"Oh, you're so right. We've only lived there about a year. My husband took an early retirement, and we came up from Sydney. It's amazing. In the Sunshine Coast area, they're either these country hicks, who have never traveled out of their backyard, or Melbourne society, up on holiday, tossing their money around, raising prices and trying to impress each other." She started to hesitate again, as if she too, felt she'd been a bit outspoken, then continued on. "But, the fishing is great and it's one of my husband's passions. It's why he likes to come to Hawaii. I must admit though, it gets bloody hot in the Queensland summers, and the shopping is really limited compared to Sydney." She seemed to be contemplating all the pros and cons, as she went on. "I'm getting more into gardening now, … I've almost finished fixing the house up. I'm still unpacking, decorating and the like, so we're slowly adjusting to it. But, do tell me, what would you both do in Australia?"

Our plans had been well thought out, so not just a pipe dream, or rattling off some quasi-ideas. "Well, there's a university, which is planning to have the same kind of intensive course for Japanese, and eventually other Asian, businessmen combined with a full international cultural program. I'm hoping to get involved, since my experience and knowledge of doing the same in Japan. My husband specialized in HVAC - Houston was quite hot and humid also, and we've made some friends in Townsville, as a possibility. He was told he'd be quite valuable, as service was … shall we say, not real reliable." I paused to get her reaction, and she nodded, as we both again chuckled. I could see, we'd quickly both built a rapport and camaraderie supportive thinking. She'd probably been a real go-getter in Sydney, definitely a different cultural group.

"Well, I'll just have to give you our address and you'll have to stop and visit us, too. We'll want to know what you've decided and how you like it all" Her machine had stopped whizzing and now digging into a small change purse. "Oh, dear, I don't have enough change for another dryer. I'll have to call Paul in our room. Oh, … that'll give you a chance to meet him. I'll tell him to bring some address cards."

As she started for the service phone, I responded, "I've got plenty of change if you want."

"No, no, I'm sure he'll want to meet you and have all kinds of questions about the *'Japs'* and what's it like living with them."

Not really shocked by her remark, for I'd discovered from our first trip to Oz, many Aussies were quite prejudiced. Some even talked about World War II, as if it had ended last week. I later learned, in Darwin, how many people had been killed, when repeatedly bombed by the Japanese. Yet, although observers had given several hours notice, the people totally ignored it, as if such a thing could not happen to them - again and again. It rather amazed me of their attitude toward the war and the Japanese. The irony I discovered, most Aussies disbelieved, not only the bombing, but even the notion Japan could have any desire or even interest in invading Australia. At the time, Darwin had been one of the most desolate outposts, with many people still regularly going stir crazy from the 'wet' - what they called the long, hot, rainy summer.

Later, also educated to the fact a lot more Aussies had participated in the Pacific war, than I realized, and many of them suffered greatly, as well dying in the brutal prisoner of war camps. To add salt to the wound, booming Japan continued to buy property in Oz, as if a fire-sale were going on, so many felt they were being invaded all over again. And, this time quite successfully. Some research I'd run across though, had shown a lot of the furor was stirred up by angry New Zealanders, who'd long been the largest investors in Oz. Since the Japanese had driven up the prices, on what had been really cheap land. There were rights and wrongs on both sides, which usually an outsider could see so much easier, as with less emotional attachments. Especially, as one who lived in Japan, I could speak from personal knowledge of how the savvy, and greedy Japanese businessman, went about his wheeling and dealing.

Though difficult to communicate with, considering all of their cultural protocols, if the negotiating was done correctly, there were usually not problems. Some things, the Japanese were just really particular about - like service, which totally catered to their every whim. They did not care how much they had to pay for it, as long as they got it. On the other hand, the proud Aussies sometimes felt as if catering to the Japanese, was more like being servants. This brought up too many bad memories for the Aussies, regarding the colonial British and their continual superiority attitude toward the laid-back, fun-loving Aussies. We'd noticed the lack of attention to detail and service, which unfortunately rather common for foreigners, to comment on. But not something most Aussies were concerned about, as status-conscious Japanese, or Americans and Europeans.

Paul brought down the change, his business card and joined us as we talked while finishing the laundry. I felt I had to bring Travis into the picture, since still trying to rescue him, and make him feel wanted and happy - part of the big-riff which eventually split us up.

Paul liked him, though I could detect Barb felt a bit uncomfortable with his six-foot-four size, dominating, and controlling presence. Perhaps, she'd intuitively detected I too, changed in his pervading space. Whenever I took the time, and thought back deeply about it, the unseen signs had been there. My subliminal reactions to be of 'the wagons circling' against the enemy, only the enemy wasn't on the outside. I was the 'Indian' trapped within, and no realized escape with my 'scalp,' or maybe even my life.

Really check? Maybe I did have something to prove to myself on this trip. Accomplishment in survival alone ... on my own?!?!?

The friendship was launched and even now had survived, after Travis had abused it by overstaying his welcome at Barb an Paul's house, while on his last, disastrous trip to Oz. He was supposed to set up the air conditioning business with the friends in Townsville. But instead, he played and walked through over twenty-five thousand in savings, we had in an Aussie bank. He'd decided he needed time away from me, to make 'his own success,' as he could no longer 'handle' Japan, or 'living under my shadow.' I'd done quite well in my position, while he'd been disappointed the Japanese had *not* made him head of engineering, or at least chiseled into stone everything he'd said.

Unfortunately, my fault from too many years cultivating his ego, which continued to need stroking, *and* I'd become too busy, as well tired of doing it. I no longer wanted to play the game of worship, though many Japanese had recognized his area of talent, which I never questioned. At the manufacturing company he worked for, some older Japanese had lavished expensive gifts on him and greatly over paid him for the limited work he'd done. Yet, it had still not been sufficient to fill his gaping-insecurities, as well lack of any language fluency.

I could now see escaping to Oz was not just a case of the 'grass being greener,' as I'd seen he had the constant need to start over, once he'd achieved some level of success. This 'self-sabotage' pattern had been perfected, with one amazing rationalization after another, over our ten years together. Yet, I too, denied the reality it was over between us, even before coming to Japan.

Reality check, AGAIN! Was it a womb-thing, or something else? Band-aids on gaping-wounds which could never heal. These were the fallacies of thinking my starting over could mean forgetting and forgiving, yet not changing the root of the past injuries.. How many women I had known who had accepted the belief of any marriage was better than no marriage at all?!?!? Or, even worse, any man was better than no man at all?!?!? Perhaps the 'old Noah's Ark, coupledom -syndrome?!?' still had some control over most of us, especially those of us over forty.

So, after pulling myself together - it had not been easy to give up my meticulously- detailed-facade, I'd created of a 'happy marriage,' without a lot of embarrassing explanations. I'd returned to Oz the following year, this one. It obviously was more than a vacation, as I'd hoped to mend-fences, while showing once again, I was a survivor, and still loved Oz, though no longer job hunting to live there. *Hope existed, too. This trip would help me find my earlier mystique of the curiosity or 'Alice in Wonderland' of my personality, which gave me enthusiasm about life. Some how my child's magic got lost in the mire of negativity, and true bullshit my marriage had become. There was no longer any other name to call it, except what it had become..*

* * * * * *

The sensation of descending, broke me out of my visual memories, while the copilot announced the turbulence was worse than expected. They had to land to take on more fuel, and this was the last 'paved- runway' airport before Alice Springs, which could accommodate a plane of this size. I'd experienced a few emergencies in my travels, but this one had no sense of danger connected to it at the time.

Glancing over, out the window the emptiness below was startling. Though, I'd seen several deserts before, this void could only make me wonder once again, what made people actually want to live in such a desolate place. I did not consider myself to be the kind of person who constantly had to have stimulus around me at all times, though I loved the movies, I was not overly attached to television. Likewise, not addicted to shopping, though I'd been in, and bargain- hunted through, some of the greatest shopping experiencers in the world from Saigon and Bangkok to New York and Paris.

In all honesty, I accepted and enjoyed these things in their perspective, but knew if I had to, I could probably live without many of them. Yet, I saw no point in purposely doing without them, when available to me, and I had the money. While I'd never actually been poor in my younger days, I'd been broke many times after my first divorce. Being a single parent, feeling my son's needs did come first, my quest for independence kept me from asking for assistance, unless really needed. I liked basic conveniences, yet had survived well in third-world countries, better than most tourists. Japan was not exactly known for its clean or accommodating public toilets, as most were unisex, which Westerns avoided unless they absolutely had to.

Also, I'd been raised to not be wasteful, so saw no need to be inundated by overly-priced, frivolous items, just because *I could* afford them. I remembered a British friend writing to me asking, after living in Los Angeles a few months with his American girlfriend - "Do Americans truly need fifty different kinds of frozen yogurt?!?" It stuck with me, as a reminder of the knee-jerk marketing which created *a need* in the States. Something, having a degree in marketing, and having worked for an advertising company, rather knowledgeable about it, sort of giving me an insider's awareness, not to buy into *needing* something. I easily lived without the frivolous.

My mind had suddenly begun to flash more memory-slides of my own desolation of an opposite kind - surrounded by people, but not the familiar things of my past. Living in Nagoya, Japan, those first few years, when the only abundance of American food products were at the international stores, which charged an arm and a leg for most items - Campbell's soup, Oreo cookies, Betty Crocker cake mixes, or Doritos Nacho chips. I saw a teacher once pay the equivalent of four dollars for a small bag of Doritos.

He responded to my criticism with, "Hey, you'll pay it too, when you've been here long enough. The money doesn't matter, as long as it can give you a taste of home." He turned out to be right, of course, for I did things just as stupid, when confronted with the desire to satisfy memories of the tastebuds. The only problem for me, the remembrances were usually more savory than the actual 'now' taste. Kind of like, my palate had put certain foods on a pedestal, which reality would never be able to gratify, even when back in the States.

* * * * * *

I stretched to stare around the young woman, also peering-out the little window at the vast rust-colored, austere landscape. The plane hit the bituminous-runway hard, as I watched the scrub bushes and trees go zooming by, as the short runway quickly eaten up by our speeding, oversized jet. The seatbelt pulled hard on my stomach, as I instinctively put my arm out in front of me, when we suddenly jerked forwarded and stopped. Carefully now, and slowly, the pilot turned this hulk, which had seemed so nimble on the large Brisbane field. I knew, if any of his tires ran-off into the sandy, red dirt, we'd definitely have a big problem.

We slowly chugged up to the small building, when the copilot came on to apologize for the landing, which he said could not be helped, considering weather conditions and lack of runway. I thought, maybe the last phrase should have been omitted, considering after fueling we'd be taking off again. After, I glanced around to see almost every passenger holding their breath, wondering if we truly would lift- off before the runway ran out. Having experienced some wild take-offs and landings, it was damn good flying which got us back into the skies safely. No one really even cared when the pilot said, we'd probably be about an hour late, reaching Alice Springs. At least we knew now we'd get there. Yes, Qantas was the best.

After racing down the bumpy tarmac, winging our way back into the belting Antarctic winter-Westerlies, it sill would not be a piece of cake for everyone. The woman next to me, had complained about feeling sick and even asked if she could de-plane, but to no avail. The flight attendants did accommodate, by moving her into Business Class, where she'd have more room to stretch out. I quickly moved over to the window, appreciating my benefit from her problem. I then strained to see all I could, of the almost forbidden countryside below. The flat expanse, almost a red-brick color, had thick dust swirling in the bright afternoon sun. I searched the small town of Charlesville, mentioned by the copilot, for some sign of life or movement. It stretched out from the airport, obviously the heart, connecting these remote inhabitants.

I wondered curiously, if our unexpected landing had caused any excitement for anyone, other than the airport crew. Perhaps, if we had gotten out and wandered the town, … but like so many things, the Aussies probably would've taken it all in stride and complacency. As much as they liked gossip and some celebrity creating a shock, I'd been told, and saw, Aussies did not take well to those who were too successful, or stood out too much, with pride or ego. In some ways, how very Japanese of them! As the Japanese proverb says, 'the nail sticking-up must be struck down.' The Aussies could really champion the underdog, but when he became the big dog, or kind of the mountain, they championed just as hard to see him fall.

After the delayed lunch, I soon returned to my magazine, only to have more feelings stirred by the next photos and story on Ayers Rock. Yes, it was dangerous. Yes, several dozen people had been killed, though usually through their own ignorance and negligence. Although, who can expect tourists to be experienced 'rock climbers?' My mind slipped in to question me about my future climb. I quickly recollected my meeting of the clairvoyant in Brisbane.

* * * * * *

The Sunday Market, at the Brisbane Riverfront was a delight for tourists and locals alike. My third time there, in as many years, and I could quickly see how it had not only expanded, but how the regular shop merchants had finally begun to keep their shops open in response to the crowds. Sundays had previously been a 'closed' day. Some were even offering specials to compete with the hundreds of discount hawkers. They did a jam-up business from booths and stalls, scattered along the sidewalks and down to the river's edge. A glorious, sunny Aussie winter day, with the temperature about twenty degrees Celsius, or in the seventies. Bright, colored, varietal flowers mushroomed everywhere like fireworks.

Brisbane, might have wet, humid springs and summers, but the autumn and winters were great, by just about anyone's standards. Too, the people were stalwart and definitely starting to develop a sense of sophistication, over the past few years with the influx of so many tourist. The Brisbanites were learning to protect their heritage, while building great high rises of style and even beauty. They'd cleaned up the river considerably and were enjoying its surroundings. The Sunday Market symbolized, not only a revitalization of the downtown sector, but the people's initiative to create their own financial rewards, since the recession and unemployment had hit them hard.

I'd visited with my dear friends, Lorraine and Graeme, a few nights earlier and now to spend most of this lovely Sunday with Lorraine and her delightful daughter, Sally. She'd been one of the teachers working for me in Japan so through our friendship, I'd met her warm parents. Close to my age, Lorraine, a quiet, lovely person with a bit of wistfulness. Perhaps this left over from missing out, or just not having done those things, she may have dreamed of so long ago. Regret never entered the conversation, nor was she prone to any kind of actual complaining. Maybe acceptance, with a certain amount of disappointment, or even a little resentment, sometimes revealing itself, seemed to be part and parcel of her life. I knew the differences between us were keyed, as to *where* we were from, as much to do with *how* we'd lived our lives. Oz at the time, outside of Sydney, had just begun to break away from its conservativeness.

Teetering on being an optimistic feminist myself, as well having only recently escaped a similar 'swallowing' of self. So, this resignation to tolerate these things, did not seem either fair or right. Only after after several annual visits, and more time spent alone together, I began to understand, Lorraine enjoyed not pushing herself. Yet, she'd made sure her daughter had explored more, simply in working in Japan, as an English teacher. Since the mother was usually the focal point of inertia in most families, this meant she could or would neither push her daughter or husband in an obvious way. Truly, as I'd seen and heard, she could have a temper, and if she really wanted something bad enough, she'd make sure she got it, as she had for their trip to the Red Centre. I still needed to accept the fact, if someone's behavior patterns worked for them, then I should not criticize or even comment upon them.

Lorraine was one of those people who loved to hear about my lifestyle ... where I'd traveled to recently, other tidbits of excitement, to fill her mind with. It satisfied some of her dreams vicariously, as I knew she loved the idea of travel and had done very little. On the other hand, I occasionally envied, yet could not bring myself to acquire willingly - a very, family-oriented suburbanite life. Yet, again, what she'd *not* done, she certainly encouraged Sally to do, if she wanted. Sally was a brilliant delight, although some would call her a bit ditzy, or even some-what *spacey*. Her bubbly, naive personality made her so endearing, everyone absolutely loved her, and laughed off her remarkable faux pas, one after another she seemed to pull off.

Sally had chosen to study Mandarin, then had gone to China for several months, before coming to Japan on a work-holiday visa. The Aussies tended to be a cheap-commodity to the Japanese administrators, looking for a 'warm body' for the classroom … an approach which was so common for many Japanese schools. The Aussies did not mind, as they looked at the situation as a *holiday,* for which they were getting paid. And, it was a lot more than they could made back in Australia, supposing they could have gotten a job.

I had a tendency to be over protective of most of my dozen or so young, naive teachers, especially those who came and went rather frequently. Sally was no exception, and possibly my favorite. Actually, being a year younger than my son, it soothed those rare motherly instincts to care for her. Sally had gregariously invited Travis and I to meet her parents, as we planned the vacation, which included the long drive down from Townsville to Brisbane. What especially enticed Travis were the photos Sally brought in, from previous fishing trips her parents had made to Frazer Island, their favorite destination. The impressive photos of great catches, were topped off with one I'd never forget of a fish's head only. The body had been snapped-off by a hungry, clever shark. Not that he was a big fisherman, but a reality, one did not think of, especially in the fished-out waters of Japan.

Our first meeting with Lorraine and Graeme, could not have gotten more 'stuffed-up' as they said, even with all of my planning. After several letters back and forth, finally set for them to meet our plane when it first arrived in Brisbane. We had several hours before our flight onto Darwin. This would give us time to get acquainted, and also plan for the few days we'd later spend together on the Sunshine Coast and Frazer Island, before we flew out again from Brisbane. Too funny, as my usual organized self, had the itinerary totally planned with hotels, tours and points of interest. I had managed to fit the schedule around our friends in Townsville, Barb and Paul in Mooloolaba, and now Lorraine and Graeme. And, as usual it did not have much time or space for delays or changes. I tended to play as hard as I worked, and a few hours or even sometimes a day of veg-out time was habitually scheduled in.

I'd also offered to take some things back to Australia for Sally, as she'd not be leaving until Christmas, so she'd piled on us several shopping bags full of *omiage* and other gifts for herself or her parents. The Qantas flight from Nagoya went straight into Brisbane, arriving at the god-awful hour of six o'clock in the morning. No problem with Lorraine, as she and Graeme were both teachers, so had arranged to take a few hours off from their classes to meet us at the airport.

Being the first in line at the airport, and one of the few non- Japanese in the crowd, the staff generously bumped us up to First Class, which always thrilled Travis. He loved having an air of money and status, which he took advantage of to act important. The flight could not have been more perfect, even with Travis playing his tiresome game of talking technical lingo with the First Class Steward, who kindly indulged him. I could see though, he was patronizing whom he thought was an important First Class passenger. It did crack me up, but I kept it all inside. How much Travis was cognizant of, didn't matter, as the facade simply gave him a bigger power surge. As it went on and on, I began to feel revulsion of the manipulation, and angry at myself for not speaking up. Yet, I didn't want him to go into one of his anger fits, or later embarrassing retribution towards me in some way. *I began to acknowledge how I'd been more and more acquiescing out of fear, from his buried resentment for me making more money, though he certainly loved to spend it.*

Sitting there, not being able to read or sleep, I kept questioning how I had continued to go on with this relationship, which had long left its love and enjoyment behind? Was it so important to me to have a husband, partner or just someone connected to, like a required facade? Yuck! Me, the so-called independent, successful business woman, did not have the guts to get out of it. I paraded the 'happy marriage' act better, than any I had performed on the amateur stage. I sat back and tried to read again, or better, even to sleep a little to remove myself from my self-created bad situation, or more truthfully, realization of my life. Beginning of a three-week vacation, so not exactly the time to break up with my husband. I also made the decision, not to allow any of his actions affect my enjoyment of my vacation. While I may not confront him, I would Not disguise so tightly my feelings, but show ambivalence regarding his actions instead.

I'd not been dozing long, with Travis lightly snoring, when the descent of the plane, as usual brought me back awake. I looked out the window, as all of the cabin lights came on simultaneously, with the announcement we'd have to make a stop in Cairns to pick up fuel.

Brisbane was cloaked with a thick, extensive carpet of fog, and the copilot expected we'd have to circle for a while before landing. The precautionary delay concerned me, as I thought Lorraine and Graeme might be anxiously awaiting us, and may even be late returning to their classrooms.

Through the velvet blackness, the stark blaring light showed the men quickly going about their unexpected chore. I wondered if they kept people on for this kind of emergency, or if they had called them in once they'd discovered the situation. My waking-brain took a moment to marvel at the technological scene unfolding, with its created circumstances and consequences donated by the whims of Mother Nature.

I enjoyed my breakfast, with sunrise as our flight traced along the coast. The rich green of the land darted back and forth, with the blue of the sea, as slices of glistening, white beaches appeared. I reveled so, at the mingling hues of turquoise and variegated greens chained together, delineating the lustrous Great Barrier Reef, sparkling like a necklace in the sun. I thought of it as a colorized-vision Claude Monet would have happily used, along with the fluffy white, whipped cream clouds. They appeared so delightful, I couldn't imagine them being ominous. As we circled around and around, the creamy cover allowed no breaks for peeking into the vast landscape, thus, one could not tell if it was field, farm, city streets or buildings below. Still, after about thirty minutes, and the uniqueness of the visions below had worn off, when the pilot announcement. Although the massive winter fog was slowly dissipating, Brisbane did NOT have the proper radar for them to land. So, we flew onto mass confusion in Sydney.

The flight crew was not thrilled, because the Japanese required more attention and explanations of things. I thought the little Japanese man and his wife across from us, were going to try to bail out. He could not understand why they could not land. He was very upset because a car was waiting to pick them up, to take them to their condo on the Gold Coast. It took several Japanese attendants to calm him down, and make him understand Qantas would bring them back to Brisbane, just as soon as they could.

This became a very long flight, for even these most capable of flight attendants, to try and keep up the pretense of their great service. On top of all the passenger problems, they were running out of food. With another hour or so on their hands, it seemed as if the attendants needed something to keep the people entertained. For me, I had now been going for over twenty-four hours, as I'd worked a full ten-hour day prior to going to the airport in Nagoya. I felt myself begin to descend into a zombie-like state. Of course, no idea how things were to be handled in Sydney - if we'd be able to get another flight direct to Darwin, or if we'd have to go back to Brisbane then on. *'Best laid plans of mice and men,'* and I chuckled to myself.

In Sydney, the staff person in charge of Brisbane passengers, said we'd have to get our luggage, process through immigration then customs. Once we had our luggage and were starting through the processing, they suddenly came and grabbed us, saying they had a plane going back to Brisbane, so we needed to hurry to get on it. These new flight attendants were just as harried as the past ones, as they'd been working since a Singapore or Hong Kong flight. They apologized for only having cake and coffee to serve, because there had not been enough time to restock the plane. It had now gone beyond the nightmare stage for all of us, and the absurdity of it was almost too funny, though Travis was not laughing. I wan't sure if he was also too tired, or simply trying to take all these delays as personal affronts, which would not be beyond his skewed emotional brain.

Finally, tromping though customs exit at Brisbane, with our luggage stacked on the cart, the last people we expected to see were Lorraine and Graeme. Almost eleven o'clock in the morning, they been waiting since six a.m.! We'd had their pictures, but I'd only given them the physical descriptions of Travis being so tall and me being blonde. But, we were easy to spot, since there were only a few 'gaijin' coming off the plane. The introductions culminated with laughs, then Lorraine followed me to the

Qantas desk to see how and when they were going to get us to Darwin.

"God," I repeated, "I really feel bad you guys waited so long for us, I certainly didn't expect you to keep waiting."

Lorraine began to slowly smile. "No, it was quite fun actually, and we kind of took advantage of the situation, to take off from school. Graeme had called them and even drove back to check if the substitutes were going, OK."

I thought what an interesting response. "But, it must have been so boring for you, just sitting here waiting. I mean airports can be quite boring sometimes, I've been stuck in some terrible ones." I'd given my paperwork, tickets, etc. to the apologetic attendant. Though our tickets onto Darwin were coach, she noted we'd come off as First Class passengers, but then never questioned me as to the difference.

Unbeknown to me at the time, Lorraine had never even flown in an airplane. For her, it reminded me of myself as a teenager, going to O'Hare airport every chance I could, once I had my driver's license. So, with much excitement, she shared. "Oh, no. Once the planes started to land, it was so exiting and interesting watching the Japanese and other foreigners come through the terminal."

I turned to look at her. "Yeah, they're a stitch … I mean really funny, in a strange way." She began to have this rather enlightened look on her face, as if she'd seen a real cultural happening, and in reality she had. For many Aussies, the Japanese were a true oddity, so opposite and not often one was in an appropriate position to simply observe them unobtrusively.

"You could see the people meeting them were obviously very happy to see them and some even had tears in their eyes, yet they'd barely touch more than maybe a

... a hand or arm or something." Lorraine then paused momentarily, as she recounted these bizarre actions. "There were all different kinds of bowing and gestures, which I didn't understand, of course." She now beamed. "No, a really wonderful experience, just to sit back and watch people's reactions. ... To see how different everyone is." She looked at me with appreciation of our lateness, having given her this chance-experience.

"Yes, I guess if not in a hurry, I must admit an airport can be a fun public place to watch people's private lives in action. Kind of like a legalized-voyeur or something." I turned to continue watching the convoluted situation now including several more attendants. Out of Japanese habit, I apologized again as if my fault for inconveniencing them. *Reality check, apologizing - gomen nasai or sumi-masen - some of the most common words spoken in Japanese. They'd become almost a natural response, to so many things now. I'd catch myself doing these habitual things, as the Japanese culture had become so ensconced into my lifestyle. So even outside of Japan, at least for the first few days of a vacation, they slipped out.*

It took a bit of haggling back and forth, since I really did not want to fly from Brisbane to Alice Springs then on to Darwin - each trip almost four hours. Qantas then finally said they'd put us up in a hotel and fly us out the next day. They even rescheduled our two Darwin tours for the next day, and I was glad I'd put a free day on the end for us as, it was now getting taken up. They wrote out a coupon packet for the hotel, food and taxis with pretty good efficiency and smiling apologies. Though we both knew they were not responsible for the weather. The real culprit was Brisbane's antiquated-airport without modern radar. I then noticed, a staff person questioned her manager, about the fact the last coupon for a taxi, back to the airport the next day, had not come out very clear. She shook her head and said it should not be a problem. Little did either of us know, the simple carbon paper *would change my life.* With hindsight, I understood how clearly Fate worked. It's always the pebbles which trip us up, never the obvious mountains.

Travis and Graeme joined us, as I informed them all was taken care of and we'd, at Qantas' expense, be spending the night in Brisbane at the Sheraton. Graeme quickly responded, it was the most expensive new hotel in Brisbane. "Well," I retorted back with a sly smile, "You'll just have to come join us for dinner. Since Qantas is paying of us, we can treat you!" Travis heartily agreed, as I knew he would, as another chance for him to play the big spender.

After numerous refusals and rebuttals, Lorraine finally tilted her head toward Graeme, "I think it will OK. What time would you like us?" She smiled broadly. I could see the casual Graeme still very uncomfortable, yet he knew the decision had been made, so he'd have to get used to the idea of 'going uppity-style,' as the Aussies said.

"How's is six thirty? Then we'll give you the rest of Sally's presents we've packed away." We slowly walked with them out to the taxi and talked while the luggage was stored in the trunk and related our 'thank yous, see you at six-thirty and good byes,' as we climbed inside. I saw Graeme shaking his head, talking to Lorraine, but she just kept quietly smiling-contentedly.

* * * * * *

Now, here two trips later, after Lorraine and I'd taken a camel ride together, shared a uniquely Aussie Christmas dinner on their verandah, and with my upcoming trek to Ayers Rock to look forward to. So, we were once again strolling through the Brisbane Sunday Market. Sally with us this time, and it had been about an hour or so of 'ohs and ahhs,' looking, touching and even trying on some things. I'd found a chunky, lapis necklace, I'd searched probably six other countries to find, and was quite pleased to get at such a bargain, plus I charged it, too. There was really nothing I needed for the trip, as I'd gotten the necessary hat and solid, hiking boots. I enjoyed thoroughly the relaxed shopping with dear friends. We may not have years of history together, nor a mutual background, but a closeness only women connected to.

Sally then said she wasn't feeling well, so Lorraine suggested we stop for something to drink. I indulged in a Cappuccino once again and offered one for Lorraine, though Sally only wanted water. We'd barely finished, when Sally decided she'd better go back home. As Lorraine got up to telephoner Graeme, I said, "Listen, if you want to go back with her, I'm fine, really. It's such a lovely day I'll finish here and just wonder around. If it's still light, I can walk back to the hotel, or if it's dark, I'll take a taxi They're cheap. It's not Japan you know where a taxi costs an arm and a leg." Sally barely smiled at my joke, and I *was* surprised at Lorraine's reaction.

"No, Sally will be fine going back and Graeme is there. I'd really like to spend the time with you, if you want." There was only the slightest hesitation in her determined response. I'd gotten to know this lady fairly well, through our letters and visits. Though we'd talked late into the night on Friday about Travis and my divorce, I realized she was grateful to have the time alone, for us to relate and bond some more. Lorraine made the call, came back, and gathered Sally up. I told her I'd be wandering around, but would keep an eye out for her.

As we went in opposite directions, the lovely, little decorated tent with the Palm Reading sign was one of the first I encountered. I stopped to read the brochure and noticed, there was another woman inside talking with the woman whose picture I was now looking at. Wanting to give them privacy, I scanned the acknowledgments, credentials, and data of this clairvoyant. I had stages in my life when I quite intrigued with astrology, tarot and even a little numerology. Yet, I still knew I attracted into my life those things I needed to learn, regardless of how good or bad, they may have seemed at the time. Likewise, I believed something good eventually comes out of even the worse situation. We all sometimes would like to know what the future holds, but then would we really want to believe it?

I finally thought, "Why the hell not?" Here I was at a rather critical point with my second divorce. Though it was a very needed and wanted situation, I still felt lost, as to who I was, or what I was going to doing with the rest of my life. At the forefront was hesitations and doubts about my age, personal lifestyle or if I wanted another relationship with a man, even if one wanted me. The confusion roiled within me, for I expected mastery, or at least a semblance of management of my own life.

Maybe, some indication of what the Fates had in store of me, would make me more accepting in finding again, who I really was to be on my own. I'd frequently felt as if I were being raised from the dead, after being deeply buried in my too long, ten-year marriage. I walked around for a few minutes and bought some natural snacks, just to keep my mind occupied during the other woman's reading. When I came back to the tent, the lovely, slim woman, who looked about my age, smiled as I thrust over my palm to her. "I'd like to have a reading, please." I was trying to sound as jovial and nonchalant as possible.

First, she looked deeply into my eyes then took my right hand, stretching out the palm, lightly tracing a few of the lines with her finger. She then carefully turned away my thumb to look at the side of my hand, and them glanced back the other way to gaze at the top. I could not see her face, as she turned back and curled my fingers into the palm while releasing my hand. "No, not now. I must see you for more than five minutes. You will be encountering danger and we must talk." As she looked up, to see the shocked look on my face, she added reassuringly. "Please call and make an appointment, as soon as possible. It is most important for you, we talk."

About to panic, as I was leaving the next morning to drive up to Mooloolaba to spend the week with Barb and Paul. "Well, … would you have some time tomorrow morning - early? See, I'm going out of town to visit some friends for a week then leaving the area altogether." I felt in a dilemma. *How could something so casual turn into something so serious? Other people's lives were usually not so complicated. Of course, I usually thought their lives were more boring. But, one pays the price for being interesting or layered, I questioned myself again. Yet, even turning my sarcastic humor on myself, did not settle this immediate impasse.*

"I'm sorry, I really don't know. You'll have to call my service to make an appointment." She seemed concerned, yet a bit detached. My choice, of course, if I wanted her advice.

"But, you can't do it just now … like for other people …?" "No …" She gently laughed, as if I didn't know. "Your
situation right now is a bit more complicated. I couldn't give you the time or details you need. All I can say is, I see some danger coming up around you, as well many changes."

Not exactly dismissed, but it was all she was going to confide at this time. Intellectually, I could understand it, but my emotional heart was pounding at race-car speed. "Thank you," I meekly mumbled, as I turned to walk away. I did not feel she was a shyster or con artist, and my gut would have warned me. Then again, one of my biggest problems, I'd not always been trusting of, nor fully understood of my intuition.

The mixed sentiments were still on my face when Lorraine caught up with me again, so I began to explain, though she'd not directly asked. Rather than questioning my whole going to a clairvoyant, I could see she was intrigued at even the consideration. As we proceeded to a shop, the next hour or so, I talked of some of my prior experiences with a psychic, the occult and my metaphysical world. Attentively, Lorraine listened more than talked, and we wandered to some rather interesting shops, she thought I may like. We then went over to the botanical gardens for a late lunch, in their foliated restaurant. The whole atmosphere along the river was so relaxing, it remained a refreshing and cherished memory.

I'd not let go of the idea of seeing the clairvoyant, as I'd finally accepted it would happen in its due course. Getting better at 'accepting those thing I had no real control over and quickly changing those I did,' to paraphrase the well-known proverb. I believed seeing the psychic, one of those things I truly would make happen somehow, even with my once again, tight schedule.

* * * * * *

The descending plane once more caught my attention, bringing me and my recent memories back to the here and now. I stretched to get a first impression of Alice Springs below. We were quite low, yet still nothing in sight but mountains, and flat empty plains, covered with weird, scraggly, bush-trees. I knew it was not a large city, but there was nothing! "What happened to *A Town Like Alice?"* I whispered to myself. Neil Shute's book, and the Australian television mini-series' referenced, had quite whetted my enthusiasm and interest in seeing the modern-day desert city. As the baggage took some time, I looked around at the emptiness of the new terminal. With no one around to ask, and no information desk within sight, I wandered out toward the 'Taxi' sign, where only a single one was waiting.

Past experience had taught me, most Aussie taxi drivers were quite talkative and sometimes even informative. Though, everything they said was the ultimate understatement of the positive. "Wher' ta Luv?" The man looked about fifty, which meant in this desert country, where skin turned almost overnight into leather, he was probably about forty. I opened the door to climb into the back seat, which I knew to some Aussie drivers was rude - the 'friendly' thing to do was to sit in the front seat next to them. On the other hand, in Japan, not only did the door automatically open for the passenger, but the taxi drive would almost faint, if a gaijin were to sit in the front seat.

"The Pacific Resort, please." I waited for his acknowledgment, which I knew would tell me how nice the place was. After his very positive response, I continued. "Gee, this is really desolate. I had no idea it was so empty and barren." I paused, then said without thinking. "I can't imagine people actually wanting to live out here. How far is it to the city?" As I heard my words, I almost began to squirm down into the seat, as I quickly tried to cover up for the negative words. "I ... I mean, it must be quite difficult dealing with the harshness and all ... I mean you only get, like seven to ten inches of rain or something, a year … don't you?" Now embarrassed and uncomfortable, I hoped he'd just write it off as a stupid tourist statement.

He slowly adjusted his rearview mirror, so he could see me better, as he pulled out onto the new two lane highway, heading for what looked like a gap in the mountains. "It's about ten kilometers or so to town. We built this new airport, so we'd have lots of room for growth. We're gettin' a lot of tourists." He paused and began to add with more pride than defensiveness, "Yeah, it takes pretty tough people live out here, … a good life, if a man's willing to work and learn… the land will give back to ya … if you put into it."

I waited through the momentary interlude knowing he, too, was now trying to choose his words, so as not to offend the 'money- paying tourist.' A category I did not like to be in, but realized I'd put myself there. "Actually, we've been pretty lucky this year. We've had some extra rain … bit of a blessin'." As an after thought, he slowly added, while glancing out his window. "Flowers 're out early." Almost with a solemn reference he said, "Desert's nice when the flowers 're out." He was again quiet, as if lost in his own contemplation of the sight then asked the expected, "You from America?"

Well, I had done it again, 'the brash, ugly, American, loses friends and influences no one.' I looked out the window at the sporadic color passing by, and realized how it would be appreciated when seen so rarely. I tried to save the situation by responding, "Yes, but I live in Japan … and it probably rains seventy to one hundred inches there, if I've computed the metric correctly. We get like fifteen hundred milliliters, I think it is. This is such a stark comparison, it's going to take a bit to get used to it." I felt a little better, as if I'd covered my mistake somewhat, and also changed to a subject I knew was dear to all Aussies' hearts.

"Japan?!? Wy do ya' liv thar'? We get a lotta them here. Never alone. Come by the bus load." He was now shaking his head. "They're a strange mob."

I decided to give him my pat answer, and perhaps it would suffice for some of my actions. "I teach business management, to people being sent overseas to work. I've been there four years and I look forward to vacations. And, getting as far away as possible to clear my mind, in order to be able to go back and handle it all. It's quite crowded and difficult to deal with, on a day-to-day basis, but they pay me well. And, I do like what I teach."

We were finally approaching what looked like the outskirts of the town. The highway and the rail tracks ran side by side through the gap, and we soon passed over what I knew to be the 'dry' Todd River. I continued to tell him of my tour plans, but now he just nodded in response, as sure they'd be quite similar to most other tourists, who he escorted to this 'Red Centre.'

The area around the golf course and resorts looked green, with some colorful blooming flowers. The older buildings and houses were basic in design and rarely more than one story. It was easy to pick out what I knew to be government-style housing, and who they'd been built for. I was not totally ready for the Aboriginal community to be so near, nor the town's response to them. There were not many cars, then I noticed a sprinkling of Aborigines walking around the park area. To me, of course, this weather was almost warm, but most people had on at least a sweater or jacket. I had yet to see a traffic signal, as we came upon a round-about, and we then continued until crossing the Todd again. Moments later the taxi pulled into the large, covered driveway of the Pacific Resort.

The meter was only $7.50, but I gave him a ten dollar bill, as he turned from placing my bag on the steps to the entrance. "Thank you, please keep the change" He looked at me with mild surprise, and nodded. He turned to go, then decided to throw out a little Outback- philosophy. "There's a lot more out thar'. .... The desert and all those bloody-rocks have got a few stories to tell … Good luck, mate." He was smiling broadly, as I knew he was telling me much more than any tourist brochure could begin to say. Truer, and more fateful words could not have been said, by even the most learned-sage.

The Weight of Potential

We look for potential in children,
as the fulfilled pride of parenting.
They may not be child prodigies,
but they have talent that can grow!

Then as adults, we grab hope.
It springs more than eternal,
in those who wait with baited-breath.
Is it a case of Great Expectations?

Have we pushed too much, or too little?
Are we living vicariously, or a fairy tale?
We cannot want more for them than they want
for themselves, or we are frustrated.

Spouses, friends or children . . .
is it right or fair to encourage more
in them, than they can truly ever
see themselves doing?

Potential is both the anchor-weighted burden of
fulfilling the expectations of others,
and the life foundation of one's talents.
Is it wantonness to waste a life's potential?

If fear is the culprit holding back one's star,
unshackle
those limiting influences to tap your power.
Anything is possible, if you choose to unleash your
energy, and the strong desire to make it happen.

Alice Parker

Chapter 2 ~ Truly, a Different World

"Hi, I'm Annie Lane Stryker … I think you have a reservation for me?

.. A single room." The new resort was truly lovely, with the front staff more than cordial and seemingly organized. Considering, we had a lot of miscommunication through the faxes I'd sent, arranging the tours and reservations. I started to take out my paperwork, just to be sure.

"Oh, yes, Ms. Lane-Stryker, we have a very nice room for you. And, how will you be paying? Oh … let's see. You'll be staying with us twice … now, and after your tour to Ayers. Is that right?" She read the details, as I filled out the form.

"I think I gave you my credit card number for a deposit. Do you want to run a impression? And, the name isn't hyphenated … I just use my full name for formal things." I smiled, so she'd know I wasn't offended. "I take it, you also have my reservations for all the tours? Should I pay you directly, or the tour company?"

At this point, an older woman sitting at the side, got up and stepped over next to the young woman. She introduced herself, as the one I had corresponded with by fax, and explained all the details to me. Afterwards, she offered to get a bellboy to take my bag, but said I preferred to tote it myself, as I looked over the grounds at my leisure.

The room, on the second floor, had a nice view and two beds, so plenty of space to spread out my maps and brochures. I decided while still light out, to walk into town, about four hundred meters away. I quickly changed my sandals to my new hiking shoes, although I considered them to be more like heavy duty sneakers. I wanted to break them in as much as possible, before the tour. Graeme had been right about the importance of having the right footgear for this area, so glad I'd bought them.

I headed down the hall in the opposite direction, as I'd seen an 'Exit' sign and knew it'd be closer to the bridge going over the Todd into town. To my surprise, the high brick wall, which I'd barely noticed at the front of the resort, completely enclosed it. I'd later learn this was not only security for the guests, but for privacy stemming from prejudice.

I quickly made the long walk back out of my building, which was at the rear of the huge compound. There, a nice little, paved pathway headed up to the Todd River Bridge. The sun had begun to set, and being a sunset 'worshipper,' I paused in the middle of the bridge to enjoy nature's soulful-symphony. The magnificent 'ghost- gum' trees, from the eucalyptus family, a familiar sight and symbol throughout the Red Centre. They seemed almost perfectly staged, as they were scattered in and along the dusty, dry river. The white bark on these giant trees reflected some lovely, soft mauves, while the pink tones danced across the few puffy clouds in the bright, blue sky. I took a moment for a long, deep breath, to enjoy finally arriving at my starting point.

Without pollution, each hue was almost too intense, with variegated purple tints, impossible to name or describe. I stared into the bright orange ball, slipping quickly below the flat horizon, only punctuated by the McDonnell Range to the south. The McDonnell's were now glowing red, as if on fire. Taking another deep breath and releasing slowly a good sign, I thought. And, saturation may come at the end of the week, if this prismatic-show was observed daily.

Movement in the bushes below, and around the trees, caught my attention, while at the same time I tried to focus my eyes into the shadows. A bit taken aback, I almost said aloud, 'Aborigines!' As if spotting Martians or something. This reminded me of how some of the Japanese reacted to the gaijin. I'd read these local Aborigines were the last to come in from the Outback - sometime in the 70s. Many had almost, selectively assimilated to the 'white man's' world. Just then I was spooked, when a shout came, but a few feet from me, quickly followed by a response from below. Snapping my head, I turned just as the large, barefooted woman walked past me, carrying a plastic store bag in one hand, and eating something with the other.

I had wanted so to see her face, which would not have been easy, as it was shadowed by the setting sun. Staring after her, the rolling gait fascinated me, as did the massive, curly head of hair, and the simple cotton dress with a sweater. All I could think of, was how difficult it must be to live between two cultures, with neither accepting them fully, nor them probably wanting all of either. They were sort of like refugees, obviously connected to the land, but not welcomed by those currently occupying it. I thought of how the Native Americans had felt, and wanting to get their quasi-independence for their reservations. This always brought up questions of my mother's own ancestry, and how she'd denied it most of the time, because of her younger life being filled with such prejudice and discrimination.

* * * * * *

I suddenly recalled my first personal 'encounter' with an Aborigine, almost four years before in Cairns, on the evening of Christmas Day. I'd made a luscious leg of lamb, enjoying the spaciousness of the kitchen, with everything else about the condominium, Travis and I had rented for the week. We had reverse, culture-shock, after almost one year in Japan. We were on the eleventh floor, high above the esplanade, on the huge balcony. We truly enjoyed the peace and quiet of the water and mountains, in the hot sleepy, little town.

I'd suggested we take a walk, not only to more closely appreciate the scenery, but also to exercise some of the big dinner off. The quickly, approaching night, had shrouded the area birds into silence. It also released the fruit-bats to their endeavors, scaring me several times in the process. We'd noticed quite a few Aborigines in the park, along the esplanade without much consideration, as to their activities or even how they may have spent the holiday.

The middle-aged Aboriginal woman walking toward us on the sidewalk, seemed intently directed, yet I had no apprehension of what she was going to do or say. She reached out to me, and took both of my hands, with me responding likewise, as if I'd expected it, like we knew each other. Travis, surprisingly, did not react, for sometimes he could come-off as if, he were a Special Forces candidate, protecting me from the *evils-lurking* all around.

The rather rough, dry, black hands gently lifted my white ones, to her thin, broad lips and softly kissed them. I looked deeply into her dark, furrowed face, which was almost indiscernible in the impending dusk. I felt a tingling-surge of electricity, along with a kind of admiration, as if we were suspended in a slow-motion scene. The whites of her eyes glowed, when she looked up at me and said, "Ya'r bles't. Be 'appy. Meri Kris'mats." The smile then went from one side to the other, of her wide, black face, with only the bright, white teeth outlining it. A park light suddenly came on behind her, illuminating the full, curly hair like a halo. She mildly squeezed my hands, released them, then continued walking up the sidewalk. I mumbled, "Thank You …" simply out of rote-response. I could slightly hear her singing something, as she drifted into the shared silhouette of a tree. I was not cognizant of the full meaning of it all, nor will I probably ever be. But, I've never forgotten our meeting, and the feelings it produced in me.

* * * * * *

Lorraine and Graeme had strongly warned me not to be out alone at night, nor to go around the bridge, where Aborigines lived. "They bother people, mainly for money and other nuisances." To me, they were not a perceived threat, as I had a soft-spot in my heart and mindset geared towards acceptance. My mother was three-quarters Native American, and I sometimes regretted I was the only one of four children who did not look like her. This was the first time I'd seen Aborigines living this close to nature, even if it was in the middle of the city. Then Travis and I'd gone to Kakadu National Park outside of Darwin, on a 'corroboree' tour.

The Aborigines had become homologous to the point, they had their own lawyers taking on the government for land rights infringement. While at the same time, running their own tours, restaurants, hotels and shops. I was aware, too, the Aborigines had the same problem with alcohol, as most indigenous people. This caused them, not only legal conflicts, but pity, prejudice and scorn as well. The subject, for me, would be learned and contemplated in numerous ways the next week, in the various areas.

Walking on into the Todd Mall - various shops and restaurants along a pedestrian street - I could see the Aboriginal art was the constant theme, while Ayers Rock ran a distant second. Strolling past one display window after another, I could not help but wonder, how much of the profits trickled-down, and how much was authentic. At the end of several blocks, after only ducking into a few open shops, I perked up to see a movie theater, merely to be disappointed, as they had nothing I wanted to see. Standing around reading the 'Coming' posters, I noticed an older Aboriginal man had come in shortly after me. A staff person moved quickly over to him, and was quietly questioning his intentions. Curiously, I watched as the Aboriginal man pulled away, mumbling in a louder voice, while the staff person kept trying, then finally succeeding in guiding him out the door.

Though there was nothing I wanted to see, a part of me questioned, did I want to contribute financially to their pervasive attitude. Logically, I did not know the city, or the problem. Yet, after three other extended visits to Oz, I felt I knew the intrinsic prejudiced belief, as it abounded also in America. Perhaps, though Japan was the worst example. Whereas most 'whites' were accepting of most other 'whites,' the Japanese were accepting of only themselves, as the purebred race. This acceptance certainly did not include other Asians. Living there, had angrily taught me an attitudinal about-face, some- thing ALL whites should experience at least once. The 'Restricted' sign on the theater door, I noted and how it used the usual peripheral language of 'appropriate attire and conduct' being required.

At a Mall cafe, the lamb dinner, half carafe of Australian red wine and pleasant talk with the staff and several customers, soothed my emotions. It mellowed me nicely for the walk back to the resort. Stopping on the bridge once again, I gloried at the sight of the diamonds sparkling in the pitch black sky, seemingly just out of my reach. Since my first sighting years before, I had gotten a thrill out of seeing the Southern Cross, along with Orion's Belt, pelting out their blue-white light. Stargazing was not something I was able to do in Japan - with the constant string of cities and pollution, one hardly could. The simple free pleasures were not always available, so I had come to cherish them. Looking out across the Todd, I could see a few fires going and a slight din of talk caught in a breeze. Personal lifestyle choices for most people is the ultimate freedom.

Back in my room, I began to plan my next full day in Alice Springs, trying to see how I could take in as much as possible of the culture and sights. The following day, I'd leave for the three-day tour to Ayers and King Canyon, with several other full-day tours planned upon my return to Alice Springs. This Red Centre turned out to have a lot more to see and do, than I'd time for, as usual. Afterwards, stretching out on the bed, I enjoyed watching Aussie TV, which surprisingly had numerous American shows. It was always local commercials which I looked forward to, as they were the most revealing of how the people, whoever, lived on a daily basis. Some were quite impressive, while others had me almost rolling off the bed with laughter. After working fifteen years in advertising, marketing and public relations, a fun pastime, no matter what country I was in.

Shortly after the light, buffet breakfast, I walked back into town enjoying the cool, breezy, morning air. The stark-brightness showed the town to be a bit more rustic, but being a Sunday, there were a number of people out and about. I planned to wait until the last day to buy souvenirs, so I'd not have to carry or store them, but it was still fun to check-out all of the shops. I'd heard the prices were much dearer, and I could certainly see it on most everything.

Many large Australian cities had the 'Wanderer' bus system, where one bought a half or all day ticket. The bus drove around and dropped tourists off at the most popular attractions, with usually about an hour's time, to enjoy before the bus returned. For most sights, the hour was more than enough, but if there were several points of interest or more time was wanted, the bus came back the next hour again. For me, it was much better alternative than a regular 'city' tour, which also cost more. With my plans set in mind, I cheerfully bought my ticket.

The cordial and hearty mini-bus driver was glad to see me, as there was only one couple abroad. Once his digital clock turned over nine o'clock, he started the bus to proceed. Then into his light, bouncy stories about Alice Springs and the surrounding area. Tour guides, though not out of the same cookie-cutter, must take the identical happy-pills every day, and truly love to hear the sound of their own voice. At the traffic circle once again, he decided to jump into it all, "So, where are all you folks from?" As if, he was addressing a full bus.

The retired couple wavered a bit, when I waved for them to go first. The man finally spoke-up, while the lady smiled, "Why, we're from Brighton, England." I was beckoning and smiling for him to tell us more. So, he turned and looked at his wife, as if he did not want to let out too many secrets. "We're here on holiday, that is … Australia." now he nodded and obviously felt he was on a roll. "We're down in Sydney, visiting the relatives, actually my wife's sister and her family, but it got so cold, … so they suggested we take a trip up here. And, that's what we did!" He seemed to take great triumph in the accomplishment, so I smiled and gestured at him.

"I have a friend from Brighton, but I never got there to visit, when I was in England a few years ago. I'm American, as you may have guessed." I looked up, at the driver and half smiled at the couple wanting to see their reaction as I said, "But, I've lived in Japan for the last … four years. I teach business and cross-cultural understanding." I paused then added, "And, this is my fourth trip to Australia."

Not unexpectedly, the couple stared at me with a 'who would have guessed she was a Martian?' Then the tour driver popped up and asked, "Do you speak Japanese? I've heard it's really difficult. I could sure use it sometimes here, because they really can't speak English."

With a rather coy grin, I replied, "Well, I'm somewhat conversational … enough to get around, shop, everyday stuff, basic conversation for the neighborhood. I've never studied the kanji." I now turned toward the couple, "You know, the characters. I've just not had the time or true inclination, as it takes a lot of dedication and practice. And, only English is allowed in my business classes." I smiled broadly, so they wouldn't think I was too crazy.

The Brits looked at each other, and the man decided to jump back in. "We had heard some Japanese companies had come into England, but we don't know anyone who works for them." He nodded to his wife, to indicate if this was true then added, "But the Brighton Council is trying to promote tourism with them, as they heard they spend a lot of money when they travel." I had just begun to give my agreement, when the guide broke-in with his bright colorful description of the 'Olive Pink Flora Reserve,' but it did not entice us, as we only looked and listened, without disembarking. We talked for a few minutes before coming to spot two, which was the 'Pritchi Ritchi Outdoor Sanctuary.' That one I had read about, and the couple was quick to follow me out the door. The driver said the 'Mecca Date Gardens' were only about 500 meters away down and around the road, so we could do both and he'd meet us there.

Interestingly, but not totally surprised, there was no one at the gate. So we just wandered in, receiving no detailed-information about the stone carvings, based mainly on the Aborigines' 'Dreamtime' series. The garden atmosphere was nicely laid-out, with flowers and trees accenting the sculptures, which were in all sizes and shapes. Many of the great rust-colored rocks had been left in a partial natural form, with the figures carved deeply into them. Quite emotionally moving how the facial points, and body shapes had been so finely cut, to depict the depth of feelings of the individual characters. I could not imagine the tremendous talent, patience or ability to truly transfer such intangibles, as these illusive myths to solid bedrock. I began, too, to sense some of the spiritualness of the legends, of these ageless-people, who had all but been destroyed. And, were only now being somewhat appreciated for their reverence, to understand their land.

The British couple sensed my need for personal space, and because the area was spread out, it was easy for us to go our way, without intruding upon each other. Some of the depictions drew me in more than others, and I'd sometimes feel myself diving into the images, visualizing them in mini-scenarios. On each trip to Australia, I'd gathered a little more information and experience about the numerous Aboriginal tribes, for they were as similar and different, as the assorted Native Americans.

A Japanese professor, in one of my discussion groups, had done extensive research on the mythical beings and characters, while living with several groups of Aborigines. He then, with much care, painstakingly translated them into Japanese to share with students and friends. I had often been amazed at his dedication, which he'd sometimes refer to as only a 'serious hobby.' The usual Japanese way of self-deprecation, while his eyes glazed over, as he spoke of them.

To me, it seemed the Aborigines had a 'living' religion, in they allowed the dictates or influences into their daily lives, for there was no doubt they were connected to the land. I had learned, too, many now were trying to get back their cultural heritage with its training, for they knew land and spirituality were inseparable, as nature was integrated into their culture.

I spent a good forty minutes contemplating the various story images, before trotting over to the date farm to enjoy some date ice cream. The bit of cool respite, under the giant palms delighted me. I learned, they'd been shipped in from the Middle East, over a hundred years before. The British couple, and perhaps a half dozen more people were now on the bus, when I joined them. We were off next to the 'Frontier Camel Farm' to see the funny-looking animals, along with some other desert creatures. When Lorraine and I had gone for our short camel trek, our first year together, the handler was a conscientious young chap. He had explained the beasts were quite amicable, when they were treated well, and he'd never had a bite, nor had any of his customers. His sincere kindness squelched the bad- mouthing, I'd always heard, as well the fear being removed, and it added greatly to our enjoyment.

I took a pass at the 'Old Ghan Train' stop, though I was able to get a fairly good photo of the old train, which had trudged across the desert and Nulabor Plain for so many years. Some say it could only be compared to the Trans-Siberian Express, with *'express'* omitted, as it was rarely on schedule, due mainly to the harsh conditions, causing continued breakdowns.

Our driver picked-up on the satire of the continuous stories, from those old days. "During one of the typical breakdowns, a very, pregnant lady came marching up to the engineer demanding to know how soon they'd reach the next town. When the engineer shook his head, saying he had no idea, she angrily responded with, "But can't you see the condition I'm in." He then retorted, "Well, Lady, you should't have gotten on the train in that condition." Her come-back was, "I wasn't in THIS condition, when I got on the train!"' So, you can see some of the delays were rather long, and they had to carry a lot of extra food and water."

We all laughed jovially, as we continued to bob up and down in our seats, having almost a carnival ride, in this land of the unusual and unexpected, being the common and accepted. Maybe part of the 'spirit' of this land, you could never take it for granted. It demanded more respect and attention, because it could quite easily and simply kill you. I looked out onto the vastness, which held so little, yet so much. No, I would not want even the mini-bus of today, to break down and we were barely ten miles from town. I could not imagine the first explores; many had tried and died in vain.

A definite part of American history, which I was somewhat proud of, the pioneering spirit of those, who braved the new world for land and a new life. Perhaps, if the military with the warring governments had stayed out of it all, the settlers and the Indians may have lived happily in peace. There was certainly enough land for them all. Then, Americans would not have the ugly scar on its history to contend with. Bad enough to have to deal with all the horrors of slavery, left over the culture and continued prejudice. The Aussies were having to do it now, as the young people had begun to acknowledge, what their forefathers had done to the Aborigines.

For me, the next stop would easily take two hours, as it had four interests in close proximity - 'Strehlow Centre,' 'Aviation/Auto Museum,' 'Araluen Arts Centre' and 'Historic Cemetery.' After a quick walk through the museum, I headed over to the Strehlow Centre. It depicted how Professor T.G.H. Strehlow had lived and worked with the Aranda Aboriginal people. I was a bit unnerved, as the realistic photography and music showed all too clearly, their lifestyle - culture as it was, and as lived now. The man himself was quite fascinating, and surprised me how honestly, both his genius and his controversial nature were portrayed.

Finally, sponging up as much as I could, I wandered into the gift shop, where several reasonably priced and totally unique items - all handmade by Aborigines from natural products - called to me, so to speak, so I bought them. The receptive designs and Earth-tone colors were beginning to grow on me, as now able to distinguish some of their meanings. My perceptions were slipping, as more and more of this art moved, danced and seeped into my soul.

In the Arleen Arts Centre, the ancient, primitive spirits, transformed themselves from the touchable to simply an essence. Appreciation of the visual statement, was my only claim to fame, and these objects from various mediums of clay, paint, material and stained glass were calling to me, in both shouts and haunting whispers. The simplicity in most designs, created intricacies as I'd never known. Moved, I absorbed it. I knew now, there were secret mysteries in this land, which I wanted to know. Getting more in touch with the 'physical' of it all, in the next few days may give me a clue.

I'd just enough time left to visit the Memorial cemetery, Alice Springs' final resting place for many of the Territory's famous and infamous. Most prominent in the area was a large sandstone sculpture, which characterized the sticky, Harold Lasseter in his most usual position, panning for gold. It was said, he'd found a 'Reef of Gold' and had returned to Alice Springs for more supplies. But apparently, lost his way and his life trying to relocate it, in the illusive duplicity of the unforgivable desert. His story was one of both greed and endurance, fighting against nature, paranoia and the Aborigines. Lassiter had gotten Sydney investors to put up a considerable amount of money in the 1930s, and though they had used airplanes, trucks and camels, all eventually succumbed to a disastrous fate.

The only other name I recognized, was of the Aboriginal painter, Albert Namatjira, who was the first native to express the essence of his land in Western style, rather than the traditional Koori style. It's referred to as 'our people,' or 'X-Ray' or skeleton paining. I experienced more of his work and life at our last tour stop.

Careening along the circuitous route, our guide kind of chuckled, as if 'telling tales out of school,' when he pointed out a particular area, where all of the houses had a high fence and barbed wire atop. "This folks is our 'American' neighborhood, for all those working out of Pine Gap, the NASA military installation. There's about one-hundred thirty of them, and they kind of keep to themselves, as you may know, this project is all secret and everything. So, be sure you don't tell nobody I told you." We all laughed rather heartily, but none with more cognizance than me, as having lived ten years in San

Antonio, with its four military bases. I knew from personal experience, how paranoid the military was about the 'spy-in-the-sky' bullshit.

I took a pass again on the 'Diorama Village,' as the day was growing short, and there were several more stops to choose from. We came next to the local 'School of the

Air,' which for the Outback children was their main source of education. Being Sunday, it was closed, but it was no loss to me, as I'd seen one on my first visit in Cairns, along with the 'Royal Flying Doctors' Base.' These two crucial facilities kept people outside of the largest cities in touch and alive, in the early days. The stop for the Old Telegraph Station was the raison d'etre, for also the sight of the artesian springs, which gave the city its name, and this desert its life.

The 'Anzac Hill,' five minute photo stop, once more filled in some gaps of my American history lessons had left out. Though Australians study about the United States government and background in high school. There was rarely a footnote in American texts about them, or other countries unrelated to our basic European ancestors. I'd been able to piece together, via my own and Travis' curiosity, just how extensively the Aussies and Kiwis (New Zealanders) had been involved in Vietnam and in Korea. For many older Aussies, there was still pride in the military, in which they spoke of such events as Gallipoli with reverence. Where history had reduced them to almost nothing more than British cannon-fodder, used and abused.

The younger Aussies had rightful resentment of the U.S., not only for dragging them into Vietnam, but more recently, the ridiculous and flashy Gulf War. To me, there was something sad and sick about so many young, unsung heroes buried on foreign soil, which never set well in my mind. I returned to force myself to enjoy the superb surrounding view of 'the Alice' - as I heard it referred to more often - and the mountains chasing off to the horizon.

'Panorama guth' was my last stop, as it took us back to the middle of the city, where I'd planned to wander around afterwards. This was a gigantic, two story '360' degree, panoramic painting of Central Australia condensed. Yet, it illustrated all of the geographic landscape in directional perspective to each other and Alice Springs. The astounding, creative feat had taken years to accomplish, and was recognized for its authenticity, as well beauty. Here, too, was displayed an extensive collection of Western style paintings of the area, along with some fascinating Aboriginal items.

I'd gotten several cheap prints of Albert Namatjira a few years before, but I never tired of looking at them. The man had been an enigma, to both populations and I felt some of his 'lostness' revealed in the way he captured the mystique of the Outback. I was told, though his vast talent had brought him great sums of money, he'd died almost penniless, as he'd followed the Aboriginal tradition of sharing his wealth with all of his relatives. Unfortunately, it was not beyond some, no matter how distant their relationship, or purposed kinship was, to constantly drain him of all his funds. Much of this money, in their inexperience and native hands, went to support their addiction to alcohol. Few, even today in Northern Territory, where the Aborigines have had less experience, living in the 'white-feller's' world, would break the tradition, although they knew how it was being abused.

Strolling into the still blistering sunlight, I meandered into the next shop more for escape, as I'd not gotten my bearings, as to what I wanted to do next. I enjoyed too, the attitude of the smiling young shop owner who had a baby 'Joey'- wallaby, hung in a cloth pouch, observing all who came in to 'ooh' and 'ah' at him. " …'is mum was killed by a car or somethin', so we took 'im in a few weeks ago. We've got all sorts-a animals, that we kind-a adopt an' cure, before we send 'em back ta the bush." When another customer asked how much work they were, she shrugged her shoulders. "Yeah, they're bloody messy an' eat everything' in sight, but they're still lots-a fun. I won't let somethin' die, just because bloody cars an' road-trains have invaded their life.'

Funny how when you least expected it, wise philosophy dropped in your lap. Regrettably, when some *people and governments* did take this attitude, it was easier to adopt it to animals, rather than humans. Especially, those whose lifestyle was alien to their own. Still, I, too, should be doing more to help with something in some way, other than donating money.

Now laden-down with several packages, I continued to ramble from one shop to another, finding bookstores, secondhand shops and souvenirs of every kind from super-tacky to high dollar collectibles. Finally, I came upon an indoor mall with a gigantic mural, which covered the entire three stories, from one end to the other. I studied it for a long time, as it depicted much of the history of the local Aboriginals, who owned it. I continued my jaunts to whatever caught my eye or nose, as I was getting hungry. Once I sat down to nibble my snacks, I realized how tired I was after all my adventures. So, gathered my stuff, and started the hike back to the resort.

Walking past another small park, I saw several Aboriginal families relaxing and enjoying their families. I decided to stop, hoping I'd not be intruding, as I really did not know how much personal interaction took place, between the white-locals and them. I knew genetically, the children kept their blonde hair, until they were eight or nine years old. The incongruity of it, framing there rich, black, smiling faces, made me want to grab for my camera. However, I wanted to respect their customs, and no picture-taking was one of them. Thus, simply observing at this point, would have to do. Their boisterous running around with their young, limitless energy, represented in some ways the generation change, since they had come in out of the bush. These children would never have to migrate with the seasons, hunting and gathering all day long for simple sustenance. Most of the Aborigines had become fat, as they took on the 'white feller's way' and nature no longer dictated diet or death.

The parents or grandparents, who had often been referred to as simply lazy, or at least-lethargic, had actually followed the inbred- rules of not wasting energy. When out in the bush, under the blazing sun, every unneeded movement was like throwing away precious food and water. Birth control, also had been controlled by nature, as the young women did not ovulate during droughts. Now becoming a problem, as the Aborigines loved children, and having them so easily with plenty of food and water, seemed a blessing to them, not something which should be 'controlled.' They attributed all life consciously to the creative forces, and everything in creation. There was a basic Aboriginal belief, which they can experience the vast creative process best through ecstatic dance and sexuality. As if to say,

"Dancing in the park is not acceptable, but producing children to dance in the park is."

After about twenty minutes, my curiosity had been somewhat fulfilled, and the children had started running toward my direction. The women had called them back in their native language, which made me begin to feel perhaps, I was disturbing their relaxation time. I rose slowly and drifted along toward my room. I'd decided to have dinner tonight in the resort restaurant, after a shower and rest. Tomorrow had an early start for my three day tour, and I wanted to repack, so I only had to take a small bag.

There's a fragment in many female brains, which sends up a red flag making them uncomfortable sitting alone, especially in a nice restaurant. Some of it for me, was being so gregarious. And, a basic component of the enjoyment of a good meal was the conversation. I really did not have a preference, as to whether male or female, as long as it was interesting. Likewise, I did not want pity pitched towards me of not fulfilling the rooted fundamental requirement of 'coupledom,' or society only accepting us 'two by two.'

On the other hand, being alone gave me the opportunity to 'people-watch,' which had sometimes been more entertaining, than the person I was with! Curious too, while sitting alone in the restaurant as to who, if any, of the other patrons, I might be spending the next three days with. Learning what countries, as well as what parts of Oz they may hail from, had a delicious anticipation all its own. Leisurely, I finished my wine and reveled in my privacy, as I continued to make up stories about almost everyone in the room. Included, too, my worn out, but still trying to smile, waitress. I'd also seen her that past morning.

Anticipation still mixed, I returned to my room, to finish preparations for my long-awaited journey, … to my real destination, true adventure and as well, 'test' of my physical or even mental-self - at 'The Rock.'

Self-Limitations

For some people, it is only for the existence of windows,
they know of other people, or
a world beyond their small lives.

They depend on their big screen TV, viewed from their
Lazy-boy chair, what-all even partially exists outside
their four walls, and select people.

They may never consider how their lives have been
controlled, or limited by the edited version being brought
to them by their TV.

None of us are the same people we were, when we were
young. Yes, we were gullible then, too. But, it was
innocent-naivety.

Back then, time and life was wastefully enjoyed,
not monitored for the money, lost or gained by its use.

It all had a totally different meaning to us - the meaning
of life,
meaning of time, and of money.

Alice Parker

Chapter 3 ~ Journey to 'The Rock'

The huge, clean blue and white tour bus sat in the driveway, as I walked out from breakfast, carrying my red, nylon tote bag. I had stored my large, gray bag, my purchases stuffed inside, with the staff. There were already several people on the bus, as I checked in with our chirpy, smiling driver, Dean. I found a nice, full window and settled in to check my tote again, for my binoculars, camera, extra film, hat, sunblock, bottled water, and the tons of wonderful 'freebie' packages of tissues, I'd collected from Japan. Passing out tissue packets, on busy street corners was the usual job for the relatively, few school drop-outs. One of those multi-purpose things, not only kept them busy, but carried advertisement - granted, sometimes of a lewd nature, with a sex-phone service or escort. Yet, since in Japanese or hysterical Japanese-English, I could care less. Tissues were so useful and necessary, since Japan's public toilets did not have paper. They also were a constant source, as a conversation-starter with people who I'd give them to.

Once we'd picked up several other people, at area hotels and we made a quick stop at the office in town to take care of paperwork, check in numbers and so forth. We then headed for the Stuart Highway, where I saw my first traffic signal in the city. Within minutes, we're out in the open, my heart geared up for action, as Dean crisply came on the mic to give us the trip it inerary, and the day's details. He knew just what patter to say to calm us down, while keeping our attention and holding the anticipation. He was good, and I knew how important a good tour driver was to make a trip even more memorable. Rolling down the highway, with several jokes under our belts, Dean now felt we were primed to introduce ourselves. "Please say your name, where you're from, and how much you've traveled in Australia.

The front seat had two short, rather slim women perhaps in their early forties who looked so much alike, it was obvious they were related. Slowly one stood, holding onto the back of the seat as she began to speak. "Hi, my name is Marta and this is my cousin Kaylin

... and we're from the Azores ... off the coast of Portugal." She smiled down at her cousin then continued, "I'm an accountant and she's a teacher ... She's a little shy and does speak as much English." She turned to look at Dean and he mumbled to coach her. "Oh, yeah, this our first trip to Australia, ... and we've been traveling for three weeks and we have one week left. It's been great so far. Thanks."

She finished with a big grin crossing her pretty olive-skinned face and her dark, shining eyes searched around for approval. As she ran her hand through her short, curly hair, I began clapping, as I knew it had not been easy for her, especially being the first. Besides, to show approval and give confidence, I'd always done it for my speech students in Japan. I was happy the rest of the bus immediately followed suit, so the next victim was not quite so afraid. The British couple, I'd met on the mini-bus the day before was next. I think he was glad he'd practiced his speech on me, for now he delivered it almost the same, but with a bit more confidence. Once he'd finished, I waved and smiled to him between claps.

Behind them, a woman by herself quickly stood up and turned slightly, as she crisply spoke, "My name is Jean and I'm also from England - York, and I'm a teacher too. I was in Australia once before many years ago, but only to Sydney and Melbourne. This time I've been to the Reef and snorkeled and travels around Queensland ... but my

main purpose for making this trip is to climb Ayers Rock!"
Said with such determination, several people including
myself cheered and clapped for her, as well for ourselves.
She let out an embarrassed laugh, as her hazel eyes
twinkled from the obvious adrenaline kick she got from
talking about it. She looked to be in her early forties and
kept her shoulder-length brown hair tied back like a
schoolgirl. In this way, her plain face was quite open,
showing great empathy for life itself. She raised her
muscular arm with her fist drawn tight, as she almost cried
out, "All Right! Let's go for it!!" She then sat down as
suddenly as she'd stood up, with the rousing applause still
going.

Dean cut in for a minute to jokingly chide us as to
who we all were, 'had he possibly gotten the wrong bus or
something? He finished up by saying he should have taken
one of those more subdued tour groups, but he always
lucks-out and gets the 'wild ones.'

Still all heartily laughing, when the lanky man, in
his thirties stood and kind of pursed his lips to speak.
"Well, I don't know if I can follow that," he lightly
chuckled. "But, I'll try. My name is Nigel and this is my
friend, Miranda." He looked around nodding his head and
went on, "We're from New Zealand and we've been to
Australia many times before, you know we're so close and
everything. Well, Australia's the only thing close.
Anyway, this our first time to … the Red Centre and we're
looking forward to it all, the climb and everything. OK,
that's it. I guess." We politely applauded, as following
Jean and Dean's renditions, a bit of a let down.

In front of me now, was an older Aussie couple.
Holding on carefully, the woman pulled herself up and
tried to speak out as much as she could. She looked at me
with great apprehension and I quickly gave her my 'you
can do it' smile and confidently as I could muster, for this

stranger. She gestured a thanks and plowed into it. "I'm Bertha and he's Charlie and he's a little lame in one leg from the war, so I'll just introduce us." She paused to catch her breath as if so far so good, and I just kept beaming at her like she was doing a starring role on Broadway. "Well, we're from Adelaide and we're on our way to visit our daughter and grandchildren up in Darwin." With just the mention of them she smiled and perked u enough to keep going. "And, we thought since we've never been her or seen Ayers Rock, we may as well go, but we certainly aren't going to try to climb it." She turned a little as if to indicate Jen's statement. "Looking will be a big enough accomplishment for us!" We were all laughing and applauding as she indicated completion and turned to lower herself back down.

A rather large, tall woman with very thick, big glasses, barely dividing her broad face, uncomfortably kneeled one leg on the seat, while holding onto the back with her ample hand. Her voice was deep, as was expected, yet almost soft and apologetic, as you knew she felt she was occupying more space than she had a right to. She'd lived with her size a long time, as she was now in her mid-thirties. I had great empathy for this woman. Though, I'd neither her size nor her looks, I had sometimes felt like I did when in Japan. She graciously smiled as she began. "Hi, my name is Trudy and I'm from Melbourne. I took an optional pay-out on my job at the bank, as they were cutting back … I figured while I had the time and money, I should travel since I'd always said I'd do it if I had the chance." She looked around realizing maybe she'd said too much personal, then figured probably 'what the hell, they're all going to think whatever they want anyway,' so she endured to finish it off. "I'm just going to try to do what I can do, and not worry about what I can't." I tried to show her some extra support, but the applause was lighter and I'm sure she had not even expected that much. I had a feeling in her own way, like Jean and myself, this trip was going to be a certain kind of turning point.

The younger of the two older women sitting across from me stood to speak. She looked to be in her early fifties, though rather fit and jovial, while the other must have been in her seventies at least. They were both slim, with lovely, short, silver-gray hair. The older woman had on bifocals and held onto her cane, but she otherwise seemed active. "My name is Rose and my mother's name is Lily, and we're from Leicester, England. We're both widowed, so we travel around together. We're here in Australia visiting children and grandchildren in Brisbane and Sydney." She smiled a little slyly, as she added. "We both needed a break from the relatives, so decided to come to Alice Springs and take this tour. We aren't planning on climbing, but we both enjoy light trekking." She smiled politely, as she concluded with, "It's nice to meet you all."

Once the applause had died down, I stood up and leaned my right knee into the seat. I had plenty of time to think about what I wanted to say, as I'd decided to gage it on the other speeches. I figured short and simple would be best, as I sometimes intimidated others without realizing it. I give a quick smile and jumped in, "Hi, I'm Annie, and I'm American, but I've lived in Japan for almost four years and teach business English. I hope to climb the 'Rock,' and this is my fourth visit to Australia. I like it, thank you." I gave another quick smile and sat down as quickly as I could. But I still noticed quite a few heads peering over and around their seats to look at me, as they applauded. Sometimes, I ate up the curiosity and sometimes I did not. With this group, I felt perhaps a lower profile would be nice. Already, I knew there were definitely some I'd look forward to getting to know better, before our return to Alice Springs.

The somewhat, good-looking, yuppie-style man behind me stood up, with some glancing ceremony, then looked directly at me as he started. "Well, we're *North American,* too," waving a slightly patronizing hand to his wife, seated by the window and his two daughters across the aisle *"But, happily Canadian,* ... from Toronto." With a definite air, to make clear his position, he drove on. "I have traveled extensively to Australia and New Zealand, but this is my family's first trip to *'Australasia.'* We were in *Tahiti,* before traveling the eastern coast of Australia. We're here to climb Ayers Rock and do *all* of the other activities." He was rather proud of his speech, until his wife tugged at his sleeve to remind him, *he'd not* introduced them. Now, a little flustered, he rattled off their names and sat down to the well-ritualized clapping.

I could not quite put my finger on it, or direct my thoughts as to what it was he said or did, which antagonized me *or* if I just felt his vibes as negative toward me. I really did not care, if he disliked *Americans from the States,* and I knew a lot of Canadians resented the comparison. I guess more than anything, I sensed his discount of his wife and daughters. I figured this either an ego or simply a sexist thing, so I'd try to avoid him, as much as I could.

The reserved and distinguished, medium built man who now stood, looked to be in his middle fifties. He spoke distinctively with a clear, solid British accent while he explained he, his wife and his sister were all from London. They were also, visiting relatives while taking this tour. As soon as he had sat down again, he retrieved the video camera from his wife. We'd all quickly learn, it was rarely out of his hands, and almost always in front of his eye, for the next two days.

Last, but certainly not least of our twenty-six, was the group of six Spaniards, who had set themselves up in the rear of the bus. I'd picked the Spanish accent up, as they'd all been chatting continuously, since they'd gotten on at the last hotel. Since a few minutes of silence, Dean had called over the mic to see if anyone would speak, or if they did not want to be introduced. He'd recognized there may be some language or communication difficulties.

"No. No, No. It is OK. I will speak for us." They all looked to be in their middle or late thirties, and well dressed in designer sports outfits, with both sexes wearing a lot of gold. In halting English he went on. "We are from Barcelona and Valencia, that is in Spain. My sister and brother-in-law with their wives … uh husband." The cackling and garbled words around him were reminiscent of a market scene, as each person interjected into his speech. "And, … this is first visit for Australia. Thank you." He sat down, then after the excited jabbering, he stood again, a bit agitated at his role for them. "Too many names. We meet you later." Most of us chuckled and clapped, as we could only feel sorry for the position they'd all put him in.

Dean then took back over the audience, "Well, thanks everyone for sharing your information. I hope we all get to know each other a bit more in the next few days, because of it. We will have ten more people joining the tour at Yulara, which is the name for the area, which includes Ayers Rock. The Aboriginal name is Uluru and The Olgas - Kata Tjuta. You need to remember and understand though, this is a national park, *and* it is Aboriginal land. We must observe their *rights,* along with the rules and the regulations of the park rangers …" Dean went on to explain rules for the bus, changing seats, especially those in front, but he was not going to force us to rotate.

As we whisked down the Stuart Highway, Dean began to give meaning to the sights whizzing by, in the fathomless array of burnt and burnished-orange-brown hues. He rattled on tidbits about the spots of flora, as we came upon it and the fauna, which we rarely saw, even he pointed them out. Fascinating how the minute trivia and specific facts filled our time and minds. If geography had been taught by tour guides like him, I'm sure a lot of kids would have more of an appreciation of nature and the environment. I slid over in my seat to take a quick peek at the Canadian girls, who looked to be eight and eleven. The younger one had fallen asleep, while the older one read a magazine and listened to her Walkmen. So much for their father's plan.

In between the set informational stuff, Dean would relate different stories about tour groups and nonsensical happenings. Only when he specifically mentioned several Japanese tours, did he ever mention a nationality. I knew too well older ones especially, tended to be so very stereotypical, so easy to deride. When he mentioned they kept asking what land was for sale and how much buildings or homestead cost, I couldn't help laughing louder than anyone else.

A little later, when the bus started to slow down, as about to have our first break, I thought I'd speak to him. Once off the paved highway, the bus churned up enough dust, to totally block the view. Dean then explained, this was a 'stretch-rest,' but we had enough time for the toilet and for a small fee, a camel ride, as we'd stopped at the Virginia Camel Farm.

Filing off the bus, I thought I'd check out the camel rides first, as I did not need the toilet, then. It turned out to be hilarious free entertainment, just watching the various sorts of people from other tour buses trying their hand at the camel rides. There was nothing much inside, but a few souvenirs and some cold drinks, so I went back out again. Dean said we had another four minutes, so I sauntered down to the corrals where a variety of camels were kept.

Wondering what a bunch of people were staring at, when I suddenly realized there were two camels having sex - quite noisily, too. I stopped, rather stunned then I could not help but laugh. The Spaniards and the British man were both videotaping the whole episode. Why, I could not imagine, except who else could brag about having such a shot. I actually felt sorry for the camels' lack of privacy, though it certainly did not stop or slow them down.

I walked back to Dean, who now tried to gather people back onto the bus. "There's a few people down there watching the camels having sex. Poor things have no privacy and subjected to being videotaped." I grabbed the handle to step up, when he commented.

"Well, I guess if you were having sex in the middle of the street, people would stop an stare and maybe even videotape the event." His satirical remark caused me to turn and laugh.

"I guess I'll have to be sure not to have sex in the streets … at least not when anyone is around to with a video camera!" I chuckled again and got on.

Back on the road again, Dean only paused before we crossed the dry riverbed of the Finke River, which archeologists had confirmed was the oldest watercourse in the world. He slowed down again, when he made the turn off Stuart Highway onto Lasseer Highway to head directly west to Yulara and the hotels. Less than an hour before, we finally stopped for our longer tea break at Mt. Ebenezer Roadhouse Outback, located on a larger cattle station. I decided to take some pictures first and use the restroom after the crowds cleared a bit, before I went on inside for my tea and scone - a large version of an American-style biscuit. I fixed up my tea, then stopped to scoop some whipped cream and jam on top of my scone to make it even more luscious. I then headed for the dinning room, where I noted Trudy sitting by herself at a table.

"May I join you?" She look up from her chewing and motioned with her hand. "Thanks." I placed the cup and plate on the table, trying to keep my tote bag from knocking everything off. "I think we've got a good tour group ... it usually makes it a lot more interesting. Have you ever been on a group tour before?" I broke off a hunk of the scone, to smothered it with my goodies.

She swallowed her tea before answering. "No, I haven't. I did take the bus up here. I mean to Alice Springs, but it's not the same." She took another swallow of tea, as if trying to make up her mind, if she should say something else or not. "I have taken some one day tours, when I've gone over to Sydney and stuff, but that's all." She'd finished her scone already, then pushed her glasses back up on her nose. It appeared out of place, as it was a small nose for such a broad, plain face. I've sometimes been concerned about being top-heavy, but complimented on my face and especially my big, blue-green eyes. She sipped her tea again with indecision of how to respond, or if it would make her feel more out of place. "What about you."

I finished swallowing and took a quick sip of tea. "Yes, several but mostly international, like this one, was in China. There were a lot of Europeans, but I think the varied backgrounds kind of builds the enthusiasm. I mean, I've been to Australia before, but the first time here and nothing is like the Red Centre, is it? And, it's just better when there are more reactions for it to feed off, ... you know what I mean?" I felt like I was rattling, and a bit confusing.

She finished her tea and just looking at me. "Well, I guess so, I never thought about it, but we might influence each other. We'll have to see." She watched me a little longer, as I finished eating then added. "Uah … I've had my second cup of tea, so I'll just go look around. I'll see you back on the bus" I nodded as she walked toward the toilets and I got up to get another cup of tea. I began to notice all of the wonderful Aboriginal artifacts, arts and crafts the Road-house had displayed. I thought I'd take a photo, as a good reference for people back in Japan to see, because I certainly was not going to be buying much more.

Since the front seat had been vacated by Marta and Kaylin, the Azores cousins, I decided to take it, as I knew within a few hours we'd be upon Ayers Rock, and the front seat was about the best view on the bus. I pulled my camera out my my bag to have it ready.

"Now, we'll have a little contest to see who can spot 'the Rock' first. The only clue I'll give you is, it's on your left …" Dean continue on about more flora and fauna until we came upon some road repair work and slowed down. The Yulara remains in the midst of Pitjantjatjara country, the Aboriginal tribe of the area, and under the 'protection' of the government's care and maintenance, as a national park. Not fully opened to tourism until 1984, when the first modern accommodations were built, and full park facilities made available. The number of visitors jumped again after 1990, when the Stuart Highway was completely sealed, from Adelaide to Darwin, making the accessibility quicker and safer for all. Lasseter Highway had been finished about the same time, but now they had found it to be quite dangerous without road shoulders.

Since, very long, and straight, many tourists pulling caravans or campers sometimes became tired, or mesmerized by the road, and lost control. Without the shoulders, the vehicles easily flipped-over, so there'd been many accidents. "We're all aware this is not an easily traversed country, with the best of options," Dean explained, "So, they're adding shoulders." It looked like a very slow, hot and tedious job, as the ground had to be built up solidly, on top of the sandy, copper-colored soil.

I slipped out my binoculars and began plying the horizon, as I thought I'd seen something jutting up in the distance. Yes, there was something protruding from all this unbroken plain. I picked back up my tour brochure to check and sure enough, the majestic, flat-topped Mt. Conner. I waited to see how soon someone else spotted it and thought it was Ayers Rock. I could see the game Dean was playing with his troop. A few minutes later, the British couple from Brighton called out merrily, they'd spotted the Rock. Dean then went into his discourse of statists, facts, real and imaginary about Mt. Conner. At 859 meters, it was higher than Ayers rock and much more difficult to climb, as the sides went straight up.

After a photo stop and stretch, we were back rolling again. I began to play my own little game of noting the weird and wonderful, animal road caution signs unique to Oz. On prior trips, I'd seen ones for koalas and kangaroos, now we encountered ones depicting camels and even wombats, the slow, nocturnal-marsupials. Not much later, we had another quick photo stop for the mysterious and vast, silvery Lake Amadeus. There was always something eerie about a dry late and this one had been dry for tens of thousands of years. Staring out, it boundlessly melted into the blaring horizon. I could see mirages of movement begin to appear, before my blurring eyes. So frightening, even in the heat, a cold chill ran down my spine.

There was a bewitching magnetism in this, which was slowly masking over me, with only my self-preservation seeming to keep it in check. Yet, the attraction even drained its influence. I almost bolted back to my seat, as if it was the only way to tear myself away from, the strange feelings this remote place was covering me with. *"Let's get this show on the road!"* I wanted to shout out, getting antsy for the main event, and not have it be anti-climatic after other spectacles.

Finally, we entered Yulara, and I need not have worried about being disappointed, or let down, as Ayers Rock dominated all of the Red Centre. Dean had said we had time for just a quick by-pass before lunch, and I knew he was simply titillating us for the upcoming events. We had now traveled 465 kilometers to Yulara, which was actually 22 kilometers to Ayers Rock and there was 32 kilometers between the Rock and the Olgas. I leaned forward, as we drove on and on foranother twenty minutes or so, as the massive, bright-orange monolith continued to grow and grow before my eyes, as if it would explode.

With the main approach road, I could no longer see it as a whole, but only its sloping, rippled sides heading toward some top point of 836 meters. My heart beat had continued to increase and now, was almost fluttering. I could not imagine such awesome power and therefore, could understand its reign over the Aboriginal people. Who could be in its presence and not be affected? I knew I was, and would be even more so, within the next twenty-four hours.

New Transitions

Out of raw truth and revelations comes huge clarity.
Another new year can bring deeper meaning, if before
from lessons, you have built
a solid foundation for your new reality.

At some time, we've all been brought to our knees,
one way or another - ourselves or loved ones.
But if you're reading this, we're both still standing.
So . . . onward and upward, we keep going.

From unprecedented endings - undeniable crossroads,
I find myself untethered, floating in-between space.
This is sometimes magical and sometimes scary . . .
I know it's transition - a natural part of being here.

What is amazingly supportive, and encouraging during
such monumental personal changes, are the few things
you can truly count on . . .
like sunrises, sunsets, the seasons - and friends.

These continue to activate me, as they reset the
zero-point of unlimited possibilities.
We all seem to be facing similarities at this time,
because we are all One, and we are all connected.

Alice Parker

Chapter 4 ~ The Rocks

Almost like a spoiled child, I wanted the prize dangled before me. "Dean, can we stop for a few minutes for a photo, please."… I hesitated, knowing we were on a schedule. "Just on and off the bus, the weather is so perfect an all?" I'd already taken several shots, as the bus swept around the entrance road, but I wanted to feel the presence of being at 'its' feet, to look into the sandstone face. Up close now, the Rock had turned a rusty, rich brown and the moving stick-figures had become discernible into the actual people. They trudged single file up the well-worn, narrow path. Once several other people chimed in with my request for a quick photo stop, Dean gave in and pulled into the parking area.

"Five minutes, that's all we have or you won't have time for lunch." Not really annoyed, as he knew we were all more enthusiastic than most of his tour groups. It took several minutes just to set up what kind of shot I wanted. Up close, the Rock was almost too mammoth to focus and get the true perspective of its size. At the same time, my fascination ran wild at the subtle smoothness of the rock sides. They accentuated the rippled effect on the crevasses, and the streaks coming from the top. It all looked as if, icing or syrup had been dribbled over a huge, lumpy mound of chocolate pudding or pancakes!

The brilliant, unreal-blue sky, blotched with puffy white clouds, tinged by silver-blue shadows, could not have made a better contrasting backdrop, to nature's testimonial of creative design and primordial splendor. Turning to get back onto the bus, I noticed across the scarce scrub, some peach sort of bumps on the horizon, in the far distance which piqued more curiosity. All so new to me, like a first trip to an art gallery, featuring only unknown works.

As I saw Dean patiently waiting at the bus door, it dawned on me how neat and fresh looking he seemed in his uniform. His perfect attire of pale blue, short-sleeved shirt, colorful insignias, dark blue shorts, long white socks and spiffy white shoes. Most of us, on the other hand, looked already disheveled, as if we had been tramping through the desert by foot for hours. Dean had put down a straw mat for us to stamp off our feet, as the red dust stuck to everything and would stain our clothes, especially when wet with sweat.

Pulling away from the Rock, I felt temporarily satisfied, both in curiosity and spiritual contact, knowing I'd be returning soon to get better acquainted. Looking back, as we continued toward the resort area, I could not get over how almost innocent-looking the Rock appeared. I then thought with sections resembling a giant folded blanket, casually tossed over a hassock. 'Rocks' were not supposed to manifest themselves into something so soft and appealing. Perhaps, part of the illusion built into the attraction. It did not come off as 'dangerous,' but I knew especially deadly, to the easily distracted.

"Dean, are you going to tell us about the plaques, off to the side?" I was well aware of them, but sure very few other people were. He glanced over at me, as if me being a bit of a troublemaker, kind of raising an eyebrow and twisting his mouth a little. He had planned to talk about it, and this probably as good a time as any.

Slowly, and deliberately, he began to explain over the mic. "Some of you may have noticed the plaques, off to the side of where you climb up. This Rock is not to be taken lightly, and I know a lot of you are planning to make the ascent tomorrow … but … please if you are not a fit or active person, or have any kind of health problems, whatsoever, please do not attempt it." He gathered his thoughts, and continue in a more organized way. "The rule is … if you can't climb to the chain *on your own*, DON'T MAKE THE CLIMB!!!"

"Now the chain is to help you, as it does get rather vertical in spots, and very windy, especially this time of year. The chain covers about half of the climb, but it is not going to save your life, if you do something stupid - like let go of it to grab your sunglasses, hat, or camera, etc." He paused again to prepare them all for what he was about to say. "Over two dozen people have died on the Rock … from simply pushing themselves too much, or … not paying attention to where they are. A year and half or two years ago, a young Japanese man had reached the top safely … then just stepped off when he moved back to take a photo."

There was a gasp from many of the people on the bus, and the hushed crowd began to mumble. To me, the black humor of the situation I'd heard before, made me cover my mouth to keep from snickering. I'd heard several other travel accident stories, of the naive Japanese and their photo obsession. Dean continue to give warnings. "It's conservatively-estimated, over fifty people have died of stroke or heart failure within *forty-eight hours* of their climb or attempt. Please

… please, don't break my record …" he now tried to lighten up the subject. "I've never 'lost' a passenger, and I don't want to start with this tour!" A light, gallows laughter rose and died from the group. He'd done his job, this was no 'picnic in the park family hike.' "The plaques were put there by a few of the families of those who died."

Nigel, the New Zealander, then called out, and asked Dean if he'd ever climbed the Rock himself. "Yes, actually three times. I feel I should have the experience of all things I take you out on, and the company feels we can't talk about something, unless we've done it. I haven't done it for several years and, I think the trail is also getting a little slick, from all the people wearing down the sandstone. Of course, the rangers close it if it rains, like in the summer, or if it gets too windy, which again, happens this time of the year."

The British man from London, then asked if they'd ever had any problems, like with rowdies or misuse. Dean appeared a little taken aback by the question, but could understand, considering the 'hooligan' situation in London. "No, no. The only sort of problem for a while, the military using the Rock, as kind of an endurance test for its trainees. They got a little too competitive and were upsetting, … psychologically more than anything, to the tourists. These guys were 'running' up the Rock, or quickly climbing it several times in a row." He stopped to shake his head, and for the group to comprehend the physical endurance of it all. "By the way, the Guinness Record is something like ten minutes."

Jean then piped in with a crucial question. "Well, how long should it take, the average person to climb it?" There was obviously a part of her who wanted to know, just how much she should be expected to endure on this quest.

Dean chose his words carefully, as he did not want anyone pushing themselves. "If you go for the sunrise tour tomorrow, you will have somewhat over three hours. Most people can make the climb in two to three hours. You do need to pace yourself, as it takes *almost as long* to come down, as to go up. We will be leaving the area around eleven. A different bus and driver will probably take you … and people from other tours, out for the sunrise. Then, I will come later with those who only want to make a partial climb, or those who want to take the nature walk around part of the base. We will then drive to another area of the Rock, for more information about the Aboriginal 'Dreamtime' stories and history."

We were now pulling into the resort area, which was laid out like a small village, with marvelous splashes of flowers generously landscaped around tidy, sparsely covered grounds. Dean went into a perfunctory dissertation on schedule, and what to expect at our specific residences, as some were upscale Four Seasons, Sheraton and some the basic Red Centre Hotel. I'd taken the latter Red Centre, as I never saw the need for modern, expensive hotels, since rarely spent time there, but I did prefer the classic, older ones. Likewise, I'd signed for the discounted-single tour, which meant I was willing to share a twin room. Not that I preferred this kind of arrangement, though it tended sometimes to be an interesting experience. Often, there was not another single for me to share with, so I'd get the room to myself.

Only a handful of us left, when Dean pulled up in front of the modern, one-story building, with simple units surrounding the parking lot. It blended nicely with numerous, interspersed green bushes and remarkable flowering plants. I found it, quite pleasant and yet surprised how basic, yet lovely it was. As I waited my turn to check-in, I looked around at the simple lobby of souvenirs, postcards and a few chairs. After the extreme, ostentatiousness of most expensive, Japanese hotels, this was refreshing. Given directions to my room, and a map to accustom me to the whole complex of buildings and facilities at Yulara, I had much to check out. Extremely well laid out, for the full enjoyment of nature, while being capable of efficiently handling four thousand people per day, it amazed me.

Outside, walking on the burnt-orange dirt paths, created little puffs of red dust. Still, I had a tremendous sensation of feeling fresh and clean. Perhaps, the release to walk after so many hours on the bus, or maybe the uncluttered open atmosphere. Strolling around past the pool and large barbecue area, I quickly found my room, which was spaciously comfortable with a view to the open khaki-toned, arid scene. I easily realized without the Rock and the Olgas, this level land truly lacked any definition.

The large, unassuming dining room was adjacent to the swimming pool, which had three, ambitious children frolicking in and out of it. The buffet lunch was generous and reasonable, as I took a table for two. Then I saw the Azores cousins, so I smiled and waved to them. I wanted to see how comfortable they'd be for me to join them. They'd stopped to look at the menu, then went over to check-out the buffet, when Jean and Trudy had come in. I'd hesitated too long, for Jean called to them, and they were soon all gathered together at the same table. I suddenly felt like my insecurities were showing. But after some thought, I knew I'd adaptively cut-back on my forwardness with strangers, since living in Japan.

I went ahead and read through more of my informational material, as I ate, then took a closer look at the Aboriginal artwork lining the walls. With a few minutes left before being picked-up again, I walked around the grounds. Soaking up more of the tranquility and space, with Uluru - the Rock, controlling it all. I touched the leaves and flowers of one of the bushes - they felt almost fake, as they looked as if sprayed with plastic or something - when Jean approached me.

"You must like Japan, since you've been there over four years. What's it all like? I can't imagine living in the Far East." Quite direct, yet endearing in her query, so I felt

I'd respond the same, as I sometimes gauged my answer on how the questions were asked.

"Honestly, it's a love-hate relationship …or maybe just a strong dislike. I love the people, but dislike the society=government, so controlling them." I chuckled lightly. "You're never truly accepted, yet as a sensei - teacher, I'm totally respected." I smiled and looked her in the eyes, "Which some times, as you know being one yourself, is much more important." She listened intently, so I continued. "I teach only adults, so they're great students, and after so many years of 'never questioning the sensei' being ingrained, it can be quite a power surge. Which means, I have to choose my teachers carefully, so they don't take advantage of the situation, or mislead the naive students. Many of them have no idea about the real world, outside of Japan, or what foreign countries think of Japan. The sheltering-government and the media gives a rather diluted and edited version of everything. It's rather a shock to there systems, so I usually move slowly when introducing controversial topics. Then I don't get defensiveness from them, since it's quite conservative, where I live and teach."

I'd gone too deep, and Jean looked a bit bewildered at this incomprehensible information. The Brits, like Americans, had learned a long time ago, not to swallow all they were told. "I know they've got that group mentality, as we see so many of them clustered in tour groups in York," she acknowledged openly. "But, what is it like living there, on a daily basis? You know … shopping, the neighborhoods …" Like so many others, the dichotomy of the workaholic image, as compared with normal, daily functions seemed strange.

"Well,…" I started and shifted my tote bag to the other shoulder. Trudy and the cousins then joined us and were listening intently. "It's crowded, more than you can believe, polluted … though I'm in Nagoya, which is not nearly as bad as Tokyo or Osaka. But, it's efficient with superb public transportation and basically safe, though some gaijin - foreign women, have been accosted." I glanced around at the shock on their faces, for safety was a really big misconception about Japan. "I've been generally accepted in my little neighborhood, yet it took a long time. It helped greatly, my landlord is a doctor and quite international in his actions. Also, I teach his children, and others in the area English. But as I said, they're quite conservative … any where outside of Tokyo or Osaka is, about anything new or different."

Marta interjected, "What about shopping? I heard it was really expensive. Do you have all kinds of products?" This question, I always relished answering.

"Unless you shop at the international stores, which are really expensive - like four dollars for a packaged cake mix, it is a bit limited, but much better than four years ago. The fruits and vegetables are usually wrapped and uniform, like they are made of plastic, but its controlled growth by hydroponics and such. They cost three to four times more than the US or Australia. Beef is usually astronomical, from five to twenty-five dollars a pound, but chicken is more reasonable and it's usually cut-up … you can hardly get a whole chicken, then they're more expensive!" I looked over to Trudy, "I can't get lamb at my local, large supermarket, only at the international store and I love lamb!" The bus was approaching and the older couple from Brighton had joined us.

Trudy leaned over to say more quietly, "What are the Japanese men like? You work and teach them, don't you? The ones I saw in Melbourne always seemed so arrogant."

She was afraid of being offensive. I laughed out loud. "Arrogant! Boy, is that putting it mildly! It's a very sexist society … not the worst I've seen, and definitely improving … but not until more of the old farts die!" The bus stopped, and the others were boarding. I turned to add a little tidbit, I thought would amuse her. "They also happen to be the most sexually-frustrated society in the world, in my opinion … the men and the women. It's funny, but sad, too." I took a seat and watched as Trudy still had a amazed look on her face, when she peered at me, before taking her seat. For a first encounter, I divulged a few good insiders about Japan.

Dean swung the bus around back to the Sheraton, where he was supposed to pick up another ten people. There were several different large groups crowded on the sidewalk, and one was a group of middle-aged Japanese. Dean looked at his roster, and by this time many had flocked over to the bus. He'd barely opened the door, when several older Japanese men began to clamor into the bus. Dean quickly held out his hand to say, "Hold on there, I don't think this is your bus!" He was not only surprised, but rather adamant about the forward physical intrusion.

To me, the little Japanese man was almost a walking-cartoon character: his kangaroo decorated cap said, "I 'heart' Alice Springs," his clip-on sunglasses lifted-up, and the ubiquitous camera around his neck, over his pink Polo shirt, not matching his bright yellow and red plaid pants. With Dean's hand almost on his camera, the Japanese man said, "You go Ayers Rock," as more of a command, than a question

Dean's pleasant demeanor slipped away, while his patience worked to control any anger. "NO, we're going to Mt.Olga!" More calmly he added, "You have the wrong bus." At that point, the Japanese man barged ahead, not listening to what Dean said, simply wanting a seat.

"That OK, Olga OK, We go there, too." Dean quickly jumped up, and grabbed the man by the back of the shoulders, to stop him from going further down the aisle. Almost as if, once he was planted in a seat, Dean would not be able to dislodge him.

"PLEASE!!" Dean tried not to yell, "THIS IS NOT YOUR BUS!! YOU HAVE THE WRONG BUS!! As gently, but firmly as possible, he turned the man around to get him off the bus. By this time though, several more Japanese men had come up the steps and were proceeding in to get seats. Dean began to lose it, as the next Japanese actually tried to pass around them, as if they were simply blocking the aisle. "PLEASE! THIS IS NOT YOUR BUS!! YOU HAVE THE WRONG BUS!! YOU MUST GET OFF THE BUS!!" He now began to guide both men, and the woman behind him back, while another lady was attempting to step up into the bus.

I slouched down in my seat laughing hysterically, as I'd seen this kind of behavior many times before. I knew Dean could not imagine what was wrong with these people. The first Japanese man began speaking rapidly to the others, and from what I could pick-up, I knew Dean would hear about this, as the Japanese man had said, Dean did not *want them* on the bus.

Many other people on the bus were laughing, and several asked me what was said and why they had acted in such a way. "The male leader thinks he is always right, and if he makes mistake, he doesn't want to lose face by admitting it. So, he told the others, Dean did not *want them* on the bus, not that it *wasn't* their bus. They always follow a leader without question." I glued my nose to the window, to watch the three-ring circus taking place outside of the bus.

Once Dean finally got the Japanese to leave, he was surrounded with another mass of people trying to get on the bus. He obviously decided there were too many, so repeated his same lines: "This is not your bus! You have the wrong bus!" When they finally dispersed, he came back into the bus to get his roster. He shook his head and sighed, "I'm going to the travel desk to try to straighten this out. If I'm not back in five minutes, go ahead and leave without me!"

We all laughed, appreciating his chagrin. He filed back about five minutes later, with several of the second group he had chased away, but no Japanese. He checked-off each name as they boarded the bus, while they nodded and said 'Hello' to those of us seated. Quite an interesting mix of young and old, women and men. With considerable jabbering, an older, slim woman, with a large hat, tied down by a bright, pink scarf came up the steps, and down the aisle. Though she seemed to be talking to both the man in front of her, and the woman behind - stopping the procession of the others by doing so - she did appear to be alone. I hoped she'd not want to share my seat. The Spaniards in the back had moved around, and reorganized them- selves, so they were only taking up three seats, leaving plenty of room for the new arrivals.

Dean stood at the front of the aisle, waiting for everyone to get settled, … then for the chattering-woman to be quiet. She got perturbed when she realized, the whole bus was staring, for her to shut up, so Dean could speak. "Well, I'm such a deadhead, I didn't know he was waiting for me …" her voice finally trailed off. What an airhead, I thought. Just what Dean needed to add to his frustration.

Dean pasted a big smile on his face, as he began. "Thank you everyone for your patience, and understand … sometimes we have a little communication problem. I apologize for being rude to any of you, but I knew we were supposed to pick up *only* ten people, and I also knew none of your names were Japanese." He kind of rolled his eyes looking over in my direction, and grinned again before continuing. "All right, the agenda for this afternoon is: we are going to the Olgas, first stopping at the viewing platform, for the best shots of them as a group. Then we will drive on to them, to take a walk together in the 'Valley of the Winds.'" He took a relaxed breath.

"You will have plenty of time at the Olgas, before we head back over to Ayers Rock for the sunset. I will then return each of you to your respective abodes, to get a good nights' rest, especially if you plan to get up for the sunrise or the climb. I'll need a count on how many will do each, but we'll talk about it later. A quick count, then I'll give you some more history and Aboriginal legends, as we get on our way." He counted, shrugged his shoulders, and returned to his drivers seat, hoping some semblance of organization was back in his hands.

"The Aboriginals call Mount Olga, 'Kata Tjuta' because it means many heads. There are six major peaks and thirty minor domes, rising to 1,066 meters and covering twenty-four square kilometers, though from a distance they appear to be attached. The Oglas occupy the western part of Uluru National Park, and roughly bounded by Lasseter Highway and the Peterman Ranges. They were first sighted by Ernest Giles, from a high hill north of Lake

Amadeus in 1872, but not until 1873, did they actually approach the base. You may also be able to see rock-wallabies, dingoes, euros (a cross between a wallaby and a kangaroo), and even some red kangaroos, if we are lucky. Of course, the number of birds and reptiles are quite large." Dean continued on with more plant descriptions, and into some folklore.

Almost fifty-two kilometers of sun-tortured highways to the Olgas - the peachy bumps, I'd previously seen. We'd stopped at the viewing platform, which was about three-quarters of the way, to try to capture the full caliber of them. On the approach, I was mesmerized by this terra-cotta and, my acclimating to it all so readily. The green splotches were dotted with minute blurs of yellows, deep purples and wisps of white. I thought how I'd never look at brown, orange and red as ordinary colors any more, after seeing their magic-hues here.

The sun was dancing interesting colors and patterns across the lumpy-looking domes, and sharper, narrower cones. There were actually some purplish-tones from the cloud-shading, which would jump to a bright, almost 'safety' orange, day-glow, when the sun burst out. Some of the mounds were shaped more like cupolas, giving the rock a surrealist, cathedral-like appearance. Slowing to pull into the viewing area, the granite began to be transformed into gigantic, soft sculptures which in a reduced form, would be wonderful to have in one's house for lounging on.

The obvious millions of years of ice floes, torrential rains and the blasting, Antarctic Westerlies, had worn off their sharp edges, but could not destroy their unyielding primitivism. Engrossed in the protruding crags, which seemed to be expressing their individuality, I could almost see ancient faces, with the crevasses being the creases, and the striations making the wrinkles. There was no question, their 'live' power and influence, to every living thing within their purview.

I bounded out of the bus with renewed enthusiasm, for trying to watch the quintessence of the Olgas in my camera, but more importantly in my mind's eye. Into this ethereal space, stepped the Canadian man. "So, ah … Yank," which I knew he used superfluously, because the Aussies often said it. "Tell me what it's like to work for the bloody Japs!" My head snapped around to meet his eyes, and there was no way to hide my dislike, and now disdain, for this arrogant bastard. My classic choice, if *I* *chose* to heartily criticize the States, Japan and the Japanese, as I felt a right to, as I knew them and lived there. He thought his money and trendy clothes brought him class, and excused his sexism, but he still had no class in my eyes.

"They're not any worse, … and even a little better than some of the NORTH American bassturrdss!" I stretched out the Aussie slang, to let him know I was onto his game. "They respect age, as experience not like Westerners, who think younger is better. They have a much higher regard for an educational background, even to the extent of putting it on a pedestal, …especially one who has both, like myself." I paused to give him the full impact of my comment. "AND, I like it there!" Setting him up for my next punch, I added. "A clever and quick person, like myself, learns to play the game, then uses the system to their advantage. I think that's how all international business people succeed, don't you?"

The question was both rhetorical and personal, yet I had no interest in his response. "Now, if you'll excuse me, I was just about to '*get-off*' on some rocks." I turned and walked away, hearing him mumble some curses under his breath. I snickered with great pride, as I was sure no woman had ever answered him or dismissed him so succinctly before, as I did. And, I doubted I'd ever learn to control my tongue, when some one pushed the wrong buttons, with discrimination - prejudice next, after sexism.

The magnificent calming of the scenery, soon drained all of the anger out of my system, as I felt the heat pouring down, as well as coming up from the baked soil. After taking shots from several different angles, and capturing a few of the chameleon color changes, I strolled around the large viewing platform to get a closer look at a new, strange and lovely flowers.

There was a scrubby bush, which looked like long, pine- needled branches stuck in the ground and had yellow blooms bursting forth, with 'fingers' spreading out to worship the benevolent sky, for sun and hopefully, rain. In another area, was a very large, round bush with the tiniest of green leaves, decorated by even tinier, yellow flowers. I looked at it and smiled, feeling its pride for producing such micro-perfection, and tenacity for living in such an arid space, producing such amazing beauty.

Totally relaxed, I sauntered back toward the bus, and turned when I heard someone running down the ramp behind me. Marta came up to me a little breathless, still holding her hat on her head. "Excuse me, I forgot your name, I am sorry. Can we talk briefly, more?" I returned her smile, and noted what an earnest, pretty face she had.

"Sure. My name's Annie and your's again, I also forgot" We beamed at each other, as we continued to slowly walk down the ramp.

"Oh, it's Marta and my cousin's name is Kaylin." She turned to look, as Kaylin was about to catch up with us, to presumably join the discussion. "I wanted to know about the Japanese school system, because we hear about how much they attend classes and how well they do at the foreign universities. Is this true? How do they accomplish so much? Are they really that much smarter?" This educational curiosity belied a certain amount of envy, and maybe even insecurity, as if her people were not up to the same par.

We were now standing in the roadside dirt, out of the way of the coming and going of other tourists. I dug the toe of my hiking shoe into the red soil, which immediately created bright orange swirls of dust. "No, it's not really the truth, as statistics, which any scientist can tell you, can be manipulated." I wasn't sure how to go about this, or even how much she wanted to know. "Yeah, they go to school more days than most countries, but a lot of the time is wasted half-days, when they take the ridiculous placement tests over and over again. The kids learn by rote-memorization for each test, then promptly forget, so they can remember the next set of whatever is to be tested. Also, the schools always only show-off the top students, not the average."

Both of their heads were cocked, with quizzical looks covering their faces. "There is no interaction between the students and teacher. As a matter of fact, the students cannot ask the teacher any questions, as it's considered a waste of time, or even rude to question any validity of what the teacher has said. The kids are given a freer reign in grade school, but this is still strictly controlled behavior, with severe punishment. Things in the States, which would have them in court on a daily basis with lawsuits." There was now a bit of shock crossing Kaylin's face, while Marta showed a repulsive reaction.

"The real sadistic stuff comes in Junior High, which is three years long, and I think a lot of the male teachers especially, almost become dictators. Schools have a real problem with older boys bullying, because the male teachers allow it, and there has even been several kids killed. The competition becomes so keen, to get into the best Junior High and Senior High school, the kids lose all of their personal time and never get to be just kids." Jean had now joined us, and I stopped to explain, "Marta asked me about the educational system in Japan."

Jean looked at the cousins, who were sadly shaking their heads back and forth. "Anyway, almost all the kids have to go to 'jukus,' the private cram-schools, which cost a fortune and take up all of their time. These again, are strictly for passing the tests. I wonder sometimes how these kids learn anything, when all they do is study shit for tests. There is definitely no arts, creativity encouraged and complete ostracism for any individual or independent thought."

All three of them had looks of horror on their faces. "I know, I feel the same way, because it's what Western culture praises the most. Anyway, I haven't gotten to the best part. They are then so exhausted, by the time they make it to college or university, they get to play for the next four years. The gaijin I know, who teach at the universities, say it is such a joke. I mean they can't flunk the students, which they blatantly cheat off of one another and sleep in class. Most of the girls are raised to be airhead, or OLs, Japanese English for Office Ladies, meaning clerks who have no responsibility. They just serve tea, make photocopies and take care of the men in more ways than you want to know about."

Jean shook her head vigorously. "I don't understand. What about all of the students we always hear about being at the top of American Universities and even in London."

"Hey, there is no doubt about it, math and science is basic, as no personal thought is required, and the top students who've had extensive private tutoring, do well. But the Chinese and Taiwanese school systems are not as archaic as the Japanese. But most of these successful students, they must be on top, to get into the best school or they commit suicide - thousands, very sad, ... every Spring after exam results are posted."

Kaylin gasped at this, while the mouths of Marta and Jean dropped open. "Yeah, it's ridiculous. Most have learned so little about things we take for granted, because the educational system is like the white collar workers. They put the time in, but it's fruitless paper- pushing and ineffective. To top it all off, these poor kids end up social-cripples, as they've never had a chance for interaction or socializing. Most still end up with arranged marriage, loveless relationships."

"Really, this day and age?" questioned Marta, "How pitiful." "But, Annie, it doesn't make sense. How can they be so ... so successful?!?" Jean raised her hands in un-acceptance of the obvious irony. "They're practically running the world with their products - cars, TVs, VCRs. You've got to acknowledge that."

I laughed loudly. "Nobody knows it better than I do. I used to teach at Toyota, and the only real efficiency in the country is in manufacturing. They learn to do *one thing* well, then they do it over and over again, perfectly. They do what they are told, they do not question and they know, they will be extensively punished for making a mistake. It all comes from the school system, which turns out these human-robots to begin with." I paused to let it be absorbed, and noticed Dean was starting to gather people back on the bus.

"The good news is, the more foreigners come into the country, Japan is slowly opening up. Things are changing, they're traveling more, even if in small groups, though still rarely in pairs or on their own. And, once they've had home-stays or even a semester of school abroad, they can see how the Western world lives. We have personal choice, not always waiting to be told what to do or think." I turned and started heading for the bus, as I continued the saga. "Even in the four years I've been there, I've seen a tremendous number of little changes. There's always hope, because they're not stupid, and the young ones certainly don't want to live the horrible, almost indentured life of their parents. But the system is so embedded in them, and the ones in power, certainly don't want it changed. Only, if this recession continues, they'll have to."

Dean greeted each of us, and asked how we enjoyed the view. We all enthusiastically responded to our relishing the environment. I trotted to my seat, and noticed how the others had gotten back to the talk of Japan. It never ceased to amaze, how the media and other powers of influence, could sway our beliefs about some people. There was nothing like traveling to or living in a country, to bust those little bubbles or misconceptions. Nothing and nobody ever really were as they portrayed. I looked out the window, to search the gigantic enigma for some answers, as to what it was all about. It was silent and secret. Funny, I thought, *I was expecting answers, and not even sure what the questions were.*

Dean brought me back to the present, with more of his fascinating information about the area, and some of the special meaning of Kata Tjuta had for the Aboriginal people. He talked about the wondrous and dangerous *spinifex* grass. I tried to imagine how these native people had learned to live so well, with what little they had been given. The spinifex could cut like a razor, yet they learned how to use it to build their original houses or *wurleys.* It produced a substance, too, they could use like a glue and sealer, which had unlimited potential. The ingenuity and creativity these people had used, for not only living off the land, but in total compatibility with the land, never ceased to amaze me.

The approach to the Valley of the Winds lay magnificently before us. The softly curved mounds of rock, actually had a sensual appeal, a yearning, almost to be touched. Serrated streaks circumscribed around many of the tumulus rises. This made them look as if, they had been cut and stacked upon one another, sometimes rather haphazardly. Before exiting, Dean reminded us of our allotted time, since Ayers sunset was next. And, to stay on the path, as the surround area was quite rough and rocky-strewn. Anxious to have this physical presence, I further soaked-up some of the legendary mystique. But then, I could not get past a beguiling spray of pink-tinge on a flowery bush. Trudy came up behind, as I bent down to get an even closer look to shoot them.

"Lovely, aren't they?" She chirped, in a much perkier mood, "Amazing how they can survive at all, much less produce so many flowers." She slowly bent down to get a better look.

"They're about the same color as the Cherry Blossoms in Japan," I said, when I looked at her. "The Japanese worship them, and have wonderful festivals in the spring to celebrate their blooming, which is called Sakura. It's always a great time, because we all go to the parks, sit under the Cherry Blossoms, eat traditional food, drink a lot and sing into the night. Nobody is considered a stranger, or unwelcome. It's marvelous!" Trudy's face was covered by confusion, as she did not comprehend my mixed emotions concerning Japan.

"Gee," she said, not knowing how to respond. "That sounds like a lot of fun. We don't have anything like that in Melbourne."

I stood up and laughed. "No, we do't have anything like that in the States either. That's one of the joys of living in a foreign culture. You experience many different things." We stopped to look at some Desert Peas, which were darling, little, wine-colored flowers with black eyes. Not too far away, more bushes with bright white blossoms seemed to brag, at their daring life.

The Valley loomed ahead of us, and we talked about Melbourne and Japan for a few more minutes, until the dominating omnipotence commanded our attention and silence. I leaned back to try and see the top of the pockmarked granite walls, black stained from rain water draining down. Trudy and I wandered apart to consume it all independently. Further into the the Valley, a whistling-wind began crying, as it whipped around and between the rock faces, curves and recesses. Like everything else in nature, it had its own native beauty, its own properties of dance. In my mind, I could hear the rhythmic drone of the Aborigine didgeridoo - a hollowed-out tree limb - which was played by blowing into it. I heard it played and demonstrated a few times, but it was a sound one could never forget. I found a rock, just right to sit on. It put me in the middle of it all, and there I perched for some time, quite intoxicated by my inner-spiritual renewal fed, from some psychic amplifiers going off in my head.

"ANNIE!... ANNIE! ... Annie!" Trudy was walking toward me, and calling my name, until I turned to acknowledge her. "We've got to get going back, it's almost time." She looked at me, as if she was not sure what she was seeing.

"Oh, Yeah. I guess I kind of zonked-out with all this …" I did not know what to say, so she'd not think I'd totally freaked. "Magnificence!" I smiled, as I got up and we started back at a faster clip, so we'd not be late. We passed by the Spaniards, who were having a great time posing one another precariously, on some giant rocks, with the massive domes as a backdrop. Each to their own, as to how we experienced the place. I thought critically, more original than Japanese who formally posed in front of a famous sign of a place, and never smiled, since it was frivolous.

When I looked back, deep purplish hues were now draped over the shadows, as the sun receded to the horizon. The sections of moss had bravely climbed up a few sides, and looked a very, eerie-green now. It looked like a squashed Earth, reaching its hands up to hold off pressure forced upon it. Suddenly, I began to feel a growing trepidation going through me, and a cold chill went down my spine. The words of the clairvoyant popped back into my head about my being in danger. An involuntary jerk went through my shoulders, reacting to a fear of the unknown.

"What's wrong?" Trudy innocently asked. "You getting cold?"

I smiled kind of shyly, back up at her. "Yeah, it's getting chilly. I'm going to have to put on my jacket for the sunset." I tried to reinvigorate myself, and clear my mind, as I did not know where all of this came from. "I'm really excited, this has been fantastic. I'm kind of a sunset buff, and this one should be spectacular."

Trudy looked around at the sky, which had been clouding up more and more. "I don't know. These clouds might get too thick. We could lose our luck on this one."

I immediately jumped on the chance to push the positive. "Oh, no. I'm sure it'll clear in time, and sometimes the best ones are with the cloud streaks. It'll be OK." I was beaming my best Crusader Rabbit - Pollyanna smile. Dean was watching a group of Japanese when we walked up, and I stopped to laugh at him. "Don't try to figure them out. I live with them, and I still get surprised, shocked and angry on a regular basis." He looked at me shaking his head.

"You know, I've been doing this job over twenty years and toured around people from just about every country, but they 'stuff it up' somehow every time, I've had to deal with them." He turned back to look at me. "How do they even deal with each other?"

I put on my most serious look and leaned over, as if to whisper some deep, dark secret. "Zen, you know, Zen Buddhism. It's the only thing that works." He looked at me, as if I had totally gone over the edge, then I cracked-up laughing.

He finally caught on, I had pulled his leg. First he smirked then he laughed. "Get on the bus before I leave you behind with them!"

I settled again into my seat and continued to study the Olgas. They were haunting, and something I'd not soon forget. They grew more and more purple as we drove away. I closed my eyes, and my mind started to play the Aboriginal music again in my head. This time, I could hear the clapping sticks, too, and I began to keep the beat with my thumb on my tote bag. I dozed several minutes, and rather surprised to wake to so many buses and cars parked around, at the sunset viewing spot. Dean pointed out some of the best spots to catch those magic rays, but he

was not holding out for a good one, as the clouds

had really backed up. I could not resist throwing him another jibe, as I jumped down on the dirt and puffed up red dust toward his perfectly white socks. "Mother Nature will NOT disappoint ME, because she knows how important this sunset is to me." I knew he could not resist my devilish smile, or the challenge.

He looked down at the dust settling on his shoes and tried to sound sarcastic, "And, just how do you know that? You have a direct line, or something?"

"Of course! Woman to Woman!" I waved my hand lightly, "You men just wouldn't understand."

He laughed, as he turned to help one of the little old ladies off the bus, and I tramped up a slight incline in search of the best spot. A group of about twenty people having beer and wine, with all the accouterments, including a waiter serving them. They had no idea how funny they looked, trying to bring the British-civility to the Outback. But, they were no stranger than the numerous people, who had chosen to *stay on their buses* to watch a once in a lifetime sunset. To me, you might as well stay home and look at postcards, as sunsets in a flat land like this, tend to affect the whole sky, with 360 degree around and 180 degrees above.

I reached the highest point on the small slope, and stepped up on one of the wooden posts, which lined the paved road area. Some thin cable connecting the posts, was to keep people out of the natural growing tract. There was not enough room for both of my big feet, so while I had time, I figured out how to balance myself, focus and shoot, without falling on my face. As the sun would be sinking behind the Olgas, I wanted to be able to get both of them into the picture, albeit separately. Several people had followed me, as they had noticed I was rather ardent in my photographing, and were also trying to copy my 'post-standing trick.' They soon found it was not easy, but for the Spaniards, it was another game to pass time and have fun with each other. They were a stitch, and made me laugh until I lost my balance.

We were all just killing time and hoping the clouds would split, at the last precious moment to reveal the magic. One of the small mini- buses, with a load of people, who'd chosen to never even disembark, revved-up its engine and pulled away, in a flurry of disgust. I could not help chuckling. They were barely down the road and rounding the bend, when the clouds began to part, as a golden sun broke through the silver, gray-blue sky. I started jumping up and down while pointing to the revelation. "WE'RE GOING TO HAVE A SUNSET! LOOK!

LOOK! I TOLD YOU SO! TOLD YOU SO!" Dean heard me and waved, as he'd probably seen a thousand of these, but the others stopped to look over their shoulders in amazement.

I climbed up on my post, to continued to swing my head back and forth, from the Olgas to the Rock, getting almost breathless with excitement, at the impending event. From the Olgas, the blues moved into a rosy-purple, layered perfectly by the clouds, so it looked like watercolor- washes. On the Rock, a dusky-purple crept up over the peachy-orange, with the intensities of each increasing, with every second of the dropping sun. With my camera clicking, first one way then the next, I could follow the progression of both, as if I were recording it for posterity.

Sunsets last an incredibly long time in the desert, and this one was no exception. As we drove back, the sky was glowing from the bright orange to a rich gold, then fading into a peach-mauve and finally dusty-rose haze. The Olgas and the Rock had taken on a dark blue and velvet-black silhouette outline, making their last statements a powerful one.

We were all rather excited and moved by the occurrence, so the bus was quite noisy on our return to Yulara. Dean gave us a few minutes to vent our adulations of nature, then he reminded us we needed to inform him of our schedule, for the big day tomorrow - sunrise, the climb, and the walk. He said we also needed to order our breakfast pack, if we were going to the sunrise, as the restaurant would not be open at four o'clock in the morning. Lastly, he strongly suggested we all get a good night's sleep. So soon, each of our groups would trundle-off to their respective beds. I personally could not wait to hit a nice, hot shower before dinner, for I had sweated as often as I'd been chilled.

Pitch black at our little hotel, beyond the small lights and a slight breeze, laced with a definite cold character. I dressed warmly following the refreshing shower, and went out hunting for food, with a stomach growling from all the exercise. I stopped to order my breakfast pack at the restaurant, and did not see anyone I knew in there. I'd decided to forsake the dinner buffet for a barbecue, I'd seen posted. With a choice of beef, chicken or kangaroo, I chose the last, as I'd not had it before. I loaded up on salads, while I waited, taking a large picnic table in the corner, hoping someone might come in to join me. The barbecue had been set up in a large tent, and I had to admit, while I sat there in my jacket, it was getting colder by the minute. Most everyone else must have opted for the restaurant, or gone to another place into the resort center.

Between my hunger and the cold, I was eating quickly, then jumped up to get my kangaroo steak when they called my number. I grabbed some more salad, and dessert before returning to the table, only to find the Canadian's wife and daughters had planted themselves at it. I did not need this kind of aggravation, and felt in a quandary, because many of the other tables had now filled up. As I returned, I moved my wine and glass to the other end, giving polite, but obvious, limited greetings to them. Hopefully, I'd finish before he joined them, for I had no real dislike of them. She got the girls up to get their salads, and order their meat, returning several minutes later. I'd dug another brochure out of my bag to occupy myself, as I ate. There was an optional flight from Ayers Rock to Kings Canyon, I seriously considered, as Dean had given it fantastic endorsements.

"Is your husband in Japan with you?" she inquired, after a few moments of talk with her daughters. She'd obviously noticed the gold- petaled ring, I wore on my left hand for camouflage from bothersome men. Not sure if she felt the necessity to make polite conversation or what, but I decided to answer directly.

"No, not any more. He couldn't handle Japan or my success there." I smiled trying not to be too sarcastic, but she was obviously stunned by the answer. "Toronto's a lovely city, I've been there a couple of times on business." I waited, then decided to plunge ahead, as disarmingly as possible. "And, what do you do?"

"Do?" She looked up a little surprised, "Oh, you mean a job? Oh, I'm a housewife, you know. I just keep busy with the house, and I have a flower garden … and a few vegetables." She tried to smile, then looked back at her food to continue eating. I knew she was uncomfortable, so I dropped it and went back to my flight brochure. "I did work, though," she unexpectedly spoke again. "I used to teach grade school, before the girls were born ... quite rewarding.." Now pleased with herself, she ate a little more vigorously. I knew it bothered her, or she would not have brought it up, to justify herself.

"When do you plan on going back, since you enjoyed it so?" Not trying to rescue her, but I thought a little awareness never hurt. Truthfully, though, I just could not handle a woman limiting herself, when she was capable of so much more.

"Oh, ... I doubt I'd go back ... I mean I am busy with the girls
... and such." She was not sure rather to go on or not, but I'd opened the door. "Well, we don't need the money now, of course, like when we were first married." To her this seemed the best answer.

I lightly laughed. "Well, most women today,... don't always work *just for the money*. Especially, when they've gotten older." I did not want to really embarrass her, so I lightly laughed again. "I guess I'm just a workaholic. It's why I get along with the Japanese so well."

I guess she now wanted to end the discussion, so she added, "It's just George doesn't want me to work. He wants me to be home for him and the girls ..." Unfortunately, at that precipitous moment, *George* appeared with a look on his face directed at me, which suggested she'd been consorting with the enemy. Or, I'd been doing an instant brain-washing on her. I did not want a showdown and embarrass the others, so I returned to finish off my dinner. His look had not gone unnoticed, though she was quite puzzled by it.

"Thank you, Dear," she said "for ordering the breakfast packs. I ordered your steak. They have a very nice selection of salads over there to choose from." I could not help but notice the change in her voice, from normal to *'sweetness and light.'* It gnawingly reminded me of the educated, intelligent, Japanese women who turned into young, simpletons girls, the instant a man, especially a Japanese man, entered the conversation. It riled me to the point of screaming.

"Did you tell them to be sure it's medium rare? You know, I won't eat it overcooked." His snappy, condescending attitude was ruining my delicious dinner, so I hurried to finish the last of it and get away before I really said something nasty."Yes, Dear, I did. Did you want me to check?"

I could not believer it, her voice had gotten even sweeter. *"Any moment"* I thought, *'we're all going to gag and die from the sugar over-load!"* I gulped down my wine and began to gather up my things without eating the last of my desert.

"No, that's OK," he whined, "I'll check myself when I get the salad. I knew we should have gone over to the Sheraton." He turned and walked up to the cooking table. I picked up my plates and trash in order to throw them into the garbage can, not far from the table.

I stepped back to grab my bag. "Good luck!" I said. I knew she did not get it, but I could not help myself for saying it. Had to be the Scorpio in me! "Have a nice time tomorrow, girls." I looked back at her, and her eyes appeared almost watery to me, but I thought, *"Maybe it's the glow from the kerosene lamps."*

She stared straight at me, with the most piteous-face

and said, "Thank you." I nodded, turned and left, as George was returning to the table. I'd been in her shoes more than once, but thank God, I no longer was, and with any courage at all, I never would be again.

Out in the briskly, cold night, I felt tears well-up in my own eyes. I quickly walked to the far corner of the parking lot, to get in touch with my own feelings. I searched for solace in the silvery moon, with the enhancing, light-show of nuggets casually tossed and strewn across the Southern Hemisphere. *Maybe this time, I was not traveling for the true experience of it, or a new culture to explore. Was I just trying to get away from who I had been, and what I had come through, to find who I was? In some ways, I had wanted to go anywhere, I did not have to stop and examine my life. Probably, not slowly running away, but literally flying as fast as I could!*

I had so many things, I wanted to tell, or even scream at the sad woman, so she'd see. Things, … poems I'd written for and to myself, even before Travis had finally left. I'd wanted him out of my life, so badly. But, totally paralyzed by the lie, I'd lived for so long. *There was an emotional price, which we usually had to pay, even when we bear- false-witness against ourselves. We must separate ourselves from the other person - recognizing what it was and what was good. For too long, I'd thought emotional satisfaction came only from making another person happy, so I never truly was satisfied within myself.*

I'd have liked to have taken the woman and shaken her to say, "No one is ever truly, 100% victim. We must take responsibility, as to our own contribution to our position. It is not stoicism, but shallowness, or even settling, accepting what we think we deserve. It keeps a person in a non-productive relationship." I breathed deeply, knowing I'd learned. We fulfill our needs either directly through choice, or indirectly through allowing fate. Likewise, we 'do' what we are meant to do in the same way - which includes all the failures, until we've had enough.

Unfortunately, sometimes mistakes were the only way, us hard- headed ones learned. I walked back to put myself to bed, without even turning on the television. I knew sleep would not come easily, but it would be delayed now, because my anticipation was leaping from one thing to the next, for tomorrow's big day.

My four o'clock wake-up call came in an instant, and I dressed methodically, checking everything I thought I'd need. Though it was quite chilly, I decided to dress for the warmer, sunny weather, as I expected to be generating a lot of perspiration with the climb. I slipped my thin, India-cotton shirt-jacket over my long-sleeved T-shirt, and packed away my heavier jacket. The bags had to be ready to go this morning, since we were checking out.

I rechecked my tote bag once again, and it felt like four-kilos, as I slung it over my shoulder, grabbed my red bag, and headed out the door. The cold blasted me unexpectedly, and almost took my breath away, as I headed for the lights of the lobby to check out, and get my breakfast pack. In twos and threes, more people finally dribbled into the lobby, complaining about the cold, and hoping it would be worth the effort. We had barely all collected, when the bus pulled up.

I intently watched the sky, for any alterations from the silky- black to a rich, dark, iridescent gray. It happened gradually, like the resurgence of my spirit. Then, memories appeared of so many other dawns, I'd risen to especially meet in other corners of the world. Thailand, Mexico, China and numerous places throughout the States. I chuckled, as I remembered the Grand Canyon with my son, David, and how he complained about the hour, then threw his arms around me with 'thanks,' after the awe-inspiring moment. Beginnings, and endings of a day should be appreciated, when we stop to think of how few we truly are given.

The sunrise spot had fewer buses than the sunset, and most everyone dragged getting off, then securing their photo place. It took me a while to find one just right, as the bushes were a bit higher. This time I wanted to get both the Rock and the Olgas together in the shots, when possible. I plunked down on a fence post, opened my breakfast pack - an apple, a plain roll, some fruit yogurt and a napkin. "Gee," I thought, " a clever person could do a land-office business here, selling hot coffee and tea. Sometimes these Aussies aren't very capitalistic!"

Facing the East, and my back to the Rock, I could keep an eye on the encroaching dawn. Marta sauntered over, followed by Kaylin, as we chatted about the Azores, and nibbled our food. A few more buses and cars bravely joined the wait, as the cloudy sky got lighter. I did not see any trash containers, so I stashed the box into my bag. Jean stopped by, as she prepared to stake out her photo spot. A nervous energy vibrated out of her, which had nothing to do with sunrise.

Several people started scurrying down the road, while others started calling out about something occurring in that direction. I left my bag to reserve my post, as it had actually become crowded, and we walked over to see what the excitement was about. Some kind of creature was walking through the group, sticking its head out looking for food. It took me a minute to realize it was an emu. Many people were now dashing up to it, taking it's picture and the bird calmly accepted it all, as it checked out their hands for something to eat.

I ran back to my bag, where I'd put most of the roll and apple core. I noticed, too, the sky was turning rosy and the sun was liable to pop up at any second. Still, I was busy trying to feed and photo this stupid bird. For several minutes, I turned into a three-ring-circus trying to toss crumbs and focus my camera at the same time. Everyone else was getting great shots of the damn bird, while I fed it, but I could not get it to cooperate and hold still for me. After several half-ass clicks, I tossed the apple at it, and returned to ascend my post to start recording the sunrise, which had no intention of waiting for us.

A golden glow now filled the sky, as shades of pink rippled across the clouds. Ayers Rock became alive, as the golden-orange took over for the rusty brown. Off in the distance, the Olgas appeared to be giant, bright pink and purple, lumpy conglomerates. Again, turning back and forth, I caught the mauve brush-stroked clouds scattered across the glowing heaven, as the sun erupted in all of its brilliance. Every scar, crease and indent in Ayers was now easily evidenced from the blasting raw light.

The Olgas grew too, respectively, as the high mounds were defined in a brighter pink, by the rising beams. At times, even us novices could see how the external world had naturally burst forth, from the Aboriginal Dreamtime creations, the cherished sanctity of it all. The glory of the day was finally in full swing, and we took our time returning to the bus, for the short ride over to the hiking entrance.

Those of us making the climb, once again gave our names and exited the bus, only to be hit by unbelievable winds. *"Shit,"* I thought, *"the Westerlies from Antarctica have returned, and I don't have my jacket! Is this a Freudian-slip or what?"* Trudy suggested we use the solar toilets before our attempt, and I was more than willing for any excuse to put off freezing. Jean ran ahead of us, and the cousins trailed behind. I looked around to see about a dozen or so people from our group. "They're bringing out another bus for more climbers, aren't they?" I held my shirt tightly around me.

"Yeah, I think so," Trudy looked at her watch. "I think around eight or eight-thirty." Almost seven-thirty, when I glanced at mine, too.

Jean came out of the toilet and took a deep breath. "Well, we all set to go?" She had a red sweater over her sweatshirt, and I saw she had another layer under it. But, I figured the wind wouldn't bothered her anyway, with her emotional excitement to keep her warm.

I looked at Trudy and she gestured with a shrug, whatever, and I said, "I kind of hope it warms up, as the sun gets higher. I didn't dress warm enough for this cold, blustery wind."

Jean was not to be put off, and she'd do this with or without our support. She smiled and lightly said, "OK, I'll either see you at the top, or catch you on my way down. Good Luck!"

As we watched her bound-off, without looking back, Trudy shook her head. "Boy, she's really determined about this." She turned and looked at me, "I want to climb it, but I'm not going to kill myself or something doing it, or if I don't., … It's not *that big* a deal." She looked at me, and I gestured for her to go ahead into the toilet. I'd not thought about not climbing it, as I really wanted to do it as an accomplishment. As another lady came out, I went in thinking, *"I'll just play this by ear, and go with the situation."*

Trudy was waiting for me down by the entrance, and we both walked up to the start of the track. There were now a few cars and buses, with the procession starting like some kind of weird traditional ritual, not quite a religious thing, such as going to Lourdes or Mecca. As we walked quietly, I wondered what made people want to climb a 'rock,' not just this one. There were no trees or bushes, flowers or even little animals to see or discover. What was the purpose, the reason? Had we brought into the PR bullshit, 'because it was *There*?'

The wind gusted around me again. I tugged at my shirt even harder. Trudy had walked a few steps ahead and could sense my hesitation, so she called 'good luck' and went on. I did not want this to be anti-climatic. I could do this. I knew I could do this.

Almost Always Counts

To attempt the climb, but not make it -- lessens neither
the mountain nor the climber. The mountain
will always be there, and the climber better prepared.

To attempt love -
and be alone in your falling does not break the fall,
or lessen the love.

The hope of love shall always be there,
not as an impossible dream,
but the practical illusion that it is.

To attempt life,
is to live every day to its fullest. For only existing,
is not really trying.

Almost always counts in life, for we are not perfect,
nor is the world. Experience is the reward,
and the force which makes us keep going.

Alice Parker

Chapter 5 - To Climb the Rock

I followed the path to the base, and looked up. With my binoculars, I spotted Jean moving up the chain. There were a few people ahead of her and fewer behind. People were scattered all over the Rock base, trying to get their footing against the intermittent gales, to make it to the prerequisite, the first chain post. I could see quite a group huddled, at some side rocks about half way to the chain. Just remaining at the base spot with my binocs, I could have had quite a captivating time watching the foibles of those trying to overcome them. *Was I afraid, lazy or just in more of a mood to be a voyeur, in one of the most classic of people 'testing' themselves against nature?*

"My wife got some sand in her contacts," the Brighton man surprised me, as I again stared into my binocs. He looked concerned. "We won't be able to go, how about you?" I smiled and pulled at my shirt again, as if keeping it tighter around me kept me warmer.

"Yeah, I was just about to start. Pretty entertaining, though, just watching them all." I put the binoculars away and snapped up my bag. "OK, I'll see you later." I started the climb, but was soon down on all fours, like so many other people, I'd seen doing to struggle up. My big tote bag had turned into a sail with each blast of wind, which I could see would be a hinderance. I tried to head for the rocks off to the side, where several were still waiting out the gales.

The Rock was rough on the hands, but slippery under the feet, as the thousands of climbers had worn quite a path, about a meter on either side of the chain all the way up. I began to laugh, as I thought of how lovely and feminine I must look from behind. My ass stuck up in the air, while I crawled and dragged my bag up this stupid rock. Somehow, all the magnificence it had from a distance, was lost in this too close of an encounter. I thought of the irony of the Aborigines, for they were never interested in climbing the Rock, to prove manhood or strength. They felt too much respect for it, and such a desecration was taboo, all those thousands of years it had been their sole possession.

I finally made it to the empty enclave of rocks, and ensconced myself away from the wind, as much as possible. I looked out at the view, and actually got some pleasure at the sight of the Olgas, glowing still pink and purple in the distance. Quite a few people came and went, recouping in the rocks then attacking with new vigor. I thought, *"What a great place to do a study - anthropology, or sociology, or even psychology of people."* I wished I had a pad and pencil or tape recorder to interview the parade, which passed me by. Some tried to make polite talk or converse, and others just wheezed and gasped, leaving once they had gotten some regular breathing back. To many of them I wanted to say, *"It's all right, you don't have to do this. No one's taking a survey or checking on your success."* To say I saw heart attacks in the making, was putting it mildly.

"This should be some fun," I thought, *"here comes a Japanese couple."* He was dressed in the *expected outfit* of an Alps-trekker, with full, high, hiking boots, rope and all. She had a jacket over her Ralph Lauren sportswear, carrying a Louis Vuitton bag, and wearing bright pink Nike shoes. I thought it would surprise them to have someone like me, perched up on Ayers Rock, speak Japanese to them, With a big smile on my face, I said,

"Ohayo gozaimasu," - Good morning,' followed by, "Genki desu ka?" - asking how he was.

"Uh, Agh?!?" The man uttered, and almost fell over backwards from the shock. I tried to keep from laughing, as I'd not meant to scare him. By the time the woman pulled herself into the rocky semi-circle, we had a regular conversation going, with me telling him I was from Nagoya - again a great shock, and him saying Shizuoka. Which when I informed him I had visited - doubled the shock again.

The conversation stumbled on for another five minutes, then the man decided to take some photos, which ended with several shots with me. In the usual Japanese manner, we would now be 'life-long friends,' and he wanted my card to send copies to me. I pretended I did not have any on me, with great regret, and they started to leave. I wished them "Gambatte," - a special good luck. They then profusely thanked me again, as the full rituals finished.

The wind calmed a little, getting tired of the game, I proceeded to stash my bag in between the rocks and go for it. I could see the first chain post, maybe fifty meters ahead, but reaching it was one of the scariest experiences of my life. The wind felt like it purposely beat me down, repeatedly moving only inches forward. Once I reached the chain, I grabbed it like a lifeline, and ploddingly began to pull my way up the side. There was no way I'd let go of the chain, as I slid one hand over the other, in my slow progress. I'd make other, faster, more agile people go around me.

Then, I'd get into some strange maneuvers, when I came head to head with someone, as frightened or clumsy as me. When the wind churned up again, I'd just sit down, holding onto the chain with both hands, and not let go for anything. It was so cold, my nipples actually hurt, from being hard so long. *I tried to laugh, telling myself this was the most excited they'd been in over a year!*

No idea how long it took me, but I finally made it to a large indented dip in the wall. I cautiously slid under the chain, and checked my footing before letting go of the chain and settling against the granite. I looked over the view, which to my surprise had not change much … only higher. I tucked my arms around, to put my hands under my armpits for warmth and protection. I'd been there about five or ten minutes when Trudy came down and joined me.

"No, enough Annie, you DO get obsessive sometimes. This has nothing to do with age, weight or showing your independence and survival without Travis. You are fine! You are OK! I love you!" I got tears in my eyes, as I realize what I sometimes did to myself. A great one for championing other people, but, I often didn't champion my own. I pulled myself up and started the descent. Somehow, still aware of the danger, I knew the fear was gone. Well, the old Rock was good for something - she'd given me an extra dose of self-confidence, and I'd not even been aware of how much I had needed it.

Very slowly and very surely, as I certainly did not want to become a statistic, much less a mess at the bottom of the Rock, I headed downward, never letting go of the chain. I barely looked up at the approaching *hoy polloy,* now increasing in numbers, trying to make their mark some where. Releasing the chain cautiously, like the lifesaver it was, I scooted on my bottom back to the cluster of rocks, where I'd sequestered myself before. Regaining my composure, I decided to once again 'people watch' the parade of parodies.

For every young, fit and agile climber, there must have been three who'd not had the same lecture, we had from Dean about safety and health. A group of three in front of me, was an excellent example. They were what most Aussies referred to as *'ockers,'* loud, rambunctious, wanna-be jocks, in their late twenties or early thirties. Each carrying a six pack of beer, and chiding each other on, not to be weak or wimpy. I thought the beer may keep them warm, while helping to support their bravery. But, I wondered if they'd considered what it might do to their balance or equilibrium. Or, even more with the peer pressure, their decisions-making abilities on the top. Likewise, would they be responsible enough, to carry the empties back down? Such drinking antics would not have been allowed in the U.S. National Park, and I began to look around for a Park Ranger, as I'd thought they protected the sight. I also was curious as to how strong the wind had to be, before they did close the Rock.

Soon distracted by three young Japanese women, perhaps eighteen to twenty, and I kept laughing. I'd seen this scene many times in the countryside of Japan. They were dressed in mini-skirts, panty- hose and dress shoes, with little heels which matched their little mini purses, with long shoulder straps. With each slip or gust of wind, they giggled, yelped or trilled in shrieks. I wanted to take their photo, but then I decided most of my friends back in Japan would not have been surprised. And, those out of Japan, would not have believed it had been taken at Ayers Rock, as no one could ever be that stupid. I thought they were going to join me, and I began to prepare what Japanese I'd say to them. Then, like bowling pins, one after the other, they just kind of plopped down as they uttered frustrations - "Sugoi!" "Yada!" "Shingirarenai!" They were better than Keystone Cops!

With it all, I really laughed, then called out to them, "Daijobu?"- asking if they were all right. A bit surprised at first, they each answered, "Yes, and thank you." I watched them for some time, as they just sat there. Amazed, I thought how sad, they had not even known how to dress for climbing the Rock. Their lack of awareness and not checking information out, always stunned me. I then looked down at myself huddled, with my lightweight clothes on and laughed again. I really did know how to criticize, too quickly.

The family now tromping up in precision, looked like a bunch of health-nuts or fitness- freaks. The little boy and girl, maybe four and severn, had hats, backpacks and very sturdy looking shoes. The tall, slim father carried a baby, perhaps a year old, in a back carrier, while the mother's backpack also seemed stuffed. It all appeared to be more of a military drill, than an outing of fun, as the father turned to verbally prep the children, probably for the umpteenth time.

How many of the children I'd seen, I wondered, would ever notice the contrasting beauty of the pale lavender Olgas in the distance, or the formidable presence of the granite under their little feet? Had they been given any nature lessons, or told any Aboriginal myths to bring more meaning to this trek? It all reminded me much too harshly, of the numerous families who traveled to the Grand Canyon, the Painted Desert or Petrified Forest in the States and spent a 'whole' twenty minutes absorbing all their glory.

I decided I'd seen enough of the disrespectful, the mobile health hazards and the ridiculous others pounding up the old Rock face. I caught sight of Trudy and several of our tour members starting the hike around part of the base. I scrambled down carefully and ran to catch up with them, as I thought this prelude could be quite experiential after all. The winding gravel path, took us close to the rock wall, revealing the sights of many ancient Aboriginal ceremonies. Park signs detailed information and referenced any legends, as to why the sight had become sacred, or was used for special rituals.

Some areas were taboo to get close to, or even take photos of, and I felt it should be respected, though I did screw-up several times, and not see the sign until after the photo. There were a few naturally hollowed out areas, where some images of rock paintings could still be discerned. They were not easily defined, for many layers had been painted over each other, during the past. Beginning to understand how these people, who felt so connected to nature, would see symbolism in these strange and varied rock formations.

One interesting granite hunk, probably split open by the ancient ice floes, resembled a gigantic jaw. The sign said many Aboriginal couples would have sex there, believing this spot could help them conceive. There was no way my claustrophobia, would have let me enjoy that experience! "I just don't think I could have been so desperate." Marta said. "And, I know having children was a very important part of their group support system." We discussed each focal point, we were women who had a strong desire to understand foreign cultures, and particularly how their women participated in them. Here, it was becoming more evident, their strength was more than solely physical, for food gathering and childbearing.

Many of the caves were still out of bounds to 'whites,' and one of them was used for secret manhood initiations, was even barred to Aboriginal women, on penalty of death. We all talked back and forth, sharing what we'd read about the Aboriginal culture of this area. To me, their whole lifestyle was a fathomed mystery of hardship and stoic survival. Yet, almost each step I took, though tenuous and brief as it was, gave me more cognizance of their attachment to this majestic, barren land, which both supported and controlled them.

Walking alongside the flank of the Rock, I began to feel as if I were peering into its secret corners. The flat, broad slope of the face, which everyone saw, and some climbed, exposed nothing but raw power and majesty. One had to go hunting for the multifaceted perspectives, which bared some of its personal historical footnotes. I did not know the scientific causes, why some sections were sheered off or others had giant 'pock' marks or gaping holes. One of the most eerie, was a section which looked like a giant, frozen wave captured forever in stone, with something which resembled a conch shell, hanging from its 'ceiling.'

The more we penetrated into this megalith, the more I began to feel vibes of a living spirit. It hit a turning point, when we came upon a huge, upper section of the Rock, where it seemed as if, part of the 'shelf' cover had been 'torn off.' The exposed underneath, looked like what I'd imagine cancer or leprosy to look like. My immediate reaction was, "Ooh, that must have hurt." Could it? Did it? Most people wanted a long life, and a quick, hopefully painless, death. For some reason this meticulously, slow erosion of this solid hunk, touched a de'ja' vu nerve of a painful, or even tortured death, or worse, helpless incapacitated state.

Heading toward the bus, I looked back to see an old, dead tree with a half-dozen birds sitting in it. Life, even for them, seemed lonely and desolate. From the scrub grass and bushes, to the scrawny trees, living here took tenacity, and the will to endure. *"A fascinating place to visit, but I wouldn't want to live here!"* I thought, with more seriousness than irony.

Once we reached the bus, we found Dean had already picked up everyone from climbing, so we headed to the other side of the Rock, for more personal encounters. Everyone looked quite wind- blown and worn out, even though it was only eleven o'clock in the morning. Dean made a check over the mic, "So, … how's everyone feeling? Ya' didn't overdo it now, did ya?" Some people moaned and groaned, while others kind of cheered at the exhilarating experience. Dean sounded relieved, "Well, that's good. No accidents or cuts, … keeps my record clean!" Some laughter came from the back, as if it had been his only concern. "And, how did everyone enjoy their experience? … Who made the climb to the top?"

Through the noise and laughter, only one voice was heard - Jean's. The only one out of thirty-six people, and especially the nineteen who *planned* to climb, to shout out - "I DID!" She was soon standing to our rousing applause, then finally she spoke. "I trained for over a year for this, and there was no way I wasn't going to do it."

She slowly looked around at all of us. "It really was hard, … and I thought sometimes with the wind blowing so piercing, I wasn't going to have enough time to make it to the top, but suddenly the wind stopped. I was able to get all the way to the summit and sign the register." Jean beamed with pride from her toes up. "This is one of my happiest days, and I think Dean should buy me a drink at dinner tonight, because I'm the only one on the bus, to make the climb to the top!" Most of us were laughing and applauding some more. I eagerly wondered what her backstory was, to prompt it all.

Dean, with a little surprise in his voice, said, "Sure, I'll be happy and proud to buy you a drink." I think he expected out of this active group, there would've been more success, or maybe he'd done his job with the cautions, too well. The chatter continued amongst us, with much of it directed toward Jean and her great personal success. For me, still curious as to its importance to her. Obviously, I'd discovered on the cold, wind-blown rock, we had different priorities. "Now," Dean cut into the clamor, to get back to the job at

hand, "we're going over to the other side, to see some areas which have waterfalls, Maggie Springs being the best known. I'll tell you some of the Aboriginal legends of the Rock's creation." (Full story in the Appendix) He went on, with more detailed information on the short drive. The base of the Rock could be driven around in fifteen to twenty minutes, but a thorough walk could take four to six hours, as there were many to choose from: Liru Walk, Mala Walk and Mutijulu - the Aboriginal Tribe Walk.

More of what I could comprehend, this area was a vast wealth of historical, as well living culture. "Before going back to the resort for lunch," he finished up, "and leaving this area entirely, we will stop at the Maruku Arts and Crafts Centre. The local tribe, which runs it, also has demonstrations."

As the bus swung into the small parking spot, I could see the Rock definitely had a 'windward' and 'leeward' side. Whereas the other walk had been rough and craggy, with broken hunks and huge boulders, this one was smooth and symmetrical from top to bottom. The rolling winds were almost voluptuous in their shapes and design, with the stains from the waterfalls and drainages outlining each crevice and crease.

Dean gathered us together at the end of a short walk, to the base of what would be the waterfalls, during the summer or 'wet' season, and pointed to two tremendously-large, opposing rock 'scars.' He began to weave the lyrical Aboriginal tale of the Rainbow Serpent, and the powers of the Great Spirit. Once he'd finished, heads were nodding'Aha' and we'd 'experienced' the visual of the Rock Dreamtime come 'alive.' Dean lead us around and emotionally-spun the magical, descriptive stories with such authenticity, it was obvious this was more than a mere job to him. He respected and loved this land and its people.

At Maruka Arts, we had a chance to see some Aborigines making a variety of crafts, from wood and bark. I slowly walked around watching them, and several times squatted to get a closer look, at those who were sitting on the ground working with, or painting the wood. Each piece seemed to have been chosen for its destined-design or pattern, and the art flowed onto it without any preceded plan. I quietly observed one older woman, methodically using a heated-rod to burn the dots, circles and other marks to delineate a particular lizard or other animal. She moved the rod back and forth, from the little fire to the piece of wood she held and turned as needed, seeming to place the marks with little forethought, and yet with such simplistic beauty.

I was mesmerized, for I knew anything which appeared so easy, must have taken years to perfect. Several times, I drew my camera up to my eye to focus and each time I withdrew, reluctantly feeling, it would be a definite invasion of privacy. I surveyed again the dozen or so Aborigines, more processing than toiling, at their creative tasks. Their connections to it all, made it seem as if they had all only recently been transformed from the Earth, as they were so rightly intertwined to its products they created. I knew I was a discerning witness, yet my presence was of totally no consequence to them.

Before we left, I made a point to talk to Dean and finalize my flight over to Kings Canyon. I'd seen so much up close, now I wanted to get the perspective from above.

"Will we be covering any new ground to Kings Canyon? I mean, I want to check to make sure I'm not missing anything important." I was somewhat hesitant, for I'd noticed a lot of clouds were banking-up, and I certainly did not want to have my view of anything blocked.

Dean looked at me and smiled a little sheepishly, "Nah, you won't miss a thing. Most of it is covering ground you've already been over. I won't even be talkin' that much," he chuckled. "It's mainly for everyone to get some sleep, since most of them got buggered from all of this exercise. It's a great flight, and you'll get a kick out of it. I'll just check they're goin' today, cause they need to have … oh, three, I think." He turned to go and telephoned from the shop, since we'd be leaving in another few minutes.

"Dean," I called after him, "would you check on the weather? It looks like it might rain." I did not want to sound scared, or stupid for I knew rain in the winter was a rarity.

He laughed back and pointed up, "Prob'ly nothin', nothin' rarely comes of it …but I'll check." Only a few minutes later and he came back smiling. "You're all set. They'll pick you up in front of the Sheraton, at one-forty-five. I'll drop you off there, when we pick up the other group at one-fifteen. The flight's a little over an hour, and they drop you off at Kings Creek Station, the cattle ranch were we stop for a break, at around three or three-thirty. You may have some time to kill, OK?" I nodded then he added, "Oh, yeah, they don't expect this to turn into anything." He gestured again into the sky. So, some new excitement for me and something to definitely look forward to. I hopped on the bus, wanting to tell someone about it.

Jean smiled up at me, so I decided to sit with her for the short ride back to the resort. "Oh, that sounds very exciting," she responded after hearing my news. "But this is the end of my trip, and I really don't have the money to spare. And, I'm honestly looking forward to taking a nap this afternoon. I'm sure tired." My nosy wonderment began to bubble again, about why this had been so important to her, and to share my own little revelation about not 'needing' to do it.

It took me a moment to come up with the right approach. "Do you do a lot of hiking or trekking in England?" I tried to sound just interested, and not probing or personal.

There was a slight indication of embarrassment in her light laugh. "Oh, no. I mean I do go walking and that, but nothing organized or formal. I don't belong to a club or anything of that sort." She glanced out the window, as we were whizzing by what was probably our last view of Ayers Rock. It had been almost twenty-four hours since 'IT' had come into our lives, yet neither one of us would ever be the same again. She studied it intensely, and gradually a smile of total satisfaction of her accomplishment slid over, to brighten her face.

I was lost too, for a moment, in may own thoughts of what it all had meant. There was still a small part of me, which was feeling something had been snatched from me, by not making the climb to the top. *"Oh, well,"* I thought, *"C'est la vie', the way my life goes."* I was sure there would soon be more opportunities of challenge, especially when I least expected them.

I brought the subject back, as I wanted to understand more about her. We talked another minute back and forth, about the great experience of the Rock, then I plunged in again. "Well, that's why I was wondering, you said you had been trying for a year. I thought maybe you had a group, which traveled around to climb famous places or something. I know the British are really into that sort of thing. So, are the Japanese, come to think of it."

She turned and peered at me, so I thought maybe I'd gotten too personal. "It didn't start out to be an obsession," she paused and glanced back out the window, studying into the open surreal expanse, as if she was still formulating it all herself. "At first, I just wanted to get in shape," she glanced back at me, "maybe you understand … middle age creeping up and all. …Changing relationships, questioning who you are,… and what you've done with your life."

Her face changed, from retrospective to perky when she announced, "So, I decided to do something that *no one else I knew* had done. Since I'd been planning a trip to Australia for several years, I thought this was the perfect place for a secret-opportunity." There was a childish glee spreading across her face. "If I failed, no one I knew would be here to witness it, and if I succeeded … well, something too be proud of and tell everybody about, … " Her face changed again into another realization. "Only now, I think it has become almost too personal to brag about … Can you understand? I became obsessed to where, it was MY Rock to climb. It's kind of funny, isn't it? I feel strange." She giggled with the same embarrassment as before.

I laughed heartily. "In some bizarre way, I guess it's *why* I decided *not* to finish the climb …" I stopped, knowing we were totally different. "What I mean is, it was an obsession, then I realized it wasn't really so important. But, I do love challenges, in fact I get easily bored doing the same things, so I'm sure I'll find something to be obsessed about again soon."

We were both quiet for a few minutes, searching for some answers out in the ochre-colored land. I got a bit of a revelation and decided to share it. "Maybe it's living all these years with the Japanese, and seeing how they are so obsessed about always doing the 'right thing,' not disappointing their families or co-workers."

She stared intently at me, as I explained. "There are many students who don't speak English, because they are afraid of making a grammatical error, like the teacher will shoot them or at least chastise them greatly in front of others. It's only when they've been overseas for home-stays or school they are able to let go of the controlling fear." I smiled slightly, and took a big sigh. "I'm sure that's part of it for me - I'm trying to break away from being so controlled, feeling I must do the right thing. What I'm trying to discover almost every day, is ... what do I want, since most of my life, up to this point, has been trying to please other people."

A slow understanding smile came across Jean's face. "Yes, I do know what you mean." There was no need to compare notes, bad experiences or even air-out our pasts. We enjoyed the quiet for a few minutes, then Dean announced times for the pick-ups after lunch. He listed off again the availabilities of restaurants in the complex, and we opted to return to the Red Centre Hotel and their buffet lunch.

Trudy, Marta and Kaylin joined us, so the talk stayed much lighter, and directed toward our enjoyment of Ayers Rock. We were walking out to wait for the bus, and I noted the pesky clouds had not only not gone away, but were building and graying even more.

Kaylin surprised me when she spoke, "Annie, how do you live?" Not sure what this was in reference to, or if it was simply her English lacking clarification. My puzzled look, prompted her to explain. "Do you live house or apartment? How big? I hear everything small and ... expensive in Japan."

I snickered, "Oh, I was wondering if this was esoteric or something." Her lost look made me shake my head, "Never mind. I live in an apartment, and I don't know the metric size, but it's about four hundred square feet, including a large balcony. It's a very open style, the way the sliding doors are set up. It's big enough for me." I gestured with my hands for more descriptive understanding, a habit I'd gotten into when I lacked the language.

"I sometimes wonder how I handled it, when my ex-husband was there, but a family with one or two small children would probably live in the same space. It costs about seven hundred American dollars. Which is rather cheap for Japan, but expensive just about everywhere else. I've gotten used to it and I don't really need a lot of conveniences like some Americans, who can't live without their large refrigerators, dishwashers, automatic washing machines snd dryers, etc. I've always been quite adaptable, as long as I have certain basics, like a western-style toilet and a good hot shower." Not sure if that was what she had in mind, but I thought she had understood most of it. "How about you? The Azores aren't exactly a sprawling country ... where do you live?"

"Oh, Marta inherit house of her mother. My aunt ... and I live there ... for three year. It is small and old, but nice view of sea."

Trudy now chimed in. "Is it one of those huge, high-rise complexes we've seen on the telly?" Her inquisitiveness sometimes bordered on the impertinent, though I knew Australian television liked to show the negative about most of the Asian countries, much like Britain usually did.

I decided not to feed any more of the negativity, by telling her how I actually lived on the edge of what had once been a popular, prostitution area and still was, to a certain extent. When I had first arrived, I had very feminist-like, pulled the photos of the naked women out of the public phone booths. But, now I just ignore them, like the rest of the female Japanese. Though seeing the porno magazines so openly read, still disgusted me, at least murder was rare.

I could have told her, too, about my petty, Yakuza (Japanese Mafia) neighbor, who was actually more frightened of me, because I had no fear of him. Also, since he knew I was from Chicago, he thought I might be mafia connected. Every country had its 'warts' and with Japan, I felt they were more of a nuisance, than when I lived in the States with its random crime, which had stirred my angry passion. I guess I believed Americans should have known better than to become complacent, whereas I tolerated most Japanese as being simply naive. Easy to report stereotypes, living in a culture you see and know the difference.

"No, actually, I'm quite lucky," I smiled, trying not to sound condescending. "It only has sixteen units, and I'm on the fifth floor with a view of a small park, and another one not too far away. We have a small post office on the ground floor, a rice store, a coffee shop, another restaurant and several other shops. It's all very convenient, and I'm only four subway stops from the downtown area." Glad to see the bus coming, as I was not in the mood for contrived talk about Japan. I was more concerned about the weather and my upcoming flight. I waited to be the last on the bus, so I could question Dean. "Will they fly if it rains?" I anxiously asked, 'I don't want to get stuck there, when the rest of the tour is over at the ranch."

Dean shook his head, "Don't worry about it. One way or another they will get you to Kings Canyon." I reluctantly went back and took a seat, not wanting to appear foolish, but I also did not want the logistical hassle of being left behind. Moments later, I jumped off the bus, while Dean had the others wait to get on. "OK," he called to me, "Have a good flight and we will see you at Kings Creek Station, later this afternoon."

I waved to everyone and got out of the way, not sure how I wanted to spend the forty minutes or so I had. I decided to go into the Sheraton to see what it was like. I headed for the gift shop and gallery, hunting for anything really unusual. Good for about ten minutes, then I decided to walk around the complex, as I'd only been driven through. I stopped to photograph some flowers and sauntered into a few shops, before wandering down past the Four Seasons to the Visitor's Centre, which had a fantastic display of flora, fauna and an explanation of how the area had developed over the past millions of years. The time in there went quickly, and soon back waiting for my pick-up. I did not want to even look at the sky, as it was now making me nervous.

The mini-bus came tooting up shortly, with a young couple inside, plus a real chirpy driver asking where we were from and what all we did. The woman spoke up first, "I work at an island resort, so I've looked forward to seeing the dry, Red Centre, after all the great rain forest and blue water." She and the driver laughed at the irony of her statement, but I thought it rather affected and inane, from her making too much artificial, small talk with tourists. She continued playing up to the driver, ignoring the lost-looking young man, presumed to be with her. My only thought about her, she had a body and mind which belonged at a resort.

The young man was getting quite nervous, and obviously did not want to be there, but he must have been doing it for her. "I've never been in *any kind* of an airplane before." He paused and looked at me, as if he had expected me to laugh. Then the poor, insecure man spoke directly to the driver for assurance. "If it starts to rain, the plane won't take off, will it? Or, if we're already flying, it will return to the airstrip … immediately, won't it?"

The driver turned to look at him, to make sure he was not pulling his leg or something. Then, a bit shocked when he saw the fear was for real. "Oh, listen mate, don't worry, you gotta good pilot. He'll take care a'you." He tried hard to fake it all, but he also accelerated to get to the airstrip faster. "And Ma'am, where you from?"

I thought, *"Oh, shit, just what I needed. I have to get to Kings Canyon, we've got a storm coming and one of the passengers has never flown before."* I turned to the young man and tried to reassure him, "Listen, the first time I flew, I went through a tornado. No problem, piece of cake … don't worry about it." He looked at me, not only as if I were a Martian, but a crazy one. *So, much for the psyching-up approach, I guess. Shit, cover your own ass, Annie!* "I'm from Japan and I'm suppose to be dropped off at Kings Creek Station, to meet with my tour group."

This time the driver almost spun around in his seat, and sure glad there was not any traffic on these roads. Not sure if his look was one of amazement, or futility at my lack of subtleness on the subject of 'forced flight.' I certainly deserved his reproached critique. "You American?" Universally, I presumed long ago, subtlety was not an American virtue.

We pulled into the tiny parking in front of the small building, and I began to wonder what size the airplane would be. We settled the payment in the little office, then introduced to another couple, so it looked like a full load. This husband and wife had only flown once in a large plane, so they, too, were nervous. The woman was quite heavy, and I thought this pilot was going to have a real chore getting us all into the six seater, single engine Cessna, much less taking off on, what I imagined would be a rather short runway.

"Well, the pilot finally said, covering much of his trepidation as possible, "we better get going, while the weather is holding."

I thought, *"Right, or my ass will be stuck here and you'll have to refund a lot of money."*

He put me in the plane first, and placed the scared young man next to me. Not happy having the smallest window, but at least we also had the back one. I avoided looking at the young man, and truly hoped he'd hold up for this test of his manhood, which I figured was at stake here for the girlfriend. The heavy-set woman was getting really nervous now, and panicked trying to get the seat belt on correctly. Her husband sat next to her, trying to soothe her as he could.

The clever pilot sat the cutesy-chatterbox next to him, so at least he'd have an enjoyable distraction, which the last thing he needed considering the weather. He quickly went through the rigamarole, with the engine turning over pretty soundly, so we were soon heading down the single runway. He took it all the way to the end of the tarmac, as he'd need every inch of it to get this load airborne.

I held my breath, and asked the Great Spirit to put a Golden Light around us and a White Light ahead of us. I could see the scraggly bushes only a few feet below us, as the wheels finally lifted off. A sign of relief was uttered by each and everyone of us. The pilot had barely turned the plane around to head for the Olgas, when the rain started to come down. I also said "Shit!" out loud, as I suddenly realized WATER! The clairvoyant had said my danger had something to do with water. *I felt as if I should apologize to these poor people, for getting them into my danger.*

I finally got hold of myself, and figured out such a thing would not happen, as it was my test, not theirs. *"Sit back, relax and enjoy the flight, Annie. You're letting your imagination run away with you!"* I said out loud again to myself. I figured no one could hear me, with the communication headsets we had been given to put on.

"It's OK, folks," the pilot crackled over the headsets, "don't worry. We'll be through this in a minute or two." In the meantime, the rain was pounding down heavier and heavier. I was sure the people on the ground were in a bit of a panic, too. This was not supposed to happen, even though any rain in this country was a blessing.

As the plane began to lightly bounce, from some turbulence which had built up, as a result of the storm. The young man grabbed hold of the seat in front of him. I stared at his white knuckles, as I'd never seen anything like them before. I barely kept from laughing, as I could only think this whole scenario would have made a wonderful Marx Brothers movie! Without turning off our headsets, the pilot called back to the base and asked if he should return. Nothing like having all of his confidence in this flight laid out before us.

I sat watching for what could happen next, then the heavy-set woman began calling for a bag, as she thought she was going to be ill. That was it! I could not hold it any longer, so I covered my mouth and pushed my face up to the window, as I giggled into a laugh. When we hit another air pocket, I turned to see the young man thrust his head between his knees, and grabbed his legs. I thought after a moment he'd passed out, or was kissing his ass good-bye, as sure he'd seen in some movie. I carefully leaned down, and asked if he was all right. There was a long pause, then slowly his head turned, until one eye was peering at me strangely. Before I could laugh right out loud in his face, I sucked my lips in, nodded and turned back toward the window, pretending to be engrossed in the view. It worked, as I finally saw the mystical scene unfolding.

In the not too far distance, the base of the Olgas had been enshrouded with clouds and mist, which made them appear to be floating. As we got closer, I became entranced by their lumpy, bumpy forms which reminded me of a huddled group of Chicago Bears, trying to play a football game during a snowstorm. The Olgas frequent obscurity by the rain, made them even more magical to me, but obviously not everyone was enjoying this 'Twilight Zone' flight.

The scene flashed in my memory of the Summer Palace in Beijing, when I saw it in April while a heavy, wet, misty snow was falling. The setting sun made it all look pink, an experience I'd never forget, like traveling back to another world … an ethereal dimension of time and space. A dichotomy which could not have possibly happened, but I had elusive photos to remind me.

The pilot's voice over the headset brought me back, "We'll go on to Ayers Rock, since there doesn't seem to be any rain in that direction. The storm is coming from this direction. Hopefully, we'll stay ahead of it." Maybe, I truly did love being on the edge of danger, and to have the opportunity to see the phenomenas of nature. How many tourists, I wagered, had seen these two glorious outcroppings from the air, … in a winter rainstorm? Very few, I'd imagine. Like the snow I saw on the Great Wall, it gave it dimension with a powerful perspective, to the bleak and rather colorless mountain terrain. I suddenly felt special and blessed, to behold this rarely seen display. Thus, I tried to sharpen my observations to not miss a single detail.

Ayers Rock soon came into view - vague and almost out of focus by the light rain. Knowing we were several thousand feet up, its immensity became even more staggering. Defined into a totally different shape from aloft, than when one was grounded and dominated, strictly by its superiority in height. The little road circumnavigating the Rock and the scattered greenery, set off each neatly furled-furrow of the distinctive knobby mass, which had been softened by the mist. A vision came to mind of a humongous, rusty- colored hound dog, stretched out and sleeping peacefully in front of the fire, on a cold winter's day. The pilot, who really was good, circled first in one direction then another, so we could all see the Rock with its many facets, from both sides of the aircraft. I had to remind myself to take photos and not just stare.

My fellow passengers had finally calmed down, and even managed to look out to enjoy the majesty laid out beneath them. Everyone satisfied, we headed on to the dry, Lake Amadeus and the almost supernatural visions it created. If I had thought it spooky from a land point of view, it was frightening from the air - so vast and impenetrable. I knew Australia was one of the largest producers of salt in the world, and most of it went to Japan. Another easy and profitable raw resource, the land had given to the people. I could not see any signs Lake Amadeus was used in this way, but perhaps it was, or would be. I pondered if they did start digging into it, what bones and stories would it reveal? Had this once been part of the 'Inland Sea,' and if they dug deep enough, would they find water again? So many mysteries and so few solved, in this land of unlimited complexities. It constantly fascinated me.

The open Outback simply went on and on. Tough green spurts supporting a meager, but persevering animal population. "Keep a look out," the pilot reminded us, "for the feral or wild camels, the brumbies, the wild horses, and even some kangaroos, dingoes and cattle. If you spot some, let us know by using the clock-hour numbers - noon, three o'clock … to describe the location, OK?"

It had just about cleared off, and he knew everyone was in a much better state to enjoy the flight. "We usually see a pretty good variety in this stretch to the Kings Creek Station." He swooped down a little lower, as a sort of pattern enveloped from one section to another, and the vegetation and indention of the land slightly varied.

Our first sighting came from the pilot, as he'd logically be able to pick out the 'different' from all this sameness. We dropped even lower to see a group of five or six camels, first running in one direction, then another. Amazing, we were so close we could see how much thinner they were, with their scruffier fur loaded with twigs and bits of brush.

"These feral males can be quite dangerous, as they are very protective of the females in their harem." The domestic ones may've had a rather boring life, toting around tourists and such, but at least they were well fed and watered. Since central Australia was so empty of people, it seemed to have been filled up, by a rather wide selection of animals with unbridled propagation.

"When their numbers get too high," the pilot went on, "they have to be thinned or eradicated, because they are taking away the limited water and grazing land for the cattle. It's usually done by helicopter or even small planes."

I remembered seeing this outside of Darwin, where the feral water buffaloes were supposed to be such a problem. The riflemen hung on the outside rung of the helicopter, and picked off the buffaloes like sitting ducks. I'd thought what a shit-job, even the most macho guy would have to get tired of doing it. Many of the Aborigines were against the program, as they culled the buffaloes for food. A definite ironic and historical ring to it, of what the railroads did in killing the buffalo, a main source of food and fur to the American Plains Indian.

A few kangaroos were spotted, and some thought they saw some dingoes, but they were quick and definitely difficult to pick out in the landscape. I got excited when I thought I'd spotted something, then pilot said, "Yes, that's cattle from the Kings Creek Station. This is one of the tributaries, and we're now over their property." He swung around to fly over the Kings Canyon Frontier Resort, where I'd be staying the night.

He explained to the others about the amenities, as it was brand new and quite impressive, especially for being totally out in the middle of nowhere. A few other facilities had even sprung up because of it. It did look quite large and I was surprised, with the obviously new highway leading up to it. The government had spent a considerable amount of money, making it so convenient and comfortable for tourists. From this angle, it was easy to acknowledge tourism was the fastest growing industry in the Red Centre, and the entire Northern Territory. I had experienced all new accommodations in Kakadu National Park, too.

The pilot swung us around once again for our final landmark, Kings Canyon. I'd seen the photos in the brochures, but I truly was not prepared for the size, or the ruggedness of it all. As different as the Rock was from the Olgas, so was this Canyon from anything else in the region. One after another of the huge sandstone walls rose up hundred of meters, and now under us was one of the spectacular, green-covered gorges with a creek snaking through it. *"Holy ... Shit!"* I whispered to myself. *"And, we're going to fucking climb THAT!"* I leaned back in my seat in total shock. I should not have taken this flight, because it showed me what we were in for tomorrow morning.

If I thought Ayers Rock was awesome and ridiculous to climb, then what the hell could I call this? I just kept shaking my head back and forth. *"Well, maybe there is an easier spot we will be ascending."* I tried to rationalize to myself, as I sat back up and stared some more in awe. The tour description had said 'the climb and walking may take up to three hours, so not for the faint-hearted or unfit ... supportive footwear is essential.' *"And, I said I was looking for another challenge - there it is and probably bigger than the last one you passed up, dummy!"* With this last remark to myself, the young man

leaned over toward me and asked if I was talking to him. I shook my head. I did not want to admit to anyone, at this time how crazy I was.

We flew around and around the Canyon until I was inundated, and it indelibly set in my mind. I was suddenly exhausted and just wanted to get back to the bus, or better yet, Alice Springs - enough of all this fitness bullshit. I was overweight and too old to be playing these games. It is not wonderful, what fear of the unknown could do for your confidence?!

Our chipper pilot was talking about the Kings Creek Station, and I realized we were about to land. I'd be able to return shortly to the bus and, in not too long a time, a lingering, hot shower. The landing was not too rough, and soon a Land Rover was racing over to greet us. *"What service,"* I thought. We all piled out, as everyone was anxious to get a stretch and their feet back on the ground, if only momentarily. I thanked them quickly, wishing them luck before running over to the waiting Rover.

A young man jumped out and came around to open the door for me. "Gidday, Ma'am. Welcome to Kings Creek." I waved to the plane, as we pulled away and I wondered if they were going to get caught in that storm on the way back. "*God what a trip,*" I ruminated to myself, in the literal, as well as the figurative. "Wher' ya from, Maiam?" He drove over the ruts toward the giant ranch gate, like on a freeway.

"I'm … American, … but I … live and … work in … Japan." I smiled, as I tried to keep my teeth from cracking together with each jostle, or my head from hitting the bar lining the roof. Not an easy new trick, for an old dog like me. I looked at his young, tanned face and could see he probably was not even as old as my son David. His clothes were covered with the fine, red dust, and most of the Land Rover had a light coating on it, with considerable build up in the edges, indents or any other place, where it could collect easily. I rolled the window down part way, and smelled the earthiness … not pungent, but a soft, freshness wafted in.

He had stopped the Rover, "That so?" He jumped out and closed the gate behind us, as I watched and giggled to myself. I began to think, I was as much a curiosity to the Aussies, as I was to the Japanese. He got back in and started to light a cigarette. "Ah, you mind, I smoke?" I gestured 'no problem' and he lit up and sat back down with the door open, watching the plane.

With the puzzled look on my face, he explained. "Oh, we've gotta wait for 'em ta take off … ya know, just in case." He stared out at the plane, which had finally finished taxing down the dirt runway then back to me.

"Whadd ya do in Japan? I had a girlfriend last year, who wanted to work there ... said ya could make a lotta money." He was somewhat uncomfortable, but I was sure he experienced many of the tourists, who had taken these plane rides.

I smiled again a little, more easily this time, as we were not moving and I gave him my usual reply. "That so? Ya' speak Jap'nese?" I shook my head 'no' and said 'only English.' "They understand ya?" When I nodded 'yes,' he was actually amazed. "They don't here. They all god 'en interpret'er." The plane was finally taking off and the second it was airborne, so were we. He shifted the Rover into gear and went charging off. He went on to tell me how busy they'd been, with some research and television people coming in, to do a story on the camels. He pointed out their plane and helicopter.

"Camels?" I questioned, "I thought this was a cattle ranch?"

He shrugged his shoulders, "Yeah, use-ta be, but th' markets bad ... an' th' camels 'er easier." He glanced over at me, as he added with some pride, though he obviously had preferred working with the cattle, "We sell 'em to th' Arabs. Ours 're the best in th' Territory," He described how messy the camels were, and how it was kind of embarrassing to be working with them. But the jobs were scarce and this was better than no job at all. He had plans, though, and was quite anxious to let me know, he hoped to get a better job come summer. "I'll head on up ta' Darwin, or Queensland, where th' cattle are."

I enjoyed this little 'slice of life' down-under, on how real people lived, those outside the tourist industry, and that they had hopes and dreams within the realm of their belief. I often wondered, if I had too much, or too little of something in my make-up... I just couldn't be very happy with the simple life, … for long periods of time.

He asked more questions about Japan, but the strangeness of it seemed too bizarre for him to comprehend, especially when I answer the 'why I was living there' question. We finally pulled up to the rest-house and general store. After I got out, I made a point to shake his hand and thank him. For some reason, it seemed to shake him up, as much as anything else I'd said. "Th'y got cold ones 'nside." He pointed to the general store, then he kind of wandered off, as if not sure what he should do next.

I got an ice cold lemon squash and sauntered down to the nearest camel pen, just to take another look at the funny beasts, while I killed time. Good to stretch my legs, as I certainly felt the morning's climb and walk. *"Ought to be in great shape this time tomorrow,"* I sarcastically said to myself. I was trying not to think about the forthcoming climb, but, of course, it would not leave my mind.

I talked to the camels for a while, watching their giant jaws just grinding away and staring back at me, with those big eyes, surrounded by their really, long lashes. I tried to guess how much they could sell them for to the Arabs, since these really were healthy looking animals, as far as I could see, by comparison to the ordinary tourist ones. I walked around the area for a while, until I found a toilet, then sat on the porch and waited for the bus.

I almost dozed off, when the bus pulled up. There was a fifteen minute tea break, so I had time to talk to Dean and many others who asked me how the fight was. As soon as I could, with out seeming too anxious, I climbed on the bus and located an empty seat to crash into. It had already been a really long day, starting with sunrise and I just did not want to deal with any kind of aggravation, or be agitated by anyone. I knew I'd feel better with a short doze.

I jolted awake, as the bus came to a full stop and started to make the turn into Kings Canyon Resort. I looked at my watch, and figured I must have dozed at least thirty or forty minutes, which surprised me, as I usually was not good at naps. I could see a gas station and a few other shops, with maybe a restaurant, across from the sprawling building complex. The Resort was truly beautiful, as it backed right up into the mountain range, blending nicely with the surroundings. They had spent the money well, preserving the area with several ghost-gum trees, prominent in the natural landscaping.

I yawned and stretched, before pulling myself up to file out. One of the last to get my bag and room assignment. It appeared to all be going like clockwork, with Dean handing me my bag and the lady manager checking off my name and giving me the key. I turned and plodded off toward the little wooden sidewalk to find the room. Then I heard the loud, drawling-voice, which had consistently drifted in and out of my ears, on and off the bus. She was the one who had been embarrassed by talking so long, after she'd been picked up yesterday at the Sheraton.

"What about me? Don't I get a room? I've paid for this!" I knew Dean did not need this aggravation, as I was sure he was probably as tired as the rest of us. I stopped a few doors down at my number, and began trying to unlock the door. I could only hear the muffled sound of Dean and the manager, but the woman's voice rang clear as a gong. "I'm on the twenty-one day tour, Dorothy ..." She gave not only her last name, but almost a case history of her life.

I kept jamming the key in the lock, jiggling it every which way I could. *Please, God, Please ... I'll be good and not be bitchy ... or cuss ... or swear so much ... please don't stick me with that woman!!!"* Finally, the door swung open and I threw my bag in and quickly shut it! Maybe I could hide under the bed or something, or pretend I am not in. *"Annie, get hold of yourself ... you're an adult ... you can handle this."* I stood with my back pressed to the door when the knock came. *"Shit,"* I cursed to myself. *"I shouldn't have been so cheap and taken the 'single' share-room option!"* All I could do, was to paste a smile on my face, turn around and open my 'protective barrier.'

"Yes?" I lied, and did the best acting job I'd done in a long time. The manager was explaining the situation, when Dorothy broke in and began apologizing, while almost demanding occupancy at the same time. Clever, how she did that! With my robot smile in place I said, "Of course, please come in." I glanced up to see Dean in the background rolling his eyes, then shaking his head, as he walked off, glad to be out of the situation. "Sure, no problem," I mumbled to the manager. What I wanted to say was, *"I have learned patience ... I've lived in Japan for four years."* But somehow, I knew this was going to be a test of my sanity, not a simple language communication problem.

I picked up my bag and walked past the bathroom and into the sleeping area. Not gigantic, but adequate for two people, with the beds

perpendicular to each other, a desk and the ubiquitous television attached to the suitcase stand and dresser. Dorothy had already opened up her very large suitcase, and placing articles in the drawers of the dresser, as if we'd be staying at least a week. She'd not stopped talking since the moment at the door, and was now talking, presumably, to me. "I'm buggered. N' dyin' for a bath. The weather's al'over the place - hot 'n cool. Whdays wear? ..."

She stopped momentarily to look at me standing

between the television and the end of what was to be my bed, still holding my small, red tote bag. She was oblivious to what, I am sure was an incredulous look on my face. "That's all you got? You travel light! I wish I could. Now, where's my pink top?" She was back digging in her suitcase which contained bags, boxes and things wrapped up, jammed, but very organized. Her hands were flitting from one thing to another - taking some thing out, looking at it then sticking it back in, or turning and putting it in a drawer. There did not seem to be rhyme or reason to any of the actions, just busy work. I could not stop from staring at the assortment of clothes so tightly packed, yet neatly folded into every corner. I thought what a case-load she'd be for any shrink.

The Trapeze Flyer

Wise-aging brings strength,
For what have we got to lose?

That inner strength brings beauty
That no make-up could provide.

I'm not a park statue, no one remembers;
Green with pigeon streaks, no one cleans.

A transformation has taken place.
The real me is alive and living well.

I am in my prime, thank you.
And, I've only begun to act.

Be passionate about life, don't fear it.
Just be like the daring trapeze flyer -

You cannot get to the other side,
Until you let go and fly over the abyss.

Alice Parker

Chapter 6 ~ A King of a Canyon

I put my bag on the bed, as I plopped down next to it. "My name's Annie and I'm just on the three-day, two-night tour. Did you want the bathroom first?" Already repeating to myself this was obviously some lesson I needed to learn. Or, more appreciative of the quiet-spoken Japanese, who rarely said more than a sentence or two at a time.

She stopped digging and looked at me with amazement, "Oh, I'm an idiot. Didn't think I'd seen you before. Of course, we're on the twenty-one. Don't feel so bad about this big suitcase. Oh, there I go again. I'm Dorothy and I'm from Queensland … Townsville actually, you've probably never heard of it. North of Brisbane … you heard of Brisbane, haven't you … yes, of course, you have or … maybe you've heard of Cairns … we're south of Cairns, a big tourist town …" She finally paused to now gape at me, as I was laughing hysterically, and almost falling off my bed, clasping my arms first behind my head then to my knees. "You OK? … I mean, what's up? … Is everything OK?" She was finally silent for a moment.

"I'm … sorry. It's just you have no idea of the irony. Of all the cities … in all of Australia, … you just had to be from Townsville!" I caught my breath, and she had even sat down on the desk chair. A look of shock came over her face, after the relief I'd not totally flipped. "My God, you've got to be kidding. That's were my ex-husband ran away to … from me and Japan" Her mouth started to drop open in amazement.

"Listen, I'm sorry…" I got some composure back. "I didn't mean to laugh at you … I mean, I wasn't laughing at you … I've been to Townsville, ah … three times, and it's delightful city … it's just … it kind of became … I guess my symbol for rejection or … lost causes or … something. Really, I still have some friends there … they own a great, little Italian restaurant on the South Bank side. Wonderful … city and I … hope to go back again … some day." I could not believe this whole scenario had happened … and was continuing to happen. I tried to watch my mouth, but a whole gamut of shock-expletives was running through my brain.

Dorothy's face was a little blank, trying to assimilate what all I had said. "… Japan? Aren't you American?" I was sure I'd confused her, because I believed *no one* was that stupid.

I sucked my lips in, to keep from laughing again, and thought, *"Boy, I'm getting good at this trick!"* I tried to keep the condescending attitude out of my voice. "Yes, I'm American, but I live and work in Japan. So did my ex-husband for a few years, but he couldn't handle it and he went to Townsville, … he was supposed to start a business with our friends."

I managed to stop myself, as I wanted to embarrass her for her stupidity. "But, … he didn't even try and just spent all of our savings, then went back to States after six months. We finally got a divorce, but I've tried to keep the friendships I have here in Australia." I wanted to add, *"Now, are you happy … you know my whole story!"* But I did not say that. I kept my face as straight as possible, trying not to show any emotion, at all.

"Oh, goodness! What do you do in Japan? The school where I work - as a bookkeeper, not a teacher," she tried to joke, "they started teaching Japanese to the students. You know, we've got to be prepared for the future." I should not have worried about the emotional effect, as obviously everything went right over this woman's head, except for what she chose to respond to. "So, do you speak *good* Japanese?"

Soon, I'd lose my patience with this woman. "I teach business English, and only speak conversational Japanese. Did you want the bath first? We need to get ready for dinner, I think they said six o'clock," She never reacted, if she caught the curtness in my voice.

She almost jumped up, "Oh, yeah, sorry. I'll get my things. Umh, ha OK, … and where is that bloody shower cap? Ah, here it is!" She said it with such a thrill in her voice, I could not help but shake my head. I'd started digging through my own bag, and pulled out some slacks and a top, I'd slated to wear. "Ta ta! Back in a jiffy," she called, as she finally headed for the shower.

I stretched out on the bed, and tried to block out the noise from the bathroom. All I could think of was my good, Aussie friend Pat, and her absolute amazement, when she heard several years back, about Travis and I planning to live in Townsville. "I can't believe it," she laughed, so lady-like covering her mouth with her hand. "I was born in Townsville, and I couldn't wait until I turned eighteen to get out of there." She'd laughed again, even heartier. "You know, we used to call it 'Clownsville!' The laugh increased again, "It was such a joke! The people were nothing but country bumpkins, who thought they were sophisticated, because they didn't live in the bush."

She then controlled herself a bit and got somewhat serious. "Oh, Annie, a well-traveled person like you! I just can't imagine your living there, having friends or not, to support you socially!" I had tried at the time, to somewhat defend it all. It had been over twenty years since she'd visited the place, and she still had no interest in doing so, either. And, now a perfect example of Pat's description of the people she grew up with in Townsville

I guess most of it was for Travis, but some of it was for me. I thought I could 'rescue' Townsville. Just like the British character in *A Town Like Alice* did, for the small town she'd moved into. In my arrogance, I'd thought 'sharing' my marketing, public relations and adverting experience would be a terrific bonus, as well as personal business venture, for the city.

Not until the third visit, had I begun to realize through, many of the newer citizens in the 110,000 or so population, were quite forward thinking. Yet, there was no way the old-timers would listen to the likes of an American, much less a female. I recognized, too, it would take a lot of work and money, with a longtime investment, to get Townsville unstuck from its 1950s - 60s mentality. Still, I gave it credit for having made numerous changes in the past few years.

But for Travis, who was a talker, not a doer, the town's laid- back attitude had been so perfect to escape to. He could always rationalize his failure as rejection, or lack of their cooperation. Unfortunately, I never heard back from the friends in Townsville, as to their side of what exactly had happened. Travis had said they said 'no,' since he no longer had the money to invest. In his arrogance, he'd thought his skills were enough, but not when they'd be sponsoring him. C'est la vie! Now long ago and far away, and almost forgotten. Interesting, how at this time with the appearance of 'Dorothy of Oz' and 'Clownsville,' it came back up again. Truly, there were no coincidences in life.

Dorothy came out of the bathroom, practically in mid- sentence, saying something about the hot water. She was fully dressed with knee-highs under her plaid pink slacks, matching pale, pink polyester sweater and floral scarf tucked around her neck into the 'V'. It did not look like what I'd consider casual, much less Outback, or Bush

Country clothing. Her sandy-colored hair was lightly flecked with gray, and done-up in what could have only been described as a 1950s 'pageboy' style - bangs and all. The pointed-rhinestone glasses, set off the plain face and pale blue steak of eye shadow. She leaned toward the mirror, over the dresser putting on the matching pink lipstick. I did not even know, you could still buy those colors of pink and blue any more! I was sure she was probably proud of her slim figure, and except for resembling some cartoon character, from a period-piece, she looked good for being in her mid-fifties.

I gathered up my clothes, "Listen, you don't have to wait for me, I can join you in the dining hall in about twenty or thirty minutes." I smiled, as I stepped into the bathroom, but she obviously did not get my clue, as I heard her say something about not minding the wait. Under the hot water, I began to relax my mind and muscles, so by the time I stepped back out, I was refreshed and ready to go, at least a few more hours before crashing.

Sitting on the bed, it felt good to slip my sandals onto my bare feet, which had been bound up in those heavy shoes all day. The light cotton pants and colorful shirt, felt crisp after the sticky-sweated ones. I quickly put on lipstick, as I usually did not were make up on vacation, and especially did not feel the need to with this tour group. Dorothy'd been talking continuously since I'd emerged from the bath, though she was supposedly reading the magazine in her hand.

Beginning to tune out her twangy-voice, but this woman was definitely the epitome of a ditzy-broad, the ultimate 'air-head' or 'space-cadet.' I was surprised her husband had let her out alone, but then it may have been his clever plan to get rid of her! It was not just her being from Townsville, or the bitter memories suddenly brought back - it was her. She was everything I disliked in a woman, all wrapped up in one package. A chatterbox, which had been a constant annoyance to many of us, with her fatuous comments, inane questions and loud complaints. There was a part of me, which thought I should feel sorry for her, because she was obviously lonely and wanted attention. But I wanted my time for myself and with those others on the tour, I could relate to. I turned and smiled, (G*ee, all those years of doing television interviews as a spokesperson sure did help*) "Shall we go. Thanks for waiting."

The wooden walkway was slightly elevated, about a meter off the ground. "I was reading they did this to preserve the natural environment, and make it easier during the rainy season," I commented to Dorothy, then realized she'd *not* taken notice of the fact, the sidewalk *was not on* the ground. She stopped to carefully look, as if to understand its importance.

"Isn't it marvelous today, what they're doing to protect the *Ozone.*" My eyes blinked, no *one could surely be that stupid* not to know where the Ozone was. I nodded, then sucked in my lips again, as I continued walking a little faster. I was sure, there had be other people we could sit and talk with. *I told myself the night would go fast, and this testing of my character strength would almost be over. I tried, but my subconscious was not buying it.*

I almost embraced Marta and Jean, when we walked in and I quickly introduced them to Dorothy, before going straight to the bar for a glass of wine. Dinner was buffet, with a nice selection … the lamb was especially tasty. Dorothy was soon anxiously introducing me to her sister and brother-in-law from Charters Towers, a small town inland from Townsville. "And, she's been to Townsville three times, and is even thinking about living there someday."

I didn't want to embarrass her, by correcting my intentions, so I just added, "I live in Japan now, and I really enjoy the open space of Australia." As usual, it was the magic trick to change almost any subject, so I was off and running with my usual spiel. Dean got our attention, and asked us to sit down as everything was ready. I called Marta to get Kaylin, as I motioned to Trudy to bring Jean, who was the star of the show tonight. I wanted to make sure, I had some interesting people around me to talk with, so I did not go for Dorothy's jugular, if her rattling-on went on too far.

The hot rolls on the table, as well the soup and salad served, and we could help ourselves to the main courses and dessert. I'd just slathered butter on a roll, and lifting the soup spoon to my mouth, when Dorothy asked, "Annie you didn't say if you had any children. I've got two myself, a son who's twenty-seven and a daughter who's twenty-four. I'm real proud of them, though my son keeps changing his mind. I mean, he's gotten two degrees in history then teaching, and now he's going to the seminary, so he's back home with us. What about you?"

I swallowed the soup and bite of roll before answering, figuring she still might keep talking. "My son's studying computers, I think it's called management information systems or something. He's quite a whiz with the computer at work, too. I hope to have him visit me in Japan this Christmas. It will be his first time to Asia." I smiled back at her, "And, what about your daughter, what does she do?"

She'd broken her roll into small pieces and buttering each piece carefully. She put both the roll and the knife down to speak. "Well, she was a real surprise" She looked around at us all, to show her genuine amazement. "My husband and I'd thought it was really nice for her to go to the Uni, you know the University in Townsville. We

144

thought she'd marry one of those nice boys she went out with. Uh, uh. She got a job with the Queensland railroad. Can you believe that?! And …" She turned to me, so I'd get the full value of this amazing story, "she's doing personnel management training down in Brisbane. First woman they ever hired for the position. But, I keep reminding her she's not getting any younger, and needs to think of her future and get married, so she can have some children. But, she keeps telling me she's in no hurry. Isn't that crazy?!"

Dorothy had no idea how sexist she was towards her own daughter, yet over protective of her son. I could not resist, "Well, good for her! Nothing like breaking the barriers of the old male bastions. It's good you're so proud of her, you should be!" I figured it should keep her quiet for a while, and it did, as her face was covered with a blank stare. She glanced down to pick up the knife and a piece of roll, with a slight smile on her face. Marta looked at me, over her soup spoon and lightly laughed..

The conversations stayed light and mixed, until just before we were getting ready for dessert. Dean called for our attention, as he was about to toast Jean, whom he'd just served a 'congratulations' drink to. He stood behind Jean, with his hand lightly on her shoulder.

"Ladies and Gentlemen, I have had tour groups where no one made it to the top, and where most of the people did, but this is the first time I've had only one person, out of the group do it!" We were all wildly applauding and calling out her name, until he finally lifted his hand to quiet us down. "What I wanted to add was, it was not the best of conditions today. In fact, I was surprised for awhile they didn't close it, because the wind was pretty cold and strong" He leaned over to look Jean in the face and she was starting to get tears in her eyes. "This is one tough, determined little lady!" he toasted her glass with his beer. "Congratulations! I wish you the best of luck, always!"

Jean lifted herself slightly, and kissed Dean on the check and whispered, "thank you." We were all calling for a speech, but she waved her hand. "No, I gave my speech on the bus before. Thank you all, for your congratulations." The wind was out of her sails, for pushing herself and what she'd done. It was something she'd have the rest of her life to reflect back on, and good she had this group, who being there understood it all, to share her moment of glory. Back in England, they would not be cognizant of the numerous details, which had shaped the event to make it so memorable an accomplishment.

I'd gotten up to for some dessert and a cup of decaf, so not sure who had kicked off the conversation, but I picked-up on the subject immediately, when I sat down. "Well, I still say, we would have some dingoes, if there had been that many before. There's something, … isn't quite right about it all, … and especially them." Dorothy had been trying to speak with authority, based on centuries of her WASPy superiority complex, that anyone, even a 'white' person who was *different, was suspect*. Or, any variation *from the norm*, no mater how slight, was not to be trusted or believed.

I decided to feign ignorance, to make sure what they were talking about, but I could see from Kaylin's wide-eyed look what it was. "What are you talking about? What dingoes?" Slowly, Dorothy ate her dinner, which she'd explained to all of us, was her usual way of enjoying every, individual morsel, one bite at a time.

Marta piped up to explain, "Dorothy was just telling us about a baby which was supposed to have been taken, and killed by dingoes at Ayers Rock." There was a nervous excitement in her voice, as if she'd been careless in a dangerous area.

"Yeah," Trudy added, "it was a really big court trial, but they let the woman off on some technically thing. But she probably did it."

"You really think a woman could kill her own baby? Weren't there witnesses, or someone who saw it all?" Marta was now almost frightened at the thought.

"Oh," Trudy spoke with more authority, "it was reported, they belonged to some cult or something, and all protected each other." Marta and Kaylin had twisted their faces with disdain and disgust.

"True blue," Dorothy chimed back in. "And, they had come originally from Mt. Ida, not too far from Townsville."

That was it, I was going to stick my foot into my mouth. "I don't want to disagree with you, but I think the media kind of misled people with a lot of exaggerations and distortions of the facts. Some of the Australian newspapers are not exactly what you'd call reliable … they tend to lean toward sensationalism, to sell papers, especially with this kind of story." Dorothy glared at me, as if I was not only a Martian, but a definite, communistic one. Trudy backed down and just peered into her cup of coffee, like it would have the answers.

Marta jumped on the chance for more comforting information. "What do you know about it, Annie? Was it in the American papers?"

"Yeah, I vaguely remember it being mentioned. I think it went back to 1980 or so, and there was some real

147

strong comments about how the Aussie media handled it. The movie came out a few years ago, with Meryl Streep. I'd talked to several of my Aussie friends about the whole thing." I glanced over at Dorothy, who was back nibbling at her food, as I continued. "It seemed to most Americans, it was a simple case of being 'hung by the media' and being guilty, until she proved herself innocent. Not that it doesn't, or hadn't happened in the States, too. The *technicality* she got out of prison on, was simply the truth. They finally found the jacket, she had said the baby was wearing, and it tested positive for the dingoes, who did do it."

I glanced over at Dorothy, but she obviously did not want to acknowledge what I was saying. "They killed all the dingoes in the Ayers area, and made sure it was kept clear, though we did see some from the airplane today. You can't run a successful tourist center, and have a danger like the dingoes around."

"I don't understand," Marta questioned. "Why didn't the people want to believe the dingo killed the baby, if they were a problem and they did it?"

The discussion continued to be bounced back and forth, with several of us expressing opinions about discrimination dealing with race, religion and even sex. Dorothy did not seem too comfortable to speak up, or express her views, when the rest of us recognized the problems on a more universal extent. She pushed her chair back and rose slowly, attracting little attention, though I could feel her vibes, she was annoyed by our liberal talk.

I laughed lightly, "If Australia had a larger population, like the States, minority groups, religious and otherwise, would probably have a larger number, then not seem so 'different.'"

"Prejudices are like comforting blankets," Jean added. "We can hide under them, or use them for protection. Look how mixed England is, especially London. We have our problems, but being non-white or non-Protestant is just not so unusual any more."

Innocently Marta spoke up, "That's terrible the media would do that to the woman."

"Australia," I continued, "is not a litigious society - meaning they don't do a lot of lawsuits, but American are, in fact too much so. But at the same time, it keeps the media in check, because if it had happened in the States, there would have been a lawsuit for millions of dollars. The real heart of the problem is prejudice. We're all prejudiced to some extent. I've really learned about it since living in Japan, but I've experienced it in many other countries, including Australia." At this point Dorothy sat back down with her cake and coffee.

"There's a difference between stereotyping and prejudice, too." Jean chimed-in, as she was getting more vocal on the subject. "We all stereotype. I mean, it's fun to talk about people, especially those who are generally different enough, to group together. No one wants to be a stereotype, but we all are, in one way or another."

"Sure," I responded."I've been stereotyping the Japanese, because they're all so similar and predictable. But of course, I don't consider any of my Japanese friends to be stereotypes." Everyone was nodding and laughing at the truth. "That's the key. Once we know someone personally, we treat them as individuals, not lumps or groups or stereotypes. We're all basically human, and come from the same maker." With this note, I glanced at Dorothy, finally listening.

Jean yawned, and it was a good signal. "Yea, Jean, my feelings exactly. It's been a really long, hard day. I saw the Canyon from above, and it's not going to be any piece of cake. We all probably need to get some sleep." Marta and Kaylin pushed their chairs back, as did Trudy. I smiled once again at Dorothy. "Take your time. I'm going to stargaze a little, before going to the room. I'll see you later." I turned to several of the others, "Good Night."

Trudy was standing outside the door when I stepped out. "I guess we shouldn't believe everything we read or hear on the telly." We slowly walked toward the long, open area where the sidewalk was several meters above the ground. "I guess Aussies are kinda backwards, in some ways. I know the Brits think we're just a bunch of lazy blokes, or at least a little cracked."

I stopped to gaze out at the darkness and started laughing. "Well, I'm not so smart, but I've tried to learn from my mistakes. Having traveled a lot, I've gotten much more objective and accepting. I've learned America is *not* such a great country, when considering how we mistreated the Blacks and the Native Americans, or our prison system. And, Americans are certainly *not* loved everywhere. In fact, in Asia we still have the tag of 'ugly American.'

The first time in Thailand, I remember our tour guide telling us at the end of our two day tour, she usually hated to guide Americans, because they were so demanding and rude, always questioning why the culture can't be like in America. We were the first, who were actually polite and enjoyed the culture, without wanting to see it changed. I know I'm outspoken, even intimidating to a lot of people, and I'd often say the wrong thing, or didn't know when to shut up. It's another thing, living in Japan has taught me. I was worse, if you can imagine?" I laughed heartily at myself.

"So, now I really notice it. Other gaijns - foreigners, when they first come to Japan, and say why can't the Japanese do this, that way or why do the Japanese do that, this was … why can't the Japanese do it the American way? I just want to scream at them. 'Because THEY ARE JAPANESE and its their damn country!!!'"

We were both laughing, then let go of it all to listen to the quiet, and enjoy the night scenery. One of the security lights had been placed in a beautiful ghost gum tree, and it gave a glow which brought out the 'ghost' essence superbly. I grabbed hold of the railing, and leaned as far back as I could to look at the magnificence. The spaciousness of the illuminated sky liberated, then humbled my Spirit. "God, this is a beautiful country!"

Trudy, without missing a beat, responded in the dry Aussie sense of humor. "Yeah, but I wouldn't want to live here. Too hard on the body." We both cracked up laughing again, then sauntered back to our rooms, because tomorrow was another day of testing ourselves.

I stretched out on the bed, looking at the television when Dorothy, still talking, came walking in "Wasn't that a great dinner, and the service was really good, too?" She had stopped in front of the television, as if I'd been staring at the wall. Curious as to what *service,* she was talking about, because the dinner had been almost all buffet. "Everything has been nice - hotels and food - this whole trip. I'm so glad my sister got me to join them. How about you? Have you enjoyed yourself so far?"

I thought, *"Boy, lady! Don't leave yourself so wide open for my answer, because I'll tell you up till now, I have had a great time."* I barely had time to agree, before she was rattling on about what they had seen and done. I clicked off the television, and sat up on the bed cross-legged, as she obviously wanted to talk. *I'd see how long*

I could put up with it.

She filled me in on Melbourne and Adelaide, as they were the only two cities she'd gone to on the tour, which I'd not seen. I listened to her making statements which were not really logical, with great authority. It suddenly occurred to me, who she reminded me of: Gracie Allen of *'Burns and Allen,'* the early radio and television comedians, then of course, Lucille Ball of *'I Love Lucy.'* I remember as a child, how funny they were on television. But, to have a walking, talking- incarnate to share space, and try to converse with, was almost frightening. "It's so educational and interesting to see other parts of the country. I've already used up two rolls of film! What about you? Your big, professional camera and fancy lens, looks really complicated. Of course, mine has the little button for close-up or far away."

While there was a momentary pause, I jumped in, "No, it's not actually professional, but it does shoot nice pictures for an old AE-1, and it's not really complicated at all. I've shot about seven or eight, thirty-six exposures so far on this trip." I let those numbers get calculated then decided to clarify. "Film is cheap, so my nephew, the photographer, says, and I never know when or if, I'd get a chance again. Besides, I like to have a lot of photos, and if I decide to sell a travel story, or something, I have them. Have you traveled outside of Australia?" *This should be revealing, as where would someone like her go, and what would her reactions be.* A 'Yahoo,' was the term my native-Italian restaurant-friend in Townsville, called people like Dorothy.

"Oh, Yes! I went to see my cousin in America. California! Aah, Bakersfield." She said it all with such pride, I tried very hard to keep a straight face, for I knew exactly what was coming next. The same as the Japanese, who make the requisite pilgrimage to Disneyland or

152

Hollywood, and think they had visited 'America,' and now knew American culture. "And you know," she was informing me, as if this was some big secret, "it's really not so different from Townsville!" I thought, *Lady, you got that one right.* Bakersfield would *not* be that much different. I just smiled and nodded, then sucked in my lips to control any laughter coming out.

"Well, on that note," I thought and leaned over to pull my nightgown out of my bag, "I guess I'll get ready for bed. We've got another long physical day tomorrow." Her talk followed me all the way into the bathroom, and for a full minute after I closed the door. When I came back out, she'd put on pajamas and in the process if putting her hair up, in *jumbo pink foam rubber* curlers. *I was about to say, I'd not seen those since high school, but was sure she'd not get the joke. There was no real need to pick on her, just because she was so different from myself.* "All yours," I said politely, and stuffed my rolled clothes back into my bag again.

I picked-up the in-room movie guide, *'Other's People's Money'* was about to come on, so I switched on the TV, to watch for awhile. We talked back and forth about movies for a few minutes, and I hoped she'd not continue to talk while it was on. Yet, I should've known better, some habits no way can some people control.

"Theres not much these days that's worth the time, or money, to go and see. They're either taking their clothes off, and doing who knows what right on the screen, or they're killing someone with lots of blood all over the place. It's just terrible … terrible." She'd finally finished setting her hair and rose to withdraw to the bathroom. "But, you can leave it on, it doesn't bother me. I can usually sleep." I thought, *"How interesting! Was she going to sleep in the bathroom, like she needed to inform me of it now?"*

Already laughing my ass off, and totally engrossed in the movie, when she came back out and sat on her bed for a few minutes. It did not take long for her to begin her comments, as Danny DeVito had not only let go of a few expletives, but also several sexual innuendos. "Oh, that's unnecessary There is no need for people to talk that way and to be so crude!" I could not help looking at her, as I'd not heard that kind of reaction for years. And, I was sure it was my mother who had said it. She pulled back her covers and was proceeding to get in, when she stopped to watch some more.

"It's just the reality of the character being portrayed. I mean … it is how a lot of business people are." I knew I was wasting my time defending it, but habits of rescuing are not easy to break. We both watched in silence for a few minutes, until Danny's abrasive character pulled a few more shots. She got up and pulled back the covers again.

"That's terrible and I can't watch that!" She was now under the covers, but her eyes were still glued to the set. Another few minutes, before she let out with a huff, turned her head away and called out to me, "Watch if you must, but I'm not gonna waste my time. Good night." I knew there was no use causing problems, and I did need my sleep, too. I turned it off and called, 'good night' to her, as I switched off the lights, and crawled into bed. Though she was probably not much older than me, I could not help feeling, we were more than a generation apart.

Our wake-up call came right on time, so I bounced up and into the bathroom as quickly as I could. Today, I was going to dress warmly with my jeans and sweatshirt, more for hiking than climbing, so nothing should limit my enjoyment. Dorothy was just finishing removing her curlers, when I came out and she had another pants outfit laid out to wear. "Should I wear my sneakers today?"

I put back on my own trekkers, straining a bit as my jeans were rather tight in the thigh and I stopped to look up at her. "I would

... the Canyon I saw I'd regard as pretty rough. That is if you're going to climb ... although I think even the riverbed walk and the Canyon floor suggests supportive footwear." I continued with the other shoe, not really wanting to contend with her this morning.

"Do you think it's going to be that difficult?" Standing in front of me with her little toiletry bag and clothes. It took me a second to decide how I wanted to answer her.

"The brochure says, 'Not for the fainthearted or unfit,' and I think it takes two to three hours, but rewards 'a spectacular view from the rim.' As I said, from the airplane yesterday, it was massive and rugged." Not about to advise her one way for the other, as I'd seen and heard how she chastised and named other people for her problems. "I'm going for a walk, so I'll see you in the dining room, OK?" I grabbed my jacket, as she tottered into the bathroom.

I loved the early morning with the dew, and I certainly needed the fresh air. And, not too late, as many of the plants were still glistening in the soft, golden sun. A little chilly, so I pulled my jacket hood over my head, and slipped my gloves on. Some flowers had closed during the night, and were now opening back up to greet the sun. I wished I'd brought my camera to record some of the lovely, dewy-reflections and color. So silent, I could hear the giant, dark- brown kite-hawk swinging in its large circles, looking for his breakfast on the run. Quiet mornings like this in a country so coarse, lusty, and refreshed my soul. I wondered if a place existed, which could give me everything - the culture and convenience of a city, adjacent to a countryside teeming with challenging, natural recreational areas.

I followed the driveway, all the way around and finally ended up back at the dining room, where everyone was waiting for the hot, buffet breakfast to be laid out. Some people had begun helping themselves to the cold dishes, as it was already after eight o'clock. I walked over, poured myself a glass of juice then went to talk to Jean and Trudy. "Good morning. How're the bodies today, ladies? I'm a bit stiff." I swallowed down the juice and put the glass on the table corner. "Well, I'm looking forward to taking it easy today," said Jean.

"It's supposed to be strenuous, but there are also some nice leisurely stretches, with a great gorge and lots of vegetation along the river. Or, I guess they'd call it a creek."

"Yeah, me too," Trudy responded, "And, I didn't even do as much yesterday, as you did."

"Hey, everyone," Dean was calling our attention, "if you want to go ahead and eat, … we're going to leave here at eight forty-four, and we need to load the luggage and things. I suggest you don't eat too much either, as the climb's easier on a lighter stomach." He took his coffee and toast, then went over to a table to sit down.

"Ugh, oh. It doesn't sound too good. I was looking forward to a nice hot breakfast and I've got to worry about making another climb." I looked at Trudy, and she just shrugged her shoulders. Jean had already started for the granola and fruit, so I followed. Though most of the fruit was canned, which was understandable, the granola and yogurt were rather refreshing, as I reminded myself how healthy they were. We separated ourselves again, somewhat away from the others, at a large table next to the floor-to-ceiling windows. The brilliant sun flooded that part of the room, bringing nature indoors. When I saw the kite-hawk again, I pointed it out to the others, though it was hard to see in the glare.

"Annie, you mentioned last night about Japanese friends ... you know, them not being stereotypes," Jean questioned, "Do you have many? ... Are they mostly teachers like yourself?"

"One of the things I like about living in Japan especially, is there is a very large, mixed foreign and Japanese community. What I mean is, say if we all lived in the States, I'd probably never have gotten to meet, or certainly not be friends with most of them. Remember, I don't come from a teaching background, but a business trainer, and now almost all of my friends work as teachers, or are somehow related to the teaching field." I paused to take a sip of coffee and recall in my mind *this was one of the main reasons why, I'd probably never live in the Midwest or Chicago suburbs again. I'd grown to really like foreigners, their vast variety of opinions and experiences.* Living in Japan had even changed a lot of the Americans, to be more objective about the world.

"I'd say, my best Japanese friend is Kazuyo, who I actually met the first day I came to Nagoya. She worked as a materials- coordinator for the same language teaching company, which hired me. Of course, I needed to spend a lot to time with her, since starting new classes and needed to know the material. Her excellent English didn't prepare me for the reality of how badly the students spoke. She'd lived in Sydney for a year going to school and had traveled around Australia, so she was quite outspoken for a Japanese woman. She was perhaps in her late twenties at the time."

"Was she married? I've read most Japanese women don't work after they're married?" Marta asked as she and Kaylin had joined us.

I gobbled down some fruit and yogurt, before answering. "No, she's still not married and it's quite upsetting to her mother. Kazuyo was put through the rituals of *omiai* - the arranged meeting for the marriage thing, on a regular basis, but so far all toads and frogs. She figures if she marries, it will probably be a foreigner, because she's too independent for most Japanese men. They'd also be intimidated by her English ability, which is now translation quality." I continued to eat some more granola, when Trudy spoke up.

"Does your friend live at home, or is she on her own?"

"She's still lives at home, though she'd love to be on her own, or at least sharing an apartment. With the recession starting to come on strong in Japan, she hasn't been able to get a real good full-time job, and it is very expensive on your own. She's expected, too, to help her mother with the cooking and cleaning, when she's not working." I took another swallow of coffee and noticed they were listening attentively, so I wanted to give credit where it was due by adding a little more.

"Kazuyo comes to a discussion class, I have in my apartment and always stays after to talk. She honestly keeps me in touch with the Japanese opinions on current topics, and how Japan has changed, even more so than my adult students. I have several other, older female Japanese friends who are married to foreigners, which I'd put in a different category than the young ones married to foreigners. These older ones were too independent for Japanese men and their foreign husbands didn't want 'yes' girls, so they're business women."

"But Annie, I was wondering how much you really socialize with the Japanese, and are they only the ones who can speak English? Jean wanted to get down to brass tacks, and see if I practiced what I preached about prejudice.

I laughed a little, "Well, in Tokyo, and maybe even Osaka, there's a large and very separate gaijin community - government, business and teachers. Many of them don't need to, or even want to socialize with any Japanese, unless they have to, like living in a foreign compound in the Middle East. But in Nagoya, it's much smaller, and the foreigners are mainly teachers, so we just sort of naturally mingle with the Japanese, especially at the schools where we work. I have to say, very few people I know are 'gaijin only' people, and some of the Japanese I know, are truly more interesting than some of the gaijin. I have two parties a year, with about fifty people, which is no small feat, considering the size of my apartment." I laughed again, but then realized the joke was lost on them, for they could not comprehend how small it was.

"Anyway, it is about fifty-fifty, Japanese-Gaijin. I have to say most of the Japanese who come speak good English. Since I'm not fluent in Japanese, it's how we talk together on a regular basis. They are my private students and friends of mine or other gaijin, but English is not a requirement, since there'd be plenty of Japanese for them to talk to. And, a lot of gaijin like to practice their Japanese, in a relaxed setting like that. In reality though, it is usually the ones who can speak good English who do come, because the others would not want to embarrass them-selves by making any mistakes talking. It's a real hang-up the Japanese have."

Several people were starting to leave the dining room, though they'd just put out the hot food. "Oh, gee, I wanted to see what they had, before we a have to go. Anybody else want to take a look?" I got up to check out the buffet, with Trudy and Marta following.

We tried a little bit of a few items then finished up, as it was past eight-thirty. I noticed, as we we're leaving Dorothy and her little group were still eating and chatting away. Marta piped up, as we walked out the door. "Does that lady, your roommate, bother you? She sure talks a lot." Kaylin and Trudy laughed, but Jean defended her.

"She's just lonely and needs attention." Spoken like a real trooper, I thought, and also someone who had been in the same boat with Dorothy's counterpart. She finally added, "My mother's the same way, since my dad died, and my brother and sister don't want to be bothered with her."

"I agree with Jean," I said, as we walked. "She drives me wacko a bit, because of the limited scope of her acceptance, but I've been able to tune her out some of the time." I snickered, "She's even a bit entertaining. She was telling me about the surprise birthday party they had for an aunt, and it all got so stuffed up, simply from disorganization and lack of communication."

I laughed at the absurdity of it, as I was coming from a bilingual situation, where it happened frequently. "And, here they are supposed to speak the same language, and she didn't even see it! They went ahead and had the party

160

without the aunt, because they didn't want the food to go bad, while the aunt was at another relative's house. The sister, or whomever didn't want to even call and tell them, because she didn't want to ruin the surprise for the aunt. So, they just sat there and waited, while, of course, nobody showed up." We were now all laughing "I couldn't help laughing at this in front of her, as the whole family must be cracked!" We had stopped in front of Marta and Kaylin's room. "OK, see you on the bus." We went to our rooms to gather our belongings.

I opened the door with my bag in hand, when Dorothy came hurrying in. "I don't like being rushed. Don't like it at all." She had put her purse down, and stopped to fix her hair in the mirror. "I hardly got a chance to eat any brekkie! Now they want us out of here in five minutes!" She turned to look at me, as I was only waiting for a space to jump in and excuse myself. "Five minutes? Fair *Dinkum!* He said it to me, himself. Believe that, will ya?" She had clothes scattered all over her bed, the dresser, the chair and an unbelievable assortment of cosmetics and bottles in the bathroom. It'd been some experience, all right, and one I'd not want to repeat, any too soon. You never really got to know anyone until you 'slept' with them!

There was nothing I could say, and certainly nothing I could, or would do. I pasted another smile on my face, as I stepped out into the hall, "Good Luck! I'll see you on the bus." I quickly closed the door, before she could pull me further into her wallow. I walked over to the bus and stood in line to give Dean my bag. When I saw the water dripping down the side of the bus, I realized Dean had washed it. With the rain and dust yesterday, it had gotten quite dirty very fast. I guess keeping the windows and the bus clean was a major job for him to keep up with. The sun was rising quite high now, and the clouds had all cleared. It promised to be a beautiful day, and it would probably even warm up. "Pacific Springs Resort," I said, when it came my turn, as he'd asked each one before me, where they were staying.

Dean glanced up at me, then asked as he was placing my bag to the far side. "Where's your roommate? She goin' to make it out here, some time today?"

I beamed from ear to ear, "Ain't my 'job, man, to watch her any more! We done finished being roomies." I cracked up laughing at my own ridiculousness. "She's all yours!"

Dean just stared at me and shook his head, "Aren't you a bloody great help? Get on the bus, before I make you sit with her."

I jumped on the bus and laughed all the way to my seat. He was not in the best of moods, as it as after nine o'clock when Dorothy and several of the others finally got on the bus. It was only a short drive over to the main entrance to the Canyon hiking trail. Dean got us started down one trail, while he led the older group over to the path for the Canyon floor and walk to the base of the waterfall. Before leaving, Dorothy questioned which group she should join, as she was still angry with Dean. "I don't want to be rushed," she finished up, pouting.

He'd had enough of it with her, and very bluntly said, "Then this is the trail for you." I could see his teeth almost grinding. We all headed in the other direction, at a rather fast clip along the flat trail. By the time he came trundling back over, most us were still struggling to get up even the first few meters of the rugged boulders. The so-called path, followed to the top … which was about one hundred meters, almost straight above my head.

I had screwed up again! I'd not expected to be doing so much climbing, and my jeans were much too tight, especially from the knees up. I could hardly lift my legs up at all, to step from rock to rock. More pulling myself up, by grabbing hold of one craggy mound after another. It helped, too, my tote bag loaded down with at least four kilos of junk - camera, binoculars, water bottle, and all the other useless things like wallet, money, tissue, etc. One after another, I let people pass me by, as I caught my breath and took off my unneeded jacket to tie it around my waist. I was going to do this, and that was all there was to it! Not so dangerous or impossible, as it was simply tedious and difficult.

Trudy was waiting and resting not too far ahead of me, "How's it going? You OK?"

"Well, besides being pissed at myself, for wearing the wrong clothes AGAIN! And, carrying too much shit!! I'll make it, slow but sure" I pulled myself up next to her, and leaned on another rock. "They're not kidding, not for the 'fainthearted or unfit.' This is serious rock climbing." About that time Dean was coming back down, as he'd noticed two of the older ladies seemed to need his help. Trudy and I watched below, as he helped them back down the rugged trail.

I looked over to Trudy, "That means you and I are the tail-end now." She turned and slowly continued up one rock after another. I was suddenly envious of her loose jeans and long, sturdy legs. I pulled myself up, took a deep breath, blew it out, and grabbed hold of another rock to haul my body up to the next level. I broke a fingernail, cursed and reached up again. Boy, was I having fun!

Only about thirty meters from the top, with the sweat beginning to pour off of me, as I stopped once again to rest. I heard Jean and Marta calling to me. "Come on Annie! We're all waiting for you. Dean said we all had to stay together."

I thought, oh great, now I'm holding up the whole group! I'm sure they're all pleased with me. I made sure I had a good hold on the ledge as at this point it could rather be mortifying to fall, and I leaned back to yell at them. "Tell then to go on, I'm slow, but I'm OK."

I could see them talking and finally Marta disappeared, but Jean and Trudy stayed watching me. I hustled myself once again, and crawled up the next boulder. *And, I thought climbing Ayers Rock was stupid! Nobody I know has probably ever even heard of this bloody Canyon. So why do it?* I paused at the next rock, and continued the debate with myself. *Because I do want to see it, as there really are some uniqued things to see here. AND, ... I did want to know I could DO IT!!!* With the renewed spirit, I went another ten meters before resting again.

As I came up the last ridge, I thought all of the others had gone, but Marta and Kaylin were merely taking some pictures with Jean, while Trudy sat under a tree.

"Yea! Here she is!" Called Marta, the first to see me.

"We knew you could make it," said Trudy, getting up to meet me, walking toward them.

"Dean said the rest of it's easy," Jean reported when I came wheezing up to her. "But, we need to get going. I sent the others ahead, but I don't want Dean to get upset with us."

I gave her a look like she could not be serious, as if Dean was gong to punish us by not letting us eat lunch or something. "I want to do this, Jean, or I wouldn't have come all the way to the top. There's supposed to be a lot of really interesting rock formations, trees and even some very rare ferns, over by the oasis. In other words, I don't want to rush through the Canyon." I shook my head, "Now, I sound like Dorothy. Truly, I do want to enjoy it and I'll hurry, but some of it has to be at my own pace. I doubt Dean would actually be upset … worried maybe, or just concerned." They were looking at me and possibly wondering why they had waited. I'd taken out my water bottle and was chug-a-lugging some down. "OK? Thank you for waiting. Let's go!" I perked up right away and threw a smile on my face. *I guess I was still rather reactionary about being controlled, even by a tour guide. Sometimes, I thought, I do better as a loner!*

I decided to tie my hair back before going on, as it was cooler off my neck, so I dug into my bag for a cotton-elastic band. "Is your hair natural curly, Annie?" The others had started walking, but Trudy stayed standing next to me. I was not sure if it was solidarity or curiosity. I knew I was a weird-bugger to her.

"No, I wish it was, it's just wavy. I get perms about every six months, when I'm traveling and sometimes it's not an easy trick." We were walking at an easy pace about fifty meters or so behind the others "I'd never have it done in Japan, or other Asian countries where there aren't a lot of Caucasians. Asian hair is usually very thick, coarse and quite straight, so when they're doing perms, they have to use very strong chemicals. which burn thinner hair, like mine. I color my hair, so its already taking some beating … I have to be careful."

I ran my fingers through the top of my hair. "I had this done in Brisbane and it's great, a really good perm. I had one done in Townsville, too, one time. I had one in Rome, which was quite an experience, and extravagance, as it was the most expensive one I've ever had. But, they insisted on putting makeup on me, too. I did look exceptional," I laughed.

We caught up with Marta, who was photographing some giant spreading ghost gums, against a backdrop of interestingly-shaped, sedimentary sandstone rock. The white-barked trees with bright green leaves did give a lovely contrast, to the sandwiched-layered, coarse ochre cliffs. We decided to take some shots and stopped to comment about the power of water, and what it had created so long ago. Everyone was more relaxed, as we drifted on following the scattered path markers, which we presumed to be the logical direction. We were eventually, supposed to cross the gorge to the other side of the canyon, in order to reach the bus. Once in a while, we would see stragglers from the main group, so it was not as if we could get lost.

The terrain varied greatly, from gigantic, granite slabs under our feet, to slabs jutting out at all sorts of angles, as if tossed around, or broken up by being dropped. At other times, there would be sand, or even slippery pebbles underfoot, as the path would converge from a wide expanse to a small opening, towered over by monstrous crags. The scrubs and plants had an ancient look of meager survival, which we all commented on as appearing to be from another time and place. Still quite raw nature, giving us the sense we were exploring, while echoing the 'ohs' and 'aha' of child-like wonderment. We saw a few informative signs, which gave both Aboriginal information and historical data on the Canyon's supposed formation. Just when we least expected it, there would be a mass of wild flowers, whose myriad colors would almost jump out at us, as we stumbled upon them. The rocky land amazed us at every turn - it seemed to change, yet aspects of the dominant weathered domes, stayed the same in their silence.

We'd been out for about an hour, when we came to a precipice which opened up back to the valley where we had come from. I took out the binoculars to check, and even discounting the height, it was easy to acknowledge we had come a long way. "No wonder I'm tired," said Marta trying to laugh as she passed the binocs to Jean. "That's really far away." She turned and gazed again. "Look at how far you can see to the horizon and how continuously flat it is, with the red showing through all the green." I took a swallow of water and rested while each one had a turn looking through the glasses. Satisfied I'd pushed myself to make this effort, such a spectacular sight with so much to see. Many of the views, I recognized from the plane.

Soon, we had reached one of the most famous spots where the Canyon not only opened wide, but the layers had shaped themselves into what looked like a camel squatted down. The Spaniards were having great fun posing around, as well in front of it, and others had their cameras clicking or videos whirring. We all seemed thrilled at this carnival-sight, which nature had so nonchalantly deposited for us. I put on my hat, as the sun was beginning to burn down, and took my jacket from around my waist to fasten it to my tote bag.

A good thing the Canyon gave us a distraction every now then, because the up and down of the rocks was wearing. There was virtually no shade, unless one stopped in the shadows of a high rock wall, or paused under the few trees which dotted the trails. Many of those, though, were situated so more difficult to get to them, than the ensuing shade likely to compensate for.

Our next excitement came not too long after, as we discovered a tree limb and rock bridge connecting two separate formations of rock. Obviously, it had been used by the Aborigines, as the distant section had a pyramid-stacked appearance, and a high point of the Canyon. It had probably been used as a ceremonial spot or something.

The gap between the two was only a few meters, but the depth of the ravine had to have been several hundred. Simply frightening to look at, and no way I could imagine the sure-footedness needed to get across it, if I had to. Glad to see it was neither in our direction, nor did the park people want us near it.

The terrain was getting much rougher, in appearance and to traverse. Jean had been left behind with me and we sometimes caught a glimpse of the others. Not sure if they had gotten bored, and just wanted to be finished with it, or if they were curious to see what was next. I was going as quickly as I could, considering watching every step, so as not to fall or slip on any of the loose stones.

Jean was standing above me, and reached down to give me a hand. "Here," I passed up my tote bag instead, "If you'll just take my bag, I can pull myself up, with this scrawny tree. I think it will hold me." She took the bag, and with great effort I hauled myself up. It was steep and the gravel kept slipping. Jean had gone ahead with my bag. "That's OK, Jean. I'll take it."

"No, let me carry it for awhile, Annie. You're getting tired and I don't mind."

I understood what she was doing, yet a part of me, just did not want her to do it. "No, Jean, please. It's my fault for binging all the junk. Really, I'll carry it…. my responsibility." She had kept walking and I was trying to hurry to keep up with her. "Please, Jean I feel bad enough dragging you behind and being so slow, because I'm so out of shape. I'd only feel worse if you carried my stupid bag, too."

She stopped and turned to look at me. "Annie, I know what's it's like to be left behind, and to be the last one. I've had that most of my life," her face was very serious and sincere. "I want to do this for you. At least for a little while, let me carry it."

I realized it was more important to her to help, than it was for me to defy my personal independence. "OK, thanks." But not sure how to convey my feelings. "When you get tired of it, just say so, or I'll say something. All right?" She smiled and nodded, as she turned up the trail.

"Don't we make a pair?" I mused. "Two 'helping' kind of women needing to express their individual states." The ground flattened out again and we marched along at a pretty good clip for a while, when I noticed some cactus plants and pointed them out to Jean. "After ten years in Texas, I got used to seeing them and I don't think I've seen them since. Strange to have such heavy, water plants like ferns in the Canyon bottom and cactus up on top." We were standing next to each other, so I reached over and retrieved the bag. "This is rather flat here. I'll take it now, thanks." It was as if I had to have an excuse to relieve her of the burden.

"May I ask you, Annie, did you meet your husband in Chicago or Texas?" She'd walked ahead again, as I lumbered along, hefting the bag onto a shoulder.

"No, it was in Texas. I'd moved down there with my son after a brief, uneventful stay in Oklahoma. I worked for an oil company, and managed to get transferred to San Antonio. But Travis was from Houston area, and had moved over there, too."

"Oh, I thought he was your son's father." As we came around the next wall formation, the Canyon rim suddenly dropped off, with the oasis valley and springs below the gorge. "Well, we have come to our goal, I guess." Jean's comment was an understatement of the vision we were about to behold. Far below, we could see a few people walking along the ledge which surrounded the two deep water holes, even further down into the layered rock. The startling greens from the numerous substantial spreading-ferns with thick trees, were both a surprise and a joy to the eyes. Across the chasm, we could see people slowly climbing the numerous stairs on the other side back up to the top. Jean turned and regarded me with surprise, covered with disappointment. "I thought we walked out from the Canyon floor. We've still got a ways to go!"

"Shit! It must be close to two hours by now. I was expecting this to be it, too." After taking a few pictures, we resigned ourselves to the reality, and got on with it. Clumping down the metal steps, I continued our conversation. "How about you, Jean. Have you ever been married?" I was trying not to pry, but I was still so curious, I was probably too open and talkative about my own personal life, which I knew some people did not want to hear.

"Yes, I was." The response was slow, and something she probably did not talk much about. "I was young and he died in an accident." She tried to sound matter of factly, but there was regret in her voice "I thought about marriage once or twice after, but I guess I was still expecting too much, or wanting some guarantee or something. I just couldn't do it again." She was quiet for a little, and I did not know if I could say something, since she'd left it hanging. "I guess, I sometimes regret I didn't, because as I'm getting older, I regret being alone."

The stairs wound down with short walkways in-between. I tried to step, so I did not bend my bad left knee too much, after the past two days of climbing, it was giving me a fit! I'd have to take a pain pill after lunch. "How about you, Annie? Do you have any regrets, or will you get married again?'

"I've tried earnestly, to make it a rule to never regret and never look back, or have any 'what ifs.' Regret ... I think is like my girlfriend, Maureen, told me about hate, 'a tremendous waste of energy.' I try to let it go and get on, but not before taking stock of how the situation happened, and thus make sure I won't make the same mistake again. I also try to see if, I need to make amends with others, then eventually with myself."

I paused to take in the glories of nature, now surrounding us as we had reached the bottom plateau. The smell was wonderfully fresh and clean, from all the ferns, palms and other strange plants, which I had never seen before. In the far distance, we could even hear the steady ripple of the creek. The two water holes must have been another one hundred meters or so, further down and still looked quite clear. "God, this is wonderful." We soaked it in for a few minutes, and took a few more photos.

"Annie?" I turned and Jean had clicked a picture of me as I laughed. "Here." she handed me her camera, "would you take a picture of me, with all of this in the background." There was suddenly a mutual feeling of schoolgirls on a day's outing, and we were capturing memories we would have to enjoy, once we were older. We finally started back up the steps, and Jean picked back up the conversation. "Well, I know what you're saying about regreets, and I try not to have them, but I think it all depends on how much you care for what you lost or don't have."

"I know, I used to think that way, too. But you've got to get on with your life. I mean my marriage was both bad and good - his obsessiveness and controlling, versus his intelligence and curiosity. And the sex was quite good, the first five years, or so. The problem was, the man I married wasn't the same man I divorced." She stopped and peered closely at me. I'd taken off my unneeded hat and sunglasses before, so I stared back at her. We both then cracked up laughing. "I guess all people change, and we sure didn't change in the same direction."

We continued moving up the steps for at least the talking, took our minds off the tedium of it all. "I realize now that's part of the reason for my trip back to Australia. I'm trying to process it all, while making amends to my friends, so I can let go of it all." Some of this talk was helping me to clarify things and feelings to myself, too. "I know this sounds strange, but it's as if I'm returning to the scene of the crime, to understand how it all happened, and to see if there was anything I could have done to prevent it." Jean stopped again and peered at me questioning. "You mean you didn't want this divorce? I though you did want it?" *I was sure she was quite amazed, at all this glaring honesty and in reality, so was I.*

"Oh, no, I mean yes. I DID VERY MUCH WANT IT!" I paused, not knowing how to explain all of the guilt complexes my mother had dumped on me, and I'd chosen to continue to carry "Hey, I'm opening veins over this … I'm opening bottles of champagne. The love came disguised as honest, and disfigured by sex." She turned and stared at me again, as I took a deep breath *and realized how devastatingly true my statement was.*

172

"I just need to make sure, so I don't feel sorry or guilty for him. I did do everything I could have done to try to make the marriage work. I know now it was basically over, before we came to Japan. We should've ended it then, but I have a real problem letting go of things, and being blamed for not trying harder. Besides that, it's never just one person's fault. I know I'm not easy to live with, because I'm kind of a perfectionist, and a definite workaholic. I want to be successful, he just wants the money and he couldn't handle it"

"Oh, I can understand all that." She turned back climbing, and I realized why she'd never remarried. I was not the only one who had the 'hope springs eternal' disease, but she did not want to be disillusioned by reality. "So what did you mean by 'scene of the crime.' Did you have some big fight here or something?"

"Yeah, I guess you could say that. I don't remember if I told you, but Travis had wanted to live here and on our second trip he was desperately, supposedly, job hunting and even had a fairly good lead. The problem was, he was so negative and actually afraid of success. As I said, I've realized a lot of this after the fact, of course. So, with his paranoia, anything even slightly, which could be construed as going against him, he attacked defensively."

She turned to glance at me, not believing my language. "I know, I know, this is all pretty heavy and psychological, but I've gone over this with several people who knew him. You know, I'm trying to clear myself here of my guilt. Anyway, he would use these things to rationalize why something didn't work out - you know, something, no matter how vague, someone else did it which caused his failure.

So, to make a very long story short, it was a poor, old schmuck of a taxi driver in Brisbane, who I was trying to pay with a voucher from Qantas, from our prior screwed up flight. The printing wasn't very clear on it, and the taxi driver had never had one before, so of course, thought we were trying to rip him off."

She turned and looked at me with pure amazement, "You're kidding? You got a divorce over a taxi fare?"

I cracked up laughing. "I guess you could say that, or the huge awareness of what came from it. Though a bit more complicated than that." We were nearing to the top of the stairs and I was relieved, as I could barely talk now for the wheezing, huffing and puffing of it all. She leaned down and took my bag. I gave her no hassles about it, as it was a relief. "Travis caused a scene at the airport, while I tried to get us checked in, and the little taxi driver had followed us in, still questioning about the voucher. I asked if he had given the driver a tip, and that's when he blew up at me. He started throwing money at the taxi driver, saying Australia didn't appreciate him and all the money spent there as a tourist. I told him he was making a fool of himself, and I'd have nothing to do with it all. So, I took the tickets and went up the to the departure lounge, leaving him still fuming at the taxi driver." We had finally reached the top and come out on other broad open stretch. In the far distance, we could see a few people, so we picked up the pace.

"So, how did you file for divorce, when you were in the middle of a vacation?"

I glanced at her, pursed my lips and giggled in embarrassment. "No, unfortunately that was over two years ago, the second day of a four-week vacation, which had a been prepaid. I was determined to have a good time and most of the rooms had two beds. Finally, after a week he apologized and asked me to forgive him, which for the up- teeth time, I did. But later, when we had our final blow-out, he cited that particular incident as to when he exactly knew I 'no longer supported him and he knew the marriage was over…'" I paused to add, "I laugh my ass off now, when I think about the irony of it, it all went on for so long, because neither one of us had the guts to get out. The charade went on and on."

I turned and looked at her, as we tromped along side-by-side on the granite slabs, having become almost oblivious to the alien surroundings. I slipped my bag back from her and heaved it over my opposite shoulder. My eyes drifted to the distant horizon, and the stark beauty of this desert geology hit me again, as to where we were. "God, I didn't mean to dump all of this on you. I guess it just comes out, as part of my processing. What started us on it all, anyway?"

"Oh, I don't know. Maybe my saying I had hesitated getting married again, after listening to other people's experiences, like yours. I'm kind of glad I didn't."

"Well, I believe good, bad or indifferent, we're meant to have all of the experiences we do, because they are part of our growing process. So, maybe in this lifetime, you do not need to have any more of those lessons." I glanced up and noticed someone walking towards us and suddenly realized it was Dean. I waved to him, he stopped, and we picked up our speed a little.

"How ya' going' ladies?" He appeared to be a little concerned, but since we saw some other people in the distance, it was not as if they were all waiting on the bus for us, or something.

"Tired, but fine," answered Jean and we kept plodding along. I just smirked back at him.

"There's about another twenty minutes or so on this last section, then it starts down." He had continued to walk with us for a few feet. "Is there anyone behind you?"

"No, we're it, and I dragged Jean back with me. Sorry, I'm so slow, but there is some great scenery to see, as well as some steep rocks to climb."

He looked at me and laughed. He'd gotten my point. "OK, it shouldn't be too difficult from here on to the end." We were just getting to another small gorge, when we heard someone calling to us, and saw one of the Spaniards across on the other side.

"YOU GUTTA COME A LOOK! IT ESE BEEUUTEEFULL!"

He was standing at the edge of the drop off and pointing down at the breath-taking view. It was as if the rock slabs had been sheared off, polished and stacked at angles to one another. All the way down the side of the small canyon area, had some water and trees growing at the bottom.

Dean was not thrilled with the Spaniard gong so far off the trail, or standing so close to the edge. Above all, he had a great concern for our safety and these Spaniards had tested it several times. "We can see it just fine from here. Now, Please come back!!!" The Spaniard threw up his arms, like it was our loss, took another photo, and turned back to join us "OK, ladies. I'll see you back at the bus. Let's hurry along now, OK?"

"Yes, Dear, I mean Dean!" I said. Then Jean and I both laughed. He shook his head and went on his way back, as the crazy Spaniard was now running in the heat to catch up. I put my hat back on and adjusted my sun glasses. Jean and I worked our way over to the last section of rock then started the descent. Steep and again slippery, with lots of pebbles and stones to watch out for. The track soon became a single file path, so we grabbed branches, bushes and outcroppings of rocks to steady ourselves. We were about half-way down, when we saw another tour group coming up the little tract. I was surprised to see them starting so late in the day, then I figured out this must be the short-cut or shorter version of the trek.

Jean and I stepped aside, as the younger, more agile, group leader bounced past, calling out "G]day." We had a reprieve to continue on our own way, before the older ones gradually began trekking up. "Annie, I'm going to try to get past them, if I can. Need to go to the toilet OK? I'll see you on the bus."

"Thanks, Jean, I really appreciated your staying with me for the hike. I know I spouted off at the beginning, but I'm still real sensitive about being controlled by other people. It's left over from the marriage, as well as living in Japan, with all of its rigidity" I beamed at her and added, "It was fun sharing all this with you." I grabbed another branch, as my foot slid a little.

"Hey, I enjoyed sharing it all with you, too, and the talk was most educational and interesting. Maybe it might come in handy one of these days." She had looked back up at me with the last comment, then back to the older heavyset man, who she was coming face to face with. "Excuse me." She slipped around him one way, and the woman behind him the other, as she made her way round them all.

I had stopped to let the man pass, and he paused to get his own breath. "Is it like this all the way, or does it get better or worse?" He was wiping his brow with a handkerchief, as he took off his 'XXXX' beer cap. I figured he must have been an Aussie from Brisbane, the home of 'XXXX'.

"Well, I laughed, "Both. It depends on how far you're going." "Why that bloke told us there was nothing to this! He'd turned
to his wife, who was also wiping her brow, though a bit more daintily, around her hat.

"Cheeky Bastard!" She mumbled under her breath. "He should not be doing this to us, in this heat. What if one of us *carks-it*?"
The way they kept looking up the path, I figured the first, young sprightly man who had first passed us, must have been their tour guide. He obviously did not have the protective nature Dean or his company had.

"Actually, this is the shorter, easier route and the Canyon is quite beautiful to see. Just take your time and you'll enjoy it all. I moved around them, "I'd better get going. I think my tour bus will be waiting for me. Good Luck!" Step by step, I worked my way down and around the people who were strung out in twos and threes, until I finally reached the bottom and jumped down to the flat ground with both feet.
Not any great feat to go into the Guinness Book of Records, but for me it had been more than a minor accomplishment. I threw my arms up in the air and shouted, "One giant step for Annie's independence, and one incredible leap for women who are FREEEEE!" As I ran over to the bus, I noticed Jean, Trudy and others waving to me. God, it was great to be me, and have supportive friends even if I was slow.

The Pulse of My Growing Was A Walking Pace

We followed the patterns of previous occupants,
whose tribes and ancestors remained,
they stayed in the original languages.
Uluru. Yorro Yorro. You Yangs.

A silence broken only via birds and cicadas.
Bushlands that swallowed. Island consciousness.

Before us, many names invoked in song cycles.
Dialects that traveled. Totems that named-spear,
woomera, boomerang. Heat meant you carried only a
dilly-bag, clap-sticks for ceremony.

All that you needed, lived in the land with you. Dig,
learn, feast! Grubs and worms, snakes, lizards,wombats,
kangaroo for meat. Minimal, yet linguistically rich.
Sing your ancestors into stories and peech.

Gather in tribes like Seasons and heat. In the stars of
fire night, you are rich.
Yabba yabba, Woollongabba. Cadabirra-warriccana.
Warana.

Sleep in the stars of a Dreamtime fire. All your
Ancestors here with you.
Hear them sing to you? Uluru. Uluru. Uluru.

Thom o Oz

Chapter 7 - Discovering Alice

Dean swung the bus around, and headed back to Kings Creek Station for lunch. The last stop of the tour, before we drove back to Alice Springs. The three days and two nights had made quite a turning point in getting in touch with myself. Though I'd known it'd have some significant insights, but not known how much. I knew, too, not to look for it to be the answer to everything. Three days, no matter where they were spent, could not 'undo' ten years of marriage. Or, more importantly, forty-some odd years of an overly adaptive and 'rescuing' lifestyle. But, I now at least took the time to examine who I was, and how I wanted to change. With those satisfying, creative and challenging thoughts, I dozed off for a few minutes, letting the hot sun bake into my brain, for relaxation and sleep.

We pulled into Kings Creek Station and all piled out, for the open-air dining room, where the lunch was doled out to us. The simple, rustic setting was surrounded by colorful bushes, and I noticed the large windowed-areas had rolled-up bamboo curtains, to keep out the wind or rain. The rough hewn benches were high-up and the matching tables quite basic, but comfortable. I sat opposite Trudy, with Jean next to me, and Marta in-between Trudy and Kaylin. "So, what is everyone up to, once we get back to Alice Springs?" My nose out six inches, from curiosity if we would run into each other again.

Trudy was the first to speak up, "I think I'm going to join the one-day trip out to Palm Valley, since it's by four-wheel drive. It's a stop at the historic Hermannsburg settlement, and an Aboriginal settlement, too. It sounds pretty interesting, and I get a discount, too, since I was on this tour." She seemed rather happy about having a plan and satisfied with it all.

"How much longer do you plan to stay in the area, Trudy?"

"Oh, I don't know, Annie. I'll have to decide when I get back from the tour. I've still got some money, and I'd been thinking about Darwin or even Perth. But, Darwin sounds more interesting, with all the Aboriginal things up there. I've really gotten interested in it, after this tour. What about you Jean? You leave this weekend, don't you?"

"Yes, I do. I just have two days in Darwin, then I fly to Singapore, then back to England. It sure has been great, … everything I wanted and more." With this, she turned and looked at each of us. "This has been the best tour I've ever been on." She smiled ear to ear.

Marta spoke up next, "Yes, I agree. We met lots of nice people, but this was the most challenging and fun. We're flying out to Darwin on Friday, then into Singapore on Sunday and back onto London and the Azores." She gestured to Kaylin, "Such a very different trip, and most exciting for us."

In the three days, Kaylin had learned to speak-up much more, not hesitating because of her limited English. "Yes, I enjoy Australia and people here are very nice." She smiled at her increased comfortableness, as the picked up her tea to drink.

"Tell me, Marta," I asked, "Is it difficult getting in and out of the Azores?"

"Oh, no. Not any more. We've become, what do you call it, 'a playground' for the Europeans, especially the British and the wealthy Spanish. There are so many flights now in and out, we have many choices of where and when we want to go someplace. We have daily flights to London or Madrid, and from there we can go anywhere."

Kaylin then spoke up again. "I think … this trip has encourage me to study … and talk more in English … for meet new tourists. This has been very good … talk to so many different people." She smiled broadly at her decision.

Marta took a swallow of her tea, then added, "It is getting so crowded with tour buses, the local people are talking about limiting the number of cars and buses, which can be brought into the island. It's unbelievable, we have traffic and pollution problems. On the other hand, of course, the tourists have brought a lot of modernization and improvements to the islands, as well as business. I'll have a lot of work waiting for me, when I get back." We all laughed and agreed, most of us had to face the same situation.

"What about you, Annie? Where are you off to next?" Jean dug into her salad, waiting for me to answer.

"I've got two more days here, or I should say in Alice Springs. I'm not planning on the Palm Valley trip, Trudy. I'm taking the half day Aboriginal Tour, then the all day canyon, gorge … whatever tour. I fly out to Cairns on Saturday and have three days there, before flying back to Japan. I've got a trip out to the Reef planned, but other than that, just relax a little."

"I thought you'd been to Cairns before?" Trudy questioned. "Yes, four years ago on my first trip, then I had a few hours stopover, about two years ago. It'll be nice to see how it's changed and do some of things I did't get to do before." I got up to get some more tea. "Does anyone want any more tea?" Marta passed me her cup, then Trudy got up to help, taking Jean's cup with her. I could feel my legs stiffening-up and reminded myself to take a few Advils, when I sat back down. Trudy and I picked up a few slices of cake and brought them back to the table for the others.

Digging in my bag for pills, Marta asked, "What's that smell?" We all sniffed our noses then laughed. Jean leaned over and whispered, "I think it's the camels. I saw them washing a few of them, when I went to the toilet. They must be shipping some of them out today, or something. It certainly gives an exotic odor." We all laughed. "So, Jean," I asked, "You looking forward to another school year and all? Marta said she had a lot work piled up, you have anything new and different to face?" I sipped my tea and took another bite of the cake.

"As a matter of fact, … I got a promotion to Vice Principal. So I'm sure I'll have a few more things I'll have to do besides teaching, though they did reduce a few classes." She looked down and held onto the thick edge of the wooden slab table for emphasis. "I was a little apprehensive, but I'm feeling much more positive about myself after this trip. So, again it certainly was all worthwhile." We all gave her a little cheer and applause.

"I know what you mean." Trudy, a bit apprehensive, … but continued on. "I've actually been thinking about maybe moving, and certainly changing the kind of work I've done. I'm going to check out the job situation wherever I travel." A smile crossed her broad face.

"Hey, what do you know! Change is always good. Great, Trudy!" I gave her a toast with my styrofoam cup and the others joined in. "I wish you the best, in all of your future endeavors."

"Anything different for you, Annie?" Marta queried, as she chuckled. "Of course, you lead the most 'different' life, any way."
I put my cup down, and placed both of my hands on it, as if it were an anchor. "I'd been hoping to start my own business - the management training program I developed in grad school. But it seems, with the recession finally

hitting Japan, they are panicking at not having all the easy-flowing cash. I really want to make a change, from working with the college. And, the clairvoyant I saw in Brisbane, told me I would, but what … I'm not sure." I paused to take a deep breath, deciding how much to share. "I'll be doing two presentations in Tokyo, at the international language conference, so who knows … Maybe I'll get some job offer, I can't refuse."

I laughed at my own joke, "Or, at least talk to someone, who can give me some insider info. I know this sounds weird, but I feel like I'm in limbo… But, I'm not worried, and I usually would be, because there's only me to fall back on, … to take care of me." Then, Annie again dug in her tote as she'd remembered prior, she purposefully put some business cards in to give to each of them, with encouragement to keep in contact if they wanted.

Everyone of them was silent and staring at me. Whether it was amazement, shock or what, I was not sure. I did know, they all had a lot more stability, security or family to fall back on. Which for me, sometimes had a price tag higher, than I wanted to pay. I really was getting to like living alone, and only being responsible for me. I loved my son, but was proud and happy for his independence, which I'd always encouraged. They were now looking at my card.

"What do you think you'll do?" Trudy asked, with such earnestness and sincerity, I tried not to laugh. Maybe this was part of my living on the edge, or my own possible fear of success.

I grabbed up my bag, and slid down from the bench. "I only know whatever is supposed to, will work out for the best. It always does." I smiled at everyone, as if to say, 'don't worry about me.' "Might as well take another look around before we have to get on the bus. It's going to be a long ride back to Alice Springs, so I'm going to 'trip' to the toilet," I joked.

Within thirty minutes of Dean heading back down the highway, the bus was almost silent with just about everyone sleeping or reading. The scenery had lost some of its mystery, as we'd gotten to know it, feel it, and even lived it for a few days. I doubted we'd ever truly understand it. That could only come with years of living through all of its seasons, trials and tribulations, which challenged man against nature. Man, of course, rarely, if ever actually won, no matter how many clever adaptations. Perhaps, it was part of it, for there was some fun and excitement in challenging ourselves against nature. For me, traversing Kings Canyon had been one such experience, while for Jean it had been the more notable Ayers Rock. I acknowledged too, it was a first for me to have personal goals and accomplishments, not connected to work or another person. It really felt good.

I dozed a little thinking of various ways this tour had absorbed most of us. I'd not clearly understood when Lorraine and Graeme had talked about their similar encounters. It was the virtue of their challenges, which had moved them so. Fascinating, how an 'area' or 'place' could have such a profound affect on people. It created indelible memories and awe-inspiring physical aspirations for some to do things, they'd probably not have done before.

Once again, the Aboriginal role in all of this was brought to mind. They have what few 'white' people would attain - the mystical bonding between themselves and the total environment of the land, through their 'Spirit life' of the Dreamtime. Even though no longer living directly off the land, they still had some innate connection, we never would or could have. It's imbued in most of them, to such an extent, it would take generations totally away from the land, for them to lose it. Fortunately now, the opposite to what had happened in the past. Both white and black had begun to realize the importance of being in touch with the land, beyond mere appreciation or appropriation or it. I dozed off again thinking about my next adventure tour, which would take me into more of the Aboriginal life.

We made a stop for tea, but after everything else, all was kind of a blur, so I only thought of my room all to myself, and a hot shower. Dean was outside the bus stretching, waiting for the others to finish and board, so we could be on our way. He looked tired and I thought, in many ways, this could not be an easy job, with all the responsibilities, memorizing of the information, dealing with the difficult people, as well the driving. I stretched myself, plunked my bag down, and questioned, "Do you get a few days off now, or do you have to go back out on another tour?"

"We're not real busy right now, so I'll get a few days off then take one of the longer tours. I prefer those actually. They're more fun, and I get more time off when they're finished. That way, if my wife and I want t get away, or if I'm working on a project - like now - it's easier to get a lot done."

"What are you working on? You building something?" Not my usual meddlesome questioning, I liked Dean. I'd not known people in his line of work, almost intimately, this way before. I wondered what he did with his free time, when he had to deal with people so much on the job. He was counter to what the Japanese were always complaining about the Aussie worker, who took too many, long tea breaks, days off and had unions defending their every move. In this way, he personified the hard-working, but easy-going Aussie.

Dean beamed with pride, so I knew I'd hit on some pet undertaking, which obviously kept his time and energy. "We've been here almost seven years, since leaving Sydney, well … it's been a bit of a change. But worth it, we think. I'm building a swimming pool!" He chuckled a little, at the amazed reaction on my face. "I know. In the middle of the desert, it sounds a bit crazy.

But, if you keep it covered, the water won't evaporate, and we can use it all year round."

"But, you're building it yourself? You know how to do something like that?" Totally surprised, as it was not the sort of thing I'd have expected this clever, energetic man to do.

"I've had help from some mates with contract-experience, and I hired-out the machinery, so it's not as if I'm digging it by hand, or anything. I got a couple of estimates from a few companies, and they wanted, something like $20,000, so I decided to do it myself." A few of the people had started sauntering out, and taking their seats in the bus for the last time. "It's been a challenge, but had a great time." Dean momentarily paused to greet and say something to several of them. He turned to me once again, "I'm hoping to finish-up before the end of next month, so it's ready before summer hits us. Be great for barbies. My wife's looking forward to it, too. After four months hard work on it, she can see how it'll look." He laughed again and another, larger group of the tourists came tottering out, most looking rather worn and ready for a rest.

I felt it was time to get on, too. "Dean, I wish you the best of luck with it, and I wanted to let you know how enjoyable you've made the tour for me. You really were terrific with all the information and stories." I started up the steps ad looked back at him. "You've got a great sense of humor, to put up with us all. Thanks." After sitting down, I could see others were stopping to thank him, and a little surprised, a few were even giving him a tip. I always did, so nice to see others, too. I scrunched down in the seat to get somewhat comfortable, and take another snooze before Alice Springs.

The largest number of us got out at the Pacific Springs Resort, so I dragged up the last, in order to have time to say good bye to the others. We'd all basically said our final words, before at Kings Creek over lunch, yet now the last of letting go of the camaraderie, we had shared was not easy. On the other hand, Dorothy and her troop, was also staying at Pacific Springs the next few days. Though not putting any energy into avoiding her, I certainly was not going out of my way to spend time with her. Interesting, how different people could be, and how much we could learn from each other, if we chose.

I retrieved my big, gray suitcase from the reception storage, and grabbed up my red tote bag again. Balancing my tote over one shoulder, with the key to my new room, I began to think of what 'experiencing' Dorothy had taught me. Probably, not much older than any of the four of us, yet our attitudes made us aeons apart from her. And also, what we'd learned from the physical accomplishments, we'd sought after and done, as well so many other things.

The fundamental divergence, and what brought me closer to the others, I believed came from the fact we'd traveled other countries and cultures, to not only enjoy them, but to learn from them. Discovering about ourselves and our own country in the process, was a surplus benefit. Again, if there was some wisdom I'd gleaned from living in Japan, there was no one 'best' or 'worst' culture, or country, or people. True, visiting or touring a country can be fun, and definitely easier than living in it. Especially if one in which 'you' the individual, were the obvious 'foreigner.' If the traveling was indeed experiential, and not too insulated - like only first class resorts in third-world countries - there were certainly things to be gained.

On a day-to-day basis, Japan living could be quite wearing, most to those who were in constant contact with the average Japanese, who had been inundated with the group 'we-ness.' Their typical response was more likely to be one to an alien from Mars. Having the language was rightly a bonus or advantage, which brought more of an acceptance. Yet, I'd heard almost as many rejection-stories from foreigners with a level of fluency, as I'd heard of those who lacked even the most rudimentary expressions.

One cannot point and say, "It's probably a racist thing,' when Parisians pride themselves on being rude to foreigners, especially English-speaking ones. It may be why, foreigners living in Tokyo for years, may not ever have the experience of the 'real' Japan. Learning Japanese was not essential in Tokyo, and associating with non-English speaking Japanese may not even happen. In the same way, this could be said about any person who goes to a foreign country with a group, and only spends time with their 'own kind.' The examples of Japanese never learning English, after years in the States, or gaijin who could not count past ten in Japanese, were numerous.

I think if research were ever done on people's tolerance of each other, the result would directly relate to how much, or little the individual had traveled internationally on their own. My group of professors, whom I had discussion classes with almost weekly, were probably the best examples of this interconnection. The more controversial our subject matter, drawn from English newspapers and magazine articles, the more they enjoyed expressing their opinions.

They'd even go as far as to disagree with one another, which was basically unacceptable in Japanese culture.

The teacher, of course, continuously was taught by her students, and for it all, I thanked them from the bottom of my heart. They all knew Japan was not perfect, and were well aware of its drawbacks, still they wanted to learn what the foreign media said about them. This did not come upon them, just because they were intelligent and articulate - they had all traveled internationally, some of them extensively. I wished I could say the same for my American countrymen, who did nothing but complain about bad press, rather than question it's relevance.

No, I did not condemn Dorothy for her provincialism, about which I'd heard scores of Aussies accuse of their New Zealand 'relatives.' Recently both had come under criticism, from their other faster-growing, adjacent countries - Malaysia, Singapore, Indonesia, and Thailand. Particularly, Australia's 'all white' immigration policy - in force until the late 1970s - which kept people like Dorothy ignorant about their 'other' neighbors, who were today their leading trade partners. They needed a conscious, cultural and political desire to be a part of the Asia-Pacific Rim, or they would remain what former Singapore Prime Minster Lee Kuan Yee called, "Asia's Poor, White- Trash."

When Dorothy told me the students at her school were studying Japanese, I later told her they should also have the choice to study Chinese, Indonesian or Malaysian, like many large city Australian schools. She responded with, "That's going a bit far! Even I know *nobody* in those countries can afford to buy any Australian products." Dorothy was simply a prime example of the average person of any nation, who had not expanded their mind, for lack of expanding their personal odometer.

I tossed my bags onto the spare bed and started stripping my clothes off, leaving them where they dropped. I could think only of the hot water beating on my sore muscles, in every part of my body. Thank God, the Advil had kicked in somewhat. I planned an evening to unwind, to take the time to sort out the things I wanted to yet see and do, before leaving on late Saturday morning. After putting on some clean underwear, I went through both bags separating out the dirties to take down to the laundromat. I figured I'd get a jump on others wanting to get theirs done, also. I slipped on my flowered culottes, with a bright pink, long-sleeved top, as it did get cool when the sun sank ... This outfit should be acceptable for dinner, too. I gathered up my bundle, key and change purse to trot down to the laundromat, on the first floor.

Glancing through a scandal-rag magazine, while leaning against one of the washers was the British guy who had video taped the tour. "Well, hi again. Getting your laundry caught-up with?" Since the dryer was running loudly behind him, he was surprised to see me, and almost embarrassed at being in charge of the wash. I placed my bundle on the empty washer.

"Oh, hello." He suddenly realized why I was there. "Umh, these two will be finished in just another few minutes." He quickly stuffed the magazine under their clothes basket, with the blaring headline and photo turned down.

I poked my clothes into the washer, not to broadcast any of it,
… as if it really mattered. "That's OK. I only need one … I haven't got much." I put the lid down and looked around for a coin-operated, washing-powder vending machine. I then noticed he had a box of detergent. "Excuse me, do you know if they have laundry soap available somewhere here?" He'd become uncomfortable, without something to do, so he was trying to appear as nonchalant as possible.

"Oh, I think they sell packets at the front desk. But, you're welcome to use some of ours." He was eager to be helpful.

I smiled at him, trying to make him more at ease, as he was obviously a fish-out-of-water. A little taller than myself, and perhaps in his late fifties. "Oh, thank you, but I'm sure your wife will need it for the rest of your trip. I'll just run down to reception. Would you mind watching my load, too, so no one takes the washer over?" He earnestly smiled and nodded. "Thank you, then I'll be right back." When I returned, he was dutifully placing their wet laundry into the empty dryer. He'd already dropped two socks n the floor. "Thanks!" I called out, not wanting to startled him … but I did.

"Oh? Yeah … sure." He noticed the socks and picked them up. He continued to remove the clothes, while I measured out about half of the soap packet … the receptionist had said it was good for two loads, if they weren't big and dirty. He finished and put his coins in the slot, just as I put mine in the washer. Before I could get away he added, "Did you enjoy the tour? Interesting, wasn't it?" I felt he truly wanted conversation, and not trying only to be polite, even though he was bored with his job. He seemed to still be wearing his clothes from the tour, so his wife must have wanted to take her shower first.

"Yes, it was wonderful. Great exercise and most educational about the Aboriginals' myths and their artwork. I'm going on another special tour tomorrow about them. What about you, and your wife, where are you off to next?" Leaning against the washer with one hand, I'd crossed my feet at the ankles to relax.

"I umh ... think we're going to a place called Palm Valley tomorrow, then Friday we leave for ... I think it's Katherine." Not planning on my question, he was a little flustered.

"Oh, that's really nice up there! I've been through the gorge, which is really spectacular and different again, from what we saw here. Then, you go on to Darwin, though you'll probably stop in Tennant Springs, if I remember right. It's on the way, too. Darwin and Kakadu National Park are fantastic. The variety of weird birds on the Yellow River ... ah, no, they call it Yellow Waters, because it's not really a river, ... anyway the birds are mind-boggling. Keep the VCR battery powered up, because you're going to need it, some of those cruises are long!" I lightly laughed now, so he'd begun to relax.

"You seem to know Australia very well. Why have you come so many times?" His curiosity was up, as he surged on.

"Mainly my ex-husband's idea to begin with, and I must admit one of his better ones. Now, I have friends here, and I honestly like the laid-back Aussies. I love the fantastic variations of the country, too."

"Do you think they're lazy, because my wife thinks so, but I feel they just like to have fun and don't worry about things, quite as much as we do in England." I had to smile at his 'cheekiness,' as the Aussies would say. Since his country had more people not working and on the dole, with more drug and crime problems than Australia had ever faced. Granted its longer history and larger population did have a considerable influence on it all.

I could not help chuckling, "It's a little more complicated than that! As my Italian-Aussie friend says of his adopted country, this government's a joke and so disorganized not knowing where it's going or what it wants, because it doesn't have any direction in trying to make all of the union factions happy. Of course, I'd rather have that, than the American government sticking their military noses where they not only don't belong, but can't afford to be… They keep telling every other country how to run their show, when America's falling apart at the seams." I shook my head, not wanting to think about it. His interest must have been piqued, as I saw his eyes grew wider.

"The Americans have their heads stuck in the telly, and keep trying to blame the Japanese for all of their problems, while the Aussie people just go, 'Oh, well, they're tryin' mate." It's like a big, almost- happy family here, with no one wanting to criticize too much, because we're kind of all in this together. It really makes my friend angry, the businesses don't demand more from the government. They've got so many laws protecting the workers, they've lost their personal responsibility, and it's easy for some to take advantage of it all." I paused to see his reaction, which I could have only called numb.

"No, I don't think they're all lazy, but then I'm a workaholic, so I try not to judge anyone with my measuring stick, because it's six feet long.... (I then realized, he may not get the analogy without meters.) Those who are ambitious, do very well, but there are many who let the system take care of them, which makes a lot of my friends here angry. I'm sure your've recognized some of the same problems in England, and they certainly have them in the States." I paused again to see if he was swallowing it all.

"Well, what I originally meant was, I like the fact they're not so status-conscious, or into making money just for its own sake, like the Americans or Japanese. The Aussies are loose and like to enjoy themselves, ... I need to learn some of that ... But to work with them on a regular basis would probably be difficult for me, because I push so much." He was staring at me with what I hoped was amazement and not fright, as sure he was not expecting a political sermon.

"I didn't mean to run on like that, I do get a bit wound up sometimes. I'll let you go, as I've got to get up to my room and write some postcards, while this wash is still going. Have a good trip, if I don't see you tomorrow."

He nodded his head and tried to smile, "Yes, thank you, ... you, too ... Nice talking to you." I grabbed my change purse and key, as I turned to go back up the stairs. I'd been told more than once, I did not know when to shut up. I just seemed to keep rattling on about whatever. Maybe I missed my true calling, as a soap-box orator, after all. Maybe also not to far from Dorothy. I stretched out on the bed and tried to let the time pass, glancing through one of the Red Centre tour promotion weekly magazines.

I waited to make sure, I returned to the laundry room when no one else was there, so I could finish quickly and go to dinner. I threw the things into the dryer, and sat up on the washer to finish reading the promotion magazine. I liked checking out the advertisements and figuring which ones were local, and which had been done out of Sydney, or Melbourne, or even Brisbane. Every few minutes, I'd slip off the washer to pluck some item out, which seemed dry, so the others would dry faster.

The marketing and advertising was to me a clear-cut measurement of how sophisticated, or even artificial and plastic a city or its people were. What I saw representing Alice Spring did not make me run in horror, as I remembered doing upon arriving in Oklahoma City, but it did amuse me. It played upon its folksy-ness and even used Outback slang to give a 'genuine' quality to what they were pushing. I could be totally off base, too, which was not uncommon. I finished folding all the clothes and traipsed back up to my room. Getting hungry, so I just plopped them on the spare bed and returned down the stairs to the dining room.

Happy not to see anyone in the dining room I knew, though I did notice a group of six in the corner which had been with our tour add-ons. I thought how little they had mingled or even talked with the original group, though we only had maybe four hours without them at the beginning. *"Isn't it funny how people cluster?"* I posed to myself.

Of course, these were the ones traveling together for something like twenty-one days. I then realized only Dorothy, her sister, brother- in-law and the one young single man, someone had said was American, were missing from the dinner party. Maybe this group had known each other before the tour. Fun to watch and guess about people, as sure they'd done about me.

I sauntered outside by the pool after dinner, but all the lights were too distracting, and the breeze rather chilly for stargazing. I went on to my room, and lost myself in watching several American programs I'd not seen for years. Only during the commercials, would I remember where I was. Though there were some Aussie programs, I opted for the familiar memories of *"Golden Girls"* and

"Murder, She Wrote." Even with my naps, I was eager to get to bed before midnight, which was rare of me to do. I knew the morning wake-up call would come quickly once again.

Morning breakfast seating had a timing-influence to it. The dining hostess sat me at a table for two next, to the windows, adjacent to the pool, glistening in the clear sunlight. I ordered my coffee, then got up to partake of the cereal and fruit buffet, almost running into Dorothy returning to her table from the hot food one. "Annie! Don't sit by yourself! Come over and join me." She was waving to the waitress, to bring my coffee and set-up over to her table. "Oh, over here, thanks. She'll sit with me" She guided me by the elbow, to make sure I knew exactly which table was hers.

"Good morning, Dorothy. Thank you, I'll be right back. I'm just going to get a plate of fruit and some yogurt for my cereal." I started to pull away and walk to the counter.

"Make sure you try some hot food, as well. It's great." The waitress had brought the things over, and Dorothy was giving her some other instructions at the same time.

I thought, *"What the hell, guess I can put up with her again."* I did feel sorry for her and that always made me a sucker. I took my time picking out the fruit, choosing the granola, but when I got back to the table she still had barely touched her plate. Not going to let her bother me, so I plowed into my food smiling once again. "I heard you're off to the Palm Valley to see all the weird plant life and rare kinds of palms. Should be fun for you all." I moved my plates around, and noticed the waitress had even brought my tote bag to the table.

Dorothy was doing her usual one, small bite at a time, then put her fork and knife on the plate, to talk each time, as well. "Oh, yes,. I'm really excited, because we're going in a four-wheel drive. How about you? What are you doing today?" She watched me cut up the fruit, then mix some of it with the granola and yogurt.

"I have the half-day Aboriginal Experience, then I'm going to wander around town to do the last of my shopping. I have an all day tour tomorrow, which will have a lot of hiking, before flying out on Saturday. I'm quite excited about the tours." I continued to eat, as I was not going to stretch-out breakfast, keeping her entertained. I also had no intentions of being late ... As she usually was. She'd resumed eating for a moment, then stopped again.

"Tell me Annie, I meant to ask you before. Are there a lot of 'mixed' marriages?" She'd leaned closer, as she spoke, and even lowered her voice when she said the word 'mixed.' This was a heavy duty topic, which rubbed a lot of the gaijin women, especial the older ones, the wrong way. I questioned how deeply I wanted to get into it with her, on this tenuously resented and wounded subject.

I took a swallow of juice, studying her face and finally answered, knowing all I said would be reported as 'secret inside information' and I truly did not like to do any Japan bashing. "It's not a simple question to answer, because in order for it not to be misconstrued, you'd have to try to understand Japanese culture in detail." I knew it was a bit of a waste of time, as she only wanted to hear the gaijin were a preferred 'catch.'

"I'll simplify it for you. The Japanese men are spoiled, and raised rather privileged, though it is changing. Marrying them means, if he's the elder son, they must live with his parents which means, she must also take care of them, kowtowing especially to the mother. Few Japanese women today want that, unless a lot of money comes with it. Many of the girls have done home-stays through their college or university, or even gone to school in English-speaking countries. Most come back changed, especially if a long stay, like a year. With a gaijin- Western man, they not only get a Green Card, but more freedom if they want to work. The gaijin pays more attention to them, and knows more about sex. Of course, in my opinion, most of these young gaijin men are not worthy of the pretty, intelligent girls, but many don't care, they just want out."

I forked a piece of melon to gather my direction, and decided not to talk about the young women's usual sexual experimenting, casual acceptance of abortion, or how the callous gaijin of all ages took advantage of their naiveté. Perhaps a different angle would help her to see the women were victims more often. "They want to do something different then, after the freedom they've had with the home-stays, rather than a traditional Japanese marriage. Contrary, a lot of the more educated ones, are simply opting not to get married at all, because they don't want to put up with society, or the men controlling their lives. It's a sacrifice many are finding worth it." I then took my vitamins, as I finished my juice.

Dorothy stared at me and sipped her tea, while her reactions varied from amazement to shock, her mouth gaped open. "I had heard, and of course, you know ..." she lowered her voice again. "We've even had a few Australian men come back with Japanese wives." She put her cup down and leaned closer again. "It's really disgusting, isn't it? I mean those girls taking all the good men away from their own kind. And, then producing those *half-breed* children!" She picked up her fork, again seeming to be satisfied to know, 'the world was going to hell in a hand-basket,' as my mother would have said.

I finished the last of my breakfast, as I made my final statement, as it was time for me to make my exit. "Well, Dorothy, I have to say, I agree and disagree with you at the same time. Some of the guys aren't so great and probably couldn't have gotten any of 'their own kind' any way, and many Japanese women, in my opinion, marry beneath themselves. Likewise, some of the marriages are truly based on love and who could ask for anything more."

I waved to the waitress, and gestured to her to bring my check.

"None of it has ever directly affected me, and if my son were to marry someone of another race, I'd simply say, he made his choice and the one who will live with her." I cackled a little, trying not too hard to embarrass her. "What the hell right, do I have to tell anyone who to marry, when I just got my second divorce?!" She pulled back, obviously offended, but said nothing. I signed the bill, giving the girl a big tip and got up. "Have a great time on the trip, and return to Townsville, … it's been 'real' meeting you." I caught her with her mouth full, and knew I had confused her totally, but I heard her call 'bye' after me as I left.

* * * * * *

There were only about twenty people on our tour, one other tour bus, and a few tourists in their own cars, joining us at the settlement area, a short distance from Alice Springs. Once assembled, a special guide, who had worked with the Aborigines and spoke their language, took over the program, to explain and have them demonstrate various areas of their lifestyle. We were given little folding stools, so we could sit and watch everything, in this traditional environment of spinifex grass, witchery bushes and a few trees giving some shade.

There were no permanent buildings or houses. At the far end of the property were solar toilets for us, as well the storage shed used by the tour guides, to keep their cooking utensils and gear. Any shelter or shade, other than provided by the sparse branches, was of a temporary nature. The Aborigines had made a few lean-tos, covered with canvas or old blankets.

A numerous variety of spears and boomerangs were laid out on the ground, with us sitting in a semi-circle around them. The guide began to detail the differences between the artifacts, compared to what we had seen as souvenirs, or had been mislead by in the movies. This was all obviously important to the guide, as he told us about the wood used for each, and how the selection of the trees were made. He finally called over, in their native language and introduced an older Aboriginal man. His gray hair was peeking out, from underneath his wide-brimmed hat and the gray mustache, helped frame the dark, deeply-creased face. Yet, his agile movements, as he eased over and physically fit body, all appeared to belie his true age. Which, while not said, I guessed anywhere from forty-five to seventy-five.

He nodded to us, while keeping his head down, and showed no notion of a smile. The guide explained most Aborigines were shy, and did not really like to do these things, in front of outside people. The man seemed to glide over to the boomerangs, and picked four different ones up out of the collection, as if he had a definite preference. They were all somewhat straight, as compared to the usual sharp angled 'returning' boomerangs. Those were commonly used more up in the Northern 'wet' country, and used to knock down birds. These boomerangs were used to break the legs of a fleeing kangaroo, or other animals which were a common source of food to the Central Bush.

There were several targets, barely seen by us, set up in the distance of the wide-open stretch in front of us. First, the guide told us what would happen, then the Aboriginall man simply did it. The follow-through movement, seemed to take no effort, or even aim. The same style, we'd admired in a talented American football quarterback, or baseball pitcher. One after another, the man would throw and the target several hundred meters away was hit. It seemed such a basic, stimulus-response action, the guide had to remind us to applaud. Only a nod of recognition again, the Aboriginal man slid effortlessly into the field to retrieve the weapons.

The demonstration turned to spears, how the holder 'launched' them and why they may have been used instead of, or in conjunction with the boomerangs. Since we were all intently watching the guide in front of us, the Aboriginal man seemed to suddenly appear out of nowhere. Several of us were distracted by this, and what I considered to be the fluidness of his motion, as he returned the boomerangs to their previous place in front of us. He again carefully chose three spears, and slipped over to his spot, to wait for the command performance. I could not take my eyes off of him, yet he appeared to be totally oblivious to us all.

Like a bullet, the spear suddenly shot from the holder, which had become an extension of his swiftly moving arm. The spear wobbled and quavered, as it vibrated itself through the air, with only a slight trill resonating in response. Each of them all hit their perspective targets. Once more, he walked away as we clapped, in awe of his flowing moves and their accomplishments.

'Amateur hour' was next, with many men thinking they could perform these simple tasks, with the same success. What the hell, the 'targets' were not even moving! The fact no one was injured was more the case. At one point, the Aboriginal man and the guide both quickly got out of the way. The overly enthusiastic tourists, performed for their own cameras and VCRs.

This time, the Aboriginal man was smiling, and eventually laughing at the antics of the 'white fellers.' As I'd tried boomerangs before, I knew how tricky they were. I remembered Travis, in his full 'John Wayne' mode, getting pissed, as he'd not been successful with it. He considered him self, of course, an 'expert' with all kinds of weapons. After sufficient numbers had embarrassed themselves, with their lack of talent in primitive hunting - we all would have starved - we moved on to other easier, more foolproof methods.

The guide lead us to a different area and taught us how to recognize the witchery bush, as well as numerous other unusual edible sources. He began to demonstrate the digging stick and the necessity of training the women, who dug for the roots. They knew to move slowly, as not to waste their precious energy or sweat. All food, and the required exertion to retrieve it, had to be weighed and balanced, as to the sustenance it delivered. Not logical, nor feasible for savoring a long life in this unforgivable, unyielding land, if one did not follow this basic rule. The intrinsic nature of gathering bush-tucker - food, was just as important as the hunter's stealth, accuracy and knowledge of the animals. They followed the season, of which the Aborigines considered six instead of four, and never took more from the land than what their tribal numbers required.

The *witchetty* grubs, which were white, thick, and four to six inches long on the average, were hidden deep inside the roots of the bush. When lucky, a bulging root might yield up several of the juicy, tasty morsels. They were not only high in fat and protein content, but when eaten raw, also had the benefit of a soluble liquid - the rarest commodity in this arid space. Using a *coolamon* - the curved, wooden carrying dish - to take the variety of food the guide had gathered … the witchetty grub, desert apple and pear … we moved to yet another area, where there were several women, men and children gathered. We then had a quick demonstration on how to make fire, using two sticks perpendicular to each other. A few, small dried sticks, leaves placed in the hollowed area, of the one stick and the other stick rotated rapidly on top, with the friction-heat creating the fire. Once the campfire was going, the grub was tossed into it and the guide began to talk about the variety of food and cooking methods.

I watched the young, bouncy child, with his locks of golden and brown curls, crawl over and around his heavy-set mother, who sat cross-legged on the ground rather motionless, leaning her downcast head on her hand. The guide then explained these people no longer lived here, because the elder of the group, a woman who had been *somewhere* between seventy and eighty, had died about six months before. They would not occupy the area for about another ten years, in respect to her. With that, I realized these people were paid to be here, and the only ones at all comfortable with the situation were the children. I truly felt for them, yet I greatly appreciated they would come and share their culture with us, strange foreigners.

The guide had poked the grub around a bit in the fire, and now gingerly removed it, and proceeded to cut it into numerous, small biters. It had turned a golden yellow, and shrank-up so when sliced, no liquid was visible. He asked how many would like to try it, as there was not enough for all of us. After cutting up the desert pear too, he then passed the *coolamon* around with the pieces, but the desert apple was untouched, as it needed more preparation before eating. I looked it over carefully, and took a piece of both the grub and pear - it was a little bitter, but the grub tasted nutty-good. Most people just photographed the 'bush' food, then questioned those of us who tried it, as to how palatable it was. Once the coolamon finished full circle, the guide offered it to the children, who scooped it up, to relish every morsel instantly.

The part many of us had anxiously waited for, came next - with traditional music and dancing by men and children, with the women finally joining in the last dance. An older man and young boy, perhaps ten or so, as his hair was fully dark, were wearing interesting-shaped head-dresses, and what could only be called a 'diaper' on their bottoms. Their bodies were covered with cotton balls, in special designs, following around a painted, yellow color on their skins.

I'd read in the past, the Aborigines used the fluff from a particular bird down, which was considered sacred for these ceremonies and dances. The boy and the man carried two spears each, and acted-out the scenarios, dancing around a large stick buried upright in the ground, and painted with various colors and designs. After circling it many times, they came in front of us, coming close,

203

sometimes dashing the spears into the ground around our feet, or between the stools. Apparently, the older man was teaching the young boy, as he would correct him, or give him instructions, as they proceeded through each story-dance. Perhaps in this way, 'performing'' for the tourists had an ultimate purpose, of training the young in their cultural heritage.

In the meantime, sitting around on the ground in a wider semi- circle, were three men with a small child and two women to the side, with another young child. They were using the clapping sticks to keep time for the dancers, and to also created a music, which was intently mesmerizing, as soon most of us felt our bodies moving in time to the rhythm. The children sat on their respective laps of the man or woman, so again they would correct or demonstrate to them, how to keep the percussion sound, while eventually letting it carry them on, via the natural din. The guide then translated the chanted songs being told in droning sounds.

The women joined in the last two dances, using their coolamon and something which looked like a thick string. Their cadence was a methodical heel-toe, with their legs rather far apart and the sway sometimes from only the waist down. Though both the men and women were pudgy or even heavy around the middle, the women's legs and arms were wiry.

These others were clothed in an assortment of old, western- mixed styles, with only two of the men and none of the women wearing shoes. Some of them also wore a variety of hats and caps. I noted only the women wore full skirts, which came to knee length, or longer, so when they sat cross-legged on the ground, their skirts could be tucked in. Again, even with rousing applause, they rarely looked at us, much less acknowledging our presence and appreciation. Curiously, many older Japanese, I'd bought handmade craft items from, had responded in an almost identical discomforting or embarrassed manner.

We were encouraged to wander around for the next half hour or so, to watch them make different art objects, purchase some for cash or just talk, and take photographs. Most of the items - bark and canvas paintings, coolamons, boomerangs - were laid out on the old blankets, while the artists continued making more of the dotted 'X-ray style' art pieces. Fascinating cultural note, one guide mentioned to us was, if we wanted to spend any time with, or watching a group or particular Aborigine, we should squat down, as they were very uncomfortable having someone standing over them. We were reminded too, to ask before taking photographs, and they did not like to speak a lot to strangers, although they did understand English well.

I squatted off to the side of one woman, who quietly painted on a boomerang, similar to the one the man sitting behind her in the shade, was patiently carving from an ordinary slice of wood. I had so many questions, I'd have loved to ask each of them, yet my own personal respect for their privacy and cultural lifestyle held me back. Enthralled, simply with this exposure to these Aboriginal people, I tried to drink-in as much as possible by just watching every movement and action, as they proceeded to produce Dreamtime images in the Earth colors. Her silent, taciturn action was distinct from the Japanese, in a peacefulness of being comfortable in solitude.

A young boy came up with his mother and she motioned for him to squat down, while she also did so. With the stillness, the seated boy responded by whispering to his mother, asking if he might have the boomerang the woman was working on. I got up to leave, and not interfere with their negotiations, happy the boy had shown regard for it. And, hoped he realized the handmade boomerang would be a much better prize, than a store-bought, mass-produced one.

For myself, disappointed I could not find anything either small and portable enough, or a design which grabbed me. The time passed quickly, as I moved among the four groups, absorbed in the variety, styles and themes, which were represented in one art form or another.

The guide then called us over to the back section, where the tour bus drivers had prepared billy tea and bush-damper - the baked, loaf-pan bread. They had mixed up some really delicious stuff with fruit and nuts in it, so we all were impressed. Once we had finished our morning tea break, the guide had us sit under some trees, while he explained about the basic clan circles and their marriage systems. An incredibly, fascinating chart he'd drawn out, explaining the involved intermarriages of the Aranda and Walpiri Tribal groups, with the individual clans within them. The mix and match was set up into a controlled scheme, so there would *never* be allowed any intermarriage of closer than probably a ninth cousin.

Most of us were truly amazed, these supposedly 'backward' people had the knowledge genetic problems came from closely, related families intermarrying. This happened in Japan, not only because it was an island, but the limitations of past class levels, and wanting to keep wealth or name within the family network, even today. Many Japanese refused to acknowledge the birth defects, and their large percentage of hemophiliacs, this practice created. Also, there was little government control of it, as they did not question any powerful family. Compared to these Aborigines, who never questioned the necessity of marrying into the proper-related clan.

Usually younger girls marrying older men too, a necessity. Based on the reality of harsh droughts restricted their diets, which in turn regulated the female ovulation, so it could some times take years for a couple to have a child. Once a girl ovulated, almost an obligation and responsibility to the tribe to produce a child. And, the older man, perhaps in his thirties, was best considered capable of providing for a family, should the Spirits grant him one.

The guide then went on to explain, though the tribal group and clan may have been controlling, most of the people knew it was this control, which kept them from chaos in the desert. This highly developed social life, was strictly built on the individual's social obligations, dictated by the complex kinship system over thousands of years. Perhaps this was why they had survived the British invasion, and almost being eradicated by the 'white feller, as the Native Americans had been.

From the beginning, the Aborigines had been treated as a nuisance, and driven away by the well-armed settlers. They were allowed to perpetuate *casual killings*, knowing they would go unpunished. Once the cattle and sheep stations were ensconced into the landscape, the well-know 'pacification by force' was an unwritten invitation, to search-out and even kill every Aborigine possible. Though the tribes tried to fight back with their skills and cunning, they were easily outgunned by the superior firepower.

It's considered, within white history, probably less than a thousand white Australians were ever killed by the Aboriginals, while conservative estimate cites at least ten times for the reverse situation. Another one hundred thousand, died from European-related disease, for which they had no immunity. There were some things their well organized, spiritual and interdependent society could not control, understand or assimilate into.

The tour ended on an upbeat note, of the Aboriginal resurgence in Australia and their numerous land rights, including environmental successes with the government. Returning to Alice Springs, I could not shake a sick feeling of how history continued to repeat itself. The white-prejudiced, Europeans went 'discovering and conquering' native, darker-skinned cultures. The few white individuals who tried to understand them and even learn from them, were always outnumbered by the masses, who only wanted to destroy those who were different.

Racing along the highway, I looked again on this almost desolate space, and realized to the Aboriginal people, it was anything but barren. They lived off the land, as well as 'in' it, knowing every creek and crevice, so to speak, from which seeds could be made into flour to unthinkable edibles. I thought, too, of how seriously the Aboriginal groups took their clan obligation, to look after the land and each 'dreaming place,' or sacred site. On its own, this relationship to their ancestors, and the adventures they may have had with a Dreamtime spirit.

How much more 'related' could one be to the ground upon which you walked? This was not the black and white history of the world's creation, but rather colorful visions of man versus mythical beasts. Then these resulted in the formations they could see stretched out before them, in rocks, canyon, animals and whatever else, their tradition celebrated, as being given to them.

Through my studies of metaphysics, I worked to develop my own 'oneness,' which I believe linked me to all living creatures, in a Spiritual relationship. Yet, it was different, since I could technically carry this personal connection with me wherever I'd go. Whereas, with the Aborigines, their 'Spirituality,' for lack of a clearer-cut word, seemed to come through the land and its direct relationship to them with their cognizance of it. The Aboriginal cultures were 'rooted,' more than just the fact of only local movement. They had millenniums of a 'presence' of their ancestors. And, what all they created for them, with the responsibility to those who preceded and who would succeed them, as well.

For many of us, this was a concept almost too difficult to accept, because it went beyond any realm of religion we knew. The Aborigines had a kind of 'shared existence' with the supernatural- powers, which 'own' their life since they ruled or controlled one's clan, or tribe, they belonged to. Thus, many Aborigines felt a direct relationship to the Dreamtime myths, as they were of their own ancestors, and their experiences with the various Spirits and Powers. These were in existence even to today, so had been entrusted to them, the descendants.

Yes, this still was Aboriginal land. No matter how many houses, or buildings, or modernizations, or rules of limitations, the 'white' man set to try to tame the land, and its people, it would not really be changed. The fact still remained, some things could never be taken away, likewise, some things could never be acquired. Though they never took it for granted, the Aborigines had a deep recognition - this land would never forfeit its power to create and astonish all those who would observe and appreciate. They knew the inestimable riches it imparted, and they could never be traded or sold. The Dreamtime stories were about the Power and the respect, with consequences of how one lived their life in balance. Something I knew I wanted to learn more about, whether or not I'd understand or have any application of it in my life.

My mind drifted around the concept of time and space - *"Nothing last forever, not even the rocks, and we are not them."* My peculiar penchant for paradoxes brought the line from one of my poems to mind. Yet, the more I learned about the Aboriginal people, the more I considered them to be timeless. They had been on the ancient, island-continent for untold millenniums, depending on which learned anthropologist or archeologist one believed, and during those times, comparatively speaking, they had changed very little. Adapted, yes, because it was survival, and what they were all about - the continued flow of life.

Curious, how now with the 'New Age' beliefs and metaphysics, we're returning to this paradigm, in which everything in life flows in a series or logical process, or natural unfolding of events. Spring follows winter, rejuvenation by procreation, or even the simple daily sunrise-sunset, as commodities of life we cannot, nor should not, control, but merely try to be a part of by living in the present. Yes, I thought the antiquities of their culture were anything but archaic. They were probably more vital today than ever. Why? Perhaps because they're all so related to one another, through their clan system and the Dreamtime - "Those who lose dreaming are lost." The succinct Aboriginal proverb abounds with meaning, more so today.

I'd decide to be dropped off in town, so I could do some shopping at the numerous stores and even check-out a few of the bookstores. I'd strolled for over an hour, and purchased half a dozen or so books, including several from a used bookstore, when I stumble across a delectable deli. Being something, which was totally non- existent to any extent in Nagoya, my stomach jumped for joy. I took my number, delighted to have the time to peruse and change my mind a dozen times, before having to make a decision. I topped off my bagel-pastrami combination with a carrot-raisin coleslaw, and the piece de' resistance of chocolate chip and Amaretto cheesecake! What a rare indulgence for me, and how delightful it all was, to sit at my little table watching the locales and tourist pass by. I'd not had so much fun since my first experience of sitting outside of a cafe in Paris, eating pate', bread and cheese.

I sauntered back out exploring one shop after another, until I'd returned to the Todd Street Mall. There were several stores there, which had some significant-looking Aboriginal pieces and I noticed a few shops said, 'Free shipping anywhere.' Since I already had collected enough stuff to fill one mailing bag, I thought it would be nice to have someone else take care of the other purchases for me. I studied the window carefully, trying to decide which shop was best and finally walked into one, which had a great display of didgeridoos, the musical instrument made from a hollowed-out tree limb.

It's played by special breathing and blowing air, while vibrating the lips. The results produces a sonorous and undulating quality, which had entranced this listener, to feel a sense of timelessness, as if I'd misplaced where I was. I could not play it myself, but I was sure I'd know some Aussies, or even my friend, Mitsuru, who'd studied with the Aborigines, could play it. There was simply an overwhelming desire for me to own one.

I opened the door to Outback and Aboriginal sounding music, playing in the background. There must have been over a hundred didgeridoos of varying lengths. Each was highly decorated with a hallmark of the symbolic Aborigine standing on one foot, with a spear or some Dreamtime animals or designs. Ever aware of my space restrictions in Japan, my choice was greatly reduced. I picked several up to handle them, and see if I got any 'vibes,' since I'd learned I could sometimes sense which one I wanted. I'd yet to check the price tags, as I knew none of them were cheap, but this was not some souvenir I'd tire of and give away later. Once my selection was made, I took it to the large desk next to the counter, where a woman sat, sorting some fascinating and unusual beaded necklaces.

"Oh aren't those intriguing? What all are they made of?" I balanced the didgeridoo on the floor with one hand, and slipped my tote bag off my shoulder, to place it on the chair next to the desk."Is it OK to leave this here a few minutes?" We were the only ones in the shop at the time, and though it was a large area, quite open with her sitting almost in the middle of it, she could see both doors.

She peered up and smiled at me graciously. Very pretty, and willowy-looking, probably in her mid-thirties with lovely, curly, long hair. Immediately evident, she thoroughly enjoyed her job and being surrounded by the Aboriginal atmosphere. "Yes, of course," she nodded toward my bag. "Aren't these just wonderful. Every time we get a new lot in, they are different from the last. I keep thinking the quality and creativity won't last, but it does." She lifted the necklace up for my inspection, and I reacted with a deep breath, showing my appreciation and amazement, as I was speechless. "These are seeds, and they've taken the time to paint these other wooden beads." I looked at each individual seed, how it had been painted and strung together, to reflect the colors of the land, yet still show its uniqueness.

"I think the women have become competitive now, as they realized we pay more for something that's colorful and really different." She watched how carefully I examined them, then realized I had the didgeridoo balanced with my other hand. Oh, I'm sorry! Let me take it for you." She stood up and leaned over the desk, as I handed it over to her.

"Oh, no problem. Everything here is so fascinating. I'm sure I'll be picking up several more things, but I'll have you ship this to me." I selected one of the necklaces and set it aside. "I'll take this too, but don't ship it. By the way, do you sell the stereo-tape playing now?" She beamed brightly, "Yes, we do. Isn't it just wonderful!

Except, we're back-ordered, and I'll have to send it to you later … Is that OK?" I nodded, as my attention had been taken up with other really unusual necklaces, which consisted of different seeds and marvelous rocks, which had been painted. I'd been looking for something unusual to give Kazuyo, as I knew when she'd come to Alice Springs as a student, she'd not been able to get many souvenirs.

"Actually, he's become really popular, and has even been performing with some of the orchestras." I glanced back at the woman, as it finally registered she'd been talking about the musician, while I'd gotten lost in the necklace.

"Yes, it's very moving music, I'll be anxious to hear the whole tape. I'll take this other necklace, too, and I'm going to look around some more." She'd sat back to write up the order, from my business card, as I wondered over to another section, which had bark paintings and canvas drawings. The collection was magnificent - I could have easily collected a dozen or more things. I selected a few earrings, as gifts, then debated a long time over one small canvas painting, which was not cheap. My space limitations won out, so I let it go.

"OK, I guess that'll do, though I could take half of your store with me! My apartment in Japan is small, compared to my appetite for the uncommon. It looks like a museum as it is, but I just can't stop myself from adding to it, when I find such unique items. I'm sure the walls will collapse one of these days, when I put one more thing up on them." I laughed at my addiction. I felt so good by the surroundings.

"We're getting a lot more Japanese tourists these days. Strange, the older men always buy the really expensive things, and the women buy lots of the jewelry like the."

I laughed at her puzzled appearance. "They've heard the Aboriginal artwork will become very valuable, and the women are buying omiage - souvenir gifts - which must be all the same for their friends or co-workers." We rattled on about so much, I'd heard before from Aussies mystified by the Japanese and I was able to answer some of her questions. She seemed merely curious and not prejudiced or critical. I tucked the small bag of jewelry in my tote, thanked her profusely for her informative help, and walked back out into the glistening sun light. I checked my watch, not sure what I was going to do, and when I glanced up again, I noticed Marta and Kaylin sitting on a bench, each eating ice creams and reading books.

Neither of them noticed me walking over to them. "Well, aren't you the natives! Sitting around eating ice cream and reading, like you've got all the time in the world." I sat down next to them, laughing at the surprise on their faces.

"Annie!" They both said almost in unison, but Marta responded first, "I thought you were on a tour today?" What are you up to?" She continued to lick her ice cream, as she turned the book over on her knee.

"Oh, it was just a half day, and now I've been out spending my hard-earned money, on collectibles to clutter up my little apartment even more. How about you two, what've you been up to today?"

"We did some sight-seeing around town today, then just shopping." She turned toward Kaylin for confirmation, as if she may have left something out. Surprisingly, she spoke.

"There is much books." She held up the book she was reading, and I could see it was about the Aborigines.

I reached over to take a look at it, as she handed it to me. All about Aboriginal myths. "Hmnh. Looks interesting Kaylin." I handed it back to her, and Marta held up her book to show me, too. "Where did you guys get these? They really look good, I was in one store, but I didn't see either of those, but I did get a couple." I dug in my tote bag and pulled a few of the ones I'd gotten, and passed them on for their perusal. After a minute or so I added. "You both would've really enjoyed the tour this morning with the Aboriginal demonstrations, and such we had. Very educational and even more enlightening for me."

I paused to think about what it had all meant. "I'm not sure I can explain the realization, which I came in touch with. It's as if I could feel the 'intimacy' the Aborigines have with the land. I want to say it's even more than the American Indians, because I don't think the Indians, in general, had such harsh living environments. Their beliefs are the same, in they also feel one can't own the land, yet the land can own them." They had finished their ice cream cones and were staring at me, while wiping their hands on the napkins.

"I mean, the land and the conditions - weather, droughts, etc. - it controls their lives, and even after they're dead. The special guide said they leave an area, after their clan leader dies, for at least ten years out of respect."

Not sure if they understood, because I'd gotten too esoteric, or what, the way they were still looking at me. I thought how they had heard me lecture, like the teacher I was, almost constantly about one thing and another most of the time they'd been around me. I tried to laugh it off, "I know I get a little heavy sometimes. I didn't mean to be spouting-off again."

Kaylin spoke to Marta in their dialect, and she explained, what I presumed was what I'd said. Kaylin then commented something to Marta, and she turned back to me. "Annie, you are amazing to us, because you see so much in things, we don't always see. Really, we feel like you have been a teacher to us, and we thank you for all of your kind patience, explaining so much and answering so many questions for us. I'm sure you are a very good teacher, and your students really appreciate you." She and Kaylin smiled, while nodding with a childlike enthusiasm.

Rather taken aback. I guess I was better and more patient with non-native English speakers, or at lest non-Americans. "Thank you both very much. I get to talking so much sometimes. I do get emotionally involved in things, I usually forget not everyone has the same passionate interest in culture and travel which I do. It's nice to meet other people, who want to know more about this world, too." I picked Marta's book up and looked through it.

"What makes you interested in the Aboriginal culture? Curiosity? Sympathy? Or, just because they're different?" I knew it was a strange question, but I wanted to know if anybody looked at things int the same vein as I did, or if I was totally bent.

Marta seemed to consider my question seriously for a few moments. "I think all of it, Annie. It's so different, when we're first introduced to it, then as we learn more, especially with good tour guides like Dean. We become interested enough to want to know the details or background information." She hesitated then continued. "I don't think I feel pity or sympathy for them, now. But, I certainly do for what I'm reading, as to how they were treated in the beginning. It was like animals, or maybe even worse." Kaylin had been listening carefully and nodding occasionally, in agreement.

"In America," Kaylin spoke slowly, choosing her words, "Indian and Black, same thing?"

"Yes, in some ways, and some things they were both treated badly,… separately and … differently, and, of course, neither were considered equal to whites. Alcohol abuse was much the same for the Indians. Europeans with their 'white supremacy' belief, slaughtered whoever went against them. I read the last, full-blooded Aborigine in Tasmania, died in 1876. What was done to them, in the name of religion, was almost as bad as the disease or murder…, as it was a kind of cultural imperialism - 'Our ideas and ways are good, and yours are bad.' More than an attitude or belief … kind of fanatic and certainly psychological." I handed the book back to Marta.

"I agree with you, they are not to be pitied, and I'm sure they don't want it, as they are a very proud people. The Northern Territory government seems to have an awareness, and they have the greatest number of Aborigines there. The resurgence of their traditional lifestyle and social organization, has given most of them the power to once again determine their own destiny. There are, of course, still a lot of white people making a lot of money off the Aborigines, their culture and naturally, the artwork. I just dropped a bit of money in that shop, and though I know they pay the Aborigines, I'd have felt better if it had been run by an Aborigine."

"But don't you think, Annie, they may feel they have to give up too much of their culture, if they are running a store, in the city area? I know what you are saying, but sometimes you can't have both things at the same time. We had one craft place run by the Aboriginal group, out by Ayers Rock, and I bought something there. But probably easier for them in their own group area." She looked at me pondering what she'd said. "I guess there will always be people making money off of others, but at least they're not killing them any more."

I looked back at her, with a sly smile on my face. "Actually, they still are, and it's still in the legal way. The percentage of Aborigines jailed for minor offenses, usually related to drinking, is many times higher than whites. And, numerous ones seem to die in jail, supposedly from suicide or accidents. There have been some investigations, but the bottom line remains, prejudice is still a killer, whether it's in this country, America or Europe. I guess not everyone looks at the Aborigines and their culture, as drawing cards for tourists." I paused to think of how strong my criticizing had become. I knew not all Aborigines were creative artists, or even the pillars of their communities. "I'm sure, if we had some local people put in a word or two, their opinions would be quite different, based on their own personal experiences with the area Aborigines. No one group is ever blameless, when cultures and races clash."

I stood up and tossed my tote bag over my should. "Well, we could talk about the world's problems all day long, but the powers that be, have no interest in our humble, yet wise, and astute opinion. I'm going to try to find that bookstore before it closes and buy those books. You guys have a great trip back, and I sure enjoyed the time we've spent together."

"Good-bye, Annie!" They both responded in unison again, with Marta adding. "Have a good trip, too." I waved back to them, as I walked off, and they returned to their reading. By the time I reached the bookstore, it had occurred to me, I already had several friends in Europe, so maybe I could plan a trip to visit them and the cousins. Again, so many wonderful moments shared, in all we did in our few days together. I then noticed the store closed in less than fifteen minutes, so just smiled, thinking some people I would not forget.

Time Travel

Our hearts are the memory keepers,
recording the imprints of our life.

We may not want to discard
the past to move forward.

Though we are also burdened by
the painful details of our story.

We do have the power to heal,
release, then let go of them.

As well, we can create new imprints,
and experiences through our new life.

Erasing those hurt memories is
sometimes easier said than done.

Setting our own lives in order,
should not put it off kilter so.

Though we may have been brought
into a deeper state of awareness.

Are we striving for self-mastery,
or ownership over our own lives?

We are meant to live in the moment.
Now is all we really are given.

Love is always the solution, and
Loving ourselves is always the cure.

Alice Parker

Chapter 8 ~ Ranges, Gorges & Chasms~Oh My!

Speckles of prism colors, from the early morning sun bounced, to reflect off the window and pool, like little iridescent mirrors. A similar vision brought back up from my memory bank. The intricate, spiral- topped temples of Thailand, which shot out arrows of light, creating the magic illusion to all, it was a glittering country by day. *"Wrong!"* The reality had shown, *"Nothing is ever as it seems,"* especially when sudden shining glints blind our true vision.

Wait. Reality check: Where was all this philosophy coming from, on this particular morning? Could it be from last night's spot reading of the two new Aboriginal books, referred by Marta and Kaylin? To keep my criticism in check here, I should consider refraining from more reading, until after I leave the country. I did not want my personal contact with the Aussies to be tainted, by what others had done in the past. Each encounter should be taken on its own ground, with each person's words and actions speaking for them. *"Good Luck,"* I mumbled to myself, *"Who of us ever totally rational and accepting of others?"*

I hopped on the bus, to finish my last tour and full day in the Red Centre. I'd again be inundated with rocks, more formations than my little, boggled-mind could probably imagine. We'd be going west from Alice Springs following the Western MacDonnell Ranges, which I supposed hid Simpsons Gap, Stanley Chasm, Mt. Sounder, Glen Helen Gorge, and Ormiston Gorge. I guess they ran out of descriptive words for rocky holes and openings.

Reality check here, again: Was I getting jaded, or how many different kinds of rocks could there be? I guessed, about to find out, in this part of the world, they were almost infinite.

Luckily, the masses from the winter tours were about gone, and any summer tour masochists were nowhere in future sight. With less than twenty people on the bus, it gave each of us our space and privacy. The guide, as usual, was quite capable and pleasant, although I'd already heard a lot of his patter and dissertations several times. For my own mental amusement, I turned it into a game of editorializing, comparing it to previous scripts, or predicting what he might say next. Outside, occasionally attracting my attention, the MacDonnell Range staunchly galloped up and down, along the left side of the bus, with long, bright rust-colored stretches. They were almost arrogant in their protrusions - "Look at ME!" There was no doubt in my mind, these 'so called' inanimate, petrified-hunks had personalities, and a rather controlling one, at that.

We'd only traveled a short distance from the city, when we had a photo stop at the memorial of Reverend John Flynn, founder of the Royal Flying Doctor Service. Sitting at the end of a short path, up the slight, beige-graveled knoll was a giant, bald boulder perched on a large rectangular cairn with a plaque cemented onto it. The life-saving service had begun in 1928, with the far-flung, ranch-stations using a pedal-operated, radio system connecting them to a medical diagnosis or treatment, made available via phone. Today, it was a nationwide network or fourteen bases, boasting twenty-eight medically equipped aircraft. In 1950, the system was adapted and expanded to two-way radios for the School of the Air, which brought together and educated over twenty-thousand students, literally scattered over two and a quarter million square kilometers.

To many, this was just another nice honoring of a single person, who made a difference in conquering the unexpected vicissitudes of the remoteness of this harsh

Outback, on its struggling inhabitants. Yet, to Alice Springs, it had made its eked-out existence, more than a historical speck in the middle of a country, too big for its limited population. Once the group had thinned, I stepped back and away, to frame my postcard shot. The clump of ghost gum trees on the right, with their chalky-white, splotched bark and feathery green leaves atop, fluttered in the breeze. They were set against the delft- blue, cloud streaked sky, broken only on the left by the jagged, ochre-cropped buttes, bursting with pride from the mountain range. The profuse, violet washed wild flowers scattering the perimeter alone, and softened this pioneer commemorative.

Standing behind me, about to finish his cigarette, was the tour driver. He was rather tall, yet pleasantly ordinary and sufficiently capable. Yes, a dull, characterless description lacking from interchange. That was solved, while also gratifying some of my insatiable curiosity.

"Is there, some sort of particular significance to the boulder?" In a land abounding in natural rock wonders, *that one* had something surreal, or at least out of place, about it.

He squashed out the cigarette, picked it up, tossed it into the trash bin, then turned to smile at me, as he knew what I was getting at, though I'd thought I'd chosen my words well. "Graffiti. It got so bad, the city fathers had the rock *sandblasted* to clean it all off." Shocked by his direct reply, and not sure what to say. "Looks a bit odd, doesn't it?" He smirked more to himself than to me, as if he had hoped someone would notice and ask. Most of the other tourists were getting on the bus, so I followed him over. He did not want to sound directly derogatory, but obviously he also felt it was a distraction, at best.

"With all the rocks available, you'd think they'd have simply replaced it." I commented.

He stopped at the door to let me step in first, and I paused for his response. "Yeah, to save money, at least." As I settled into my seat, he said over the mic, "Looks like it's going to be great weather for pictures and hiking."

I clearly remembered the first sweltering, humid summer Travis and I had come to Australia. In all the public parks, we had not seen one drinking fountain, or drink-vending machine, much less any abundance of public telephones. When we finally asked the landlady at the condo in Cairns, she had sharply replied, the extensive vandalism had simply made the constant repair and replacement prohibitive. We were both shocked, as we'd expected the Aussies to be much more stable, than American juveniles. Again, there was something to be said for the benefits of the controlled-society in Japan. The vending machines and public telephones were as ubiquitous as the bicycle, or the noise pollution and even the smallest park I'd been to, had at least one drinking fountain.

We zipped on to Stanley Chasm, and delightful to see only a few cars with no other tour bus or people to clutter up the narrow crevice. I vividly recalled the photos Lorraine and Graeme had, with people practically on top of one another, trying to enjoy the spectacles of nature. As I entered the park path, the formations were more like sheered slabs, stacked as if left over inventory. With ferns, shrubs and trees growing out of them, like dust or mold from the past millennium. Which, of course, one could say was exactly what they were.

I could slowly feel the temperature dropping, as I got closer to the actual towering sides of the chasm, it quite easily blocked-out all but the most piercing rays of light. I was sure the little sparse greenery probably burst forth, once the sun was overhead and flooded them for those precious moments with its blessing.

The path was replaced with the remains of loose gravel, rocks and enormous boulders, the dry season exposed. One could imagine the rushing waters and torrents, which had swept through this narrow break thousands of times, creating, manipulating and depositing the granite fragments. We mere humans could simply stand in awe of. I had the feeling, I was viewing the survivors of an ongoing battle, of the dominating powers of nature - sun, wind, and rain. There were no absolute 'winners' or 'losers' … Perhaps it could simply be described as seasonal rites of passage, one succumbing to the other, as its paramount peaked, then waned to the next.

Having saturated myself in this visage of raw omnipotence, I slowly worked my way back, crawling and climbing over the naturally, quarried rubble. I stopped frequently to appreciate the wild myriad of plant life, which had not easily yielded its stance on the infertile slopes. Those numerous ones cast aside had surrendered, and were again a testament to the rigid rules of endurance. The cool respite, suddenly became a quirky chill down my spine, as my nerves barely twitched, with a kind of ominous fear at the aftermath of 'normal' rage from nature. Firsthand, I'd witnessed a 'mild' tornado in Illinois, and a bit stronger one in Oklahoma, but both had been at safe distances, and neither had personally touched me in any way. I turned and walked quickly to rejoin the bus, thinking it was a good awareness and another point of consideration about this Territory.

Our guide had made some Billy tea, which was hot and good, served up with some tasty box cookies. The few other tourists at the surrounding tables were eating snacks, or preparing for lunch. We were soon on the bus destined for Glen Helen Gorge and a barbecue lunch at the old homestead, On The Way. Fascinated, how once again the rolling scenery changed to gentler hills, with what seemed to be outbursts of a jagged, spiked narrow rock hedge. The driver then stopped to point out and let us photograph, what definitely looked like rock remains of a prehistoric, dinosaur or dragon, depending on one's imagination. It reminded me, Mother Nature had a sense of humor after all, not only to produce such a thing, but make it readily accessible to appreciate.

We had one more diversion to Ellery Creek Gorge, to see the beautiful water hole, framed by ghost gums and multi-colored stacks of granite. The crystal clear water, the magic ingredient which gave the verdant hues life form, shifted the boulders, and added character to the rock formations. I was sure, too, in the summer it refreshed the body like nothing else ever could. The guide pointed out water stains on the rocks, from the annual 'wets' which gave this placid point and serene scene a totally different perspective.

Not sure what I was expecting the 'homestead' to be like, but was pleasantly surprised as its homeyness mixed with general store and museum. Somehow, one would think it could not be pulled off, yet in Australia, those things just worked. We had an hour to hike and explore before lunch, which seemed a little presumptuous until I stepped out on the wide open verandah. Smack in the middle of what one would call a 'backyard' was the Glen Helen Gorge!

I took off almost at a trot down the path toward the mauve- colored sand, chartreuse variegated reeds and bright blue water, still separating the high roan stone forms. As I got closer, I could pick out the water marks, both from run-off and basic flooding, and saw how it bleached out the color, as well as defined the configurations.

I felt within me a recognition of the delineations, as if during these past few days, I'd developed an intimacy with this inherent crust.

Perhaps, brought on by personally solving the mystification - only from a distance did it all look the same. I'd never considered myself to be any kind of a 'rock-hound,' but I'd yet to be bored as each new massive array intrigued and beckoned me.

"God," I suddenly said out loud. "There truly is more to life than being successful in a job." It felt as if the workaholic, in me just cringed, as the human in me jumped for joy. I had surely shucked some kind of brittle old shell. An armadillo, I thought, all wound up in self-sacrificing, and not living life to its fullest. I stretched and moved to feel this new freedom, realizing I could breathe more deeply. I looked up, the sky was a sharper blue, the air was pungent and the details of rock, with slivers of green, were focusing clearer.

My awakening made me feel full of life-juices, energy and a hunger for more. I wanted to laugh out loud for no reason, other than being happy with my life 'now.' Interesting, when and where a stroke of genius hits upon you, and suddenly nothing will ever be quite the same again. If I'd planned this sensation, it could not have taken place in a stranger, or better place. I smiled from ear to ear, then plopped down to play in the coarse auburn sand for ten minutes or so before pushing myself back up.

I poked and ambled, registering the nuances of shades, shapes and survival techniques for every nook, cranny or ridge, which had some plant hanging on and flourishing in some way. It finally leaked into my pea brain, I could learn some things from nature, if I knew how to listen to what she was trying to say. The teacher can be taught when she wants to … and she certainly needs to.

I took off my hat and let the light breeze cool my head, as I tossed my curly-mass to keep it from sweating up. The sun was bright and hot … winter or not. I glanced at my watch and started back, yet forced myself not to be compelled by the time to hurry along, and miss any of the things I'd come out to see. My lunch hour, and I'd learned food service was one of the more relaxed things on an Aussie tour.

There were few enough of us and other tourists, I still was able to get a good seat at one of the picnic tables, right at the edge of the verandah. Nothing blocked my spectacular view of the massive almond ridge staring back at me. Appropriately enough, a black and white Magpie crow flew in, and began parading back and forth, as if doing an inspection of us.

One of the children threw a crumb of bread out to it. It glanced almost sullenly, then finally walked over and pecked it momentarily as if, "You've got to be kidding?" The Magpie then turned and walked away, insulted by such poor offerings. I cracked up laughing and several people stared, not understanding why, and I could not have cared less. It felt great.

I finished up my barbecue steak and sausage, I'd not bothered with the hot dog, and even had seconds on the salads. "Real Food," as my friend Justine would say, as never a great lover of the Japanese variety. I smiled again thinking of how much she'd have loved, all this countrified air, people and surroundings, since originally from West Virginia. Lost in thoughts of how she'd have appreciated everything here, I had another glass of ice tea, and savored the moment by taking mental photographs. Each scene was framed, focused and stored to be frozen in my file memory. I tucked them away in my computer box of a brain, to be pulled out on those lonely, wet or cold days, when I needed some warmth, which these sunny remembrances could give me. Or, if encouraged, I'd verbally repaint the image for friends.

Our driver brought me back to the present, with his announcement we'd be departing in fifteen minutes. I drank up, wanting a few minutes to explore the rest of the Homestead, abundantly decorated with dated memorabilia. Outside was the old smoke-house, refurbished with the traditional equipment and material intact. One reflected on the living conditions, easily measured by the fact, many Outback places still had only self-generating electricity.

Though the lifestyle on the cattle stations may be a part of the 'white fellers' mythology, it was not the story today. Most drovers, though enshrined in Australian history, as the pioneers who opened up the virgin country by their own initiative. But now worked for national meat companies of even British, American and Japanese multi-national concerns. The horse had not yet been replaced, but it was extensively augmented by both fixed-winged aircraft and helicopters, to drive and search-out the cattle for mustering. Perhaps only the road train, truck drivers were the last image of the dying breed of lone, independent men on the range.

Back on our circuitous trip, we stopped to view the dramatic intensity of Mt. Sounder, rising out of the Finke River bed and contrasted by the ruling plains. The drifting circles of kite-hawks distracted the idyll setting, the puffs of clouds had framed. Beautiful visions, no doubt about it, easy, pleasant living: Get Real - even a novice could see the reality of it all, and I no longer felt like one. Our guide was dispatching some repetitive profundities, about the challenging life within the natural setting.

I could have dazzled him with some witty repartee, as I'd already rehearsed this tune back on Ayers Rock, but it was neither the time, nor my place to break him on a roll. I glanced at my spellbound cohorts, realizing many were hanging onto his words of wisdom, about sussing as much out of the land as possible, taking for granted it owed them a livelihood. Trying to move unobtrusively, I got our of earshot, for now this 'conquering' of the land, began to disturb me. I took photos, attempting to become enthralled in my own contemplations, but not easy.

The long, harder hike of the day was at Ormiston Gorge, which had a new informative, though small, park-ranger station, explaining about the fauna and flora, as well the creation of the formations We had an hour to climb the Gorge, and by this time, it did not seem so difficult to me, though it was tedious in the later heat of the day. The views from the several high points were sprawling tundra, with no flat- out horizons this time, but a continuous crisscross of ranges, seeming to conflict in their directions.

The creek splayed into several directions, creating dark, blue- ink blotches of ponds neatly graced in several of the curves, with flowing gum trees. The rare and famous black swans were said to have made their home amongst it all, and a reward I felt well worth climbing for. On the other hand, they could have been reached by taking the other flat path, so perhaps back into the challenging and testing myself.

Last again, of the few of us who climbed, I could see several of the others at the end of the pond snapping photos of the swans so graceful, while displaying their deserved arrogance. I hurried to find my own spot, which was not easy, as by this time of day, the swans blended well into the shadows. I'd move and focus, then they'd paddle off ignoring me, with only a simmering refection of their feathers, to catch my attention once again. We played the game several minutes, until the only one chasing around trying to get them posed was me. Barely satisfied with the yielded cooperation I got, I ambled toward the bus, stopping for yet another wild flower photo.

The driver made me happy once again, by making an unscheduled stop at the ochre pits. They had been taken off the usual route, because too many tourists had disturbed them, again lacking resect for what was not public property. The Aboriginal people still used them and, of course, they had a right to. There was a more than adequate viewing platform, yet one of the men had insisted on climbing down to get a closer look. With promises he'd not touch anything, the guide had not said anything to him. I felt angered, then realized it took my energy away from thoroughly enjoying it all.

The subtle vertical hues and shades looked like toned rainbows. Exquisite, how nature had created this streaked and variegated palette, for the imaginative artists of yesterday and the creative ones of today. Though the few mounds were only three or four meters high, and sequestered away among ordinary rocks, their discovery and use was a balanced bonus. I could not help but wonder which came first - the desire to leave designs or messages on the rocks, thus find a way to do so; or having found a material which easily lent itself to leaving marks, making them as creative or informative as possible. This was based on a theory, which some of the original rock paintings were signs left by one Aboriginal tribe to another: "Good kangaroo, here." …"Water near here." Of course, they used stylistic hieroglyphics, rather than words.

Back on the bus heading for our last stop, I stared back at the pits for my mind was still boggling at what the Aborigines had realized they had at their fingertips. Survival in this outland may not have been so difficult for them, when one considers they still had time left over for developing 'the arts' - song, dance, musical instruments, mythology, paintings and crafts for utilitarian, and aesthetic appreciation. Definitely, a converted worshiper of them.

Truly so easy and common for the 'white man' to castigate the Aborigines, for their lack of finesse, not wearing a three-piece suit, or going to church on Sundays. Time was a pitfall, test, snare or even a trial which we fail, when we don't foresee our ignorance of the future.

My thoughts were whirling when we pulled into Simpsons Gap. It could have been the first park we visited, as it nearest Alice Springs, but the wise, tour company tried to make the route circular, to avoid the long, dry-run back into town. Our trusty guide gave us vague promises of Rock wallabies scampering through the white sands, or up in the giant boulders or rock-shelf themselves. It'd be unfair to say they'd chosen to leave the best for last, as each stop had been unique and fascinating in its own way. Yet, once again, not prepared to be as amazed and thrilled, as I was.

The creamy beige and white sand, belonged along at shoreline with waves breaking against them, giving meaning to their existence. Inland sea or not, this incongruity made me almost want to search the sky for sea gulls. Just in case, there really was some expansive water beyond those massive rock formations and leftover minute creek.

Climbing over the strewn megaliths, I could only ponder what this would be like in the middle of the wet season. I certainly would not be walking around or playing in the sand. I suddenly became cognizant of the fact, not only did the whole perspective of the land change, but the living conditions for the animals did, too. I began to study the ridges and cliffs for those elusive rock wallabies, who'd be smart enough to hide in the growing shadows thrown raggedly across them, by the late afternoon.

The camouflage seemed to jump and move, the longer I stared unaided by my binoculars, as I knew not to trust my dwindling eyesight. I gave up to walk on to the remaining creek water. It looked so clear and inviting, I bent down to rinse my hands of the sandy residue shed by the rock. I quickly jerked both hands back, as it was ice cold. Now feeling the chill of the shade, I snapped back again to reality - one might enjoy drinking it, but certainly not bathing in it.

Although, the return ride to Alice Springs was not long, it did have a definite closure to it. I came here looking for more than a tourist's experience and I certainly received it. More than I expected, and in some ways, more than I wanted. All the subtle meanings and realizations would have to be sorted and filed in their appropriate mental or emotional places, to be drawn back out when I was ready to analyze, reflect or just use. The closer our approach, the more I accepted how much I liked this town. Not great by any city standard, but it certainly was comfortable. I watched long, lazy shadows stretch over sections of the neatly organized city, as if it was aptly content to get ready to be tucked away for another night. The sun, about to drop from the sky and the luminous peach light would once again settle over the somber, red desert. I sighed.

I knew Alice Springs could be rousing, as it had some rather infamous celebrations, which I certainly would not mind some day coming back to experience. The Henley-on-Todd Regatta, held annually in October, one could call the piece de' resistance of a dry sense of humor. "Henley,' rightly came from the celebrated boating center on England's River Thames, and the 'Todd,' was naturally, Alice's own river, which was usually dry.

It's a race with *bottomless*-'yachts,' which the competitive teams supported or carried, as they ran along the dusty riverbed. As if not ironical enough, each year the organizers took out insurance against rain, for water definitely spoiled the river race! From the extensive photo collections seen, the boats had grown considerably in size and creation, limited only by one's sense of ridiculousness. Scull- races along rails, with the oars digging into the sand to propel them had also been added, to further the preposterous 'boating' celebration.

The Camel Cup, another equally well-known happening, had come quite upscale from its humble beginnings in the dry Todd, to being held in the legitimate race park. From the 1870s to the late 1920s, camel-trekking inland was for commerce, not tourists. Common for their Afghan masters to have both spontaneous and organized races for entertainment, as well sport. Now the Cup sponsored by the Lions Club to raise money, and have a good time.

Like many other Territory and Outback towns, Alice Springs also had a rodeo and several other festivals.

One could say, most events had begun in order to break the monotony of the lifestyle, and had continued to simply celebrate another year of survival there. These people dealt with their 'testing' of themselves against it all, if not on a daily basis, then certainly on an annual one. Barely a year went by without old mother nature tossing out another acid test for them. Many won the touchstone, a few lost the ultimate, their lives and others just toss in the towel. Thus, interesting how many of those survivors in Alice Springs faced the harshness with such social humor. I may not want to join them, but I certainly did admire them.

Back in my room, pack-up time, and collecting all I had to mail in my last box back to Japan. I certainly appreciated the Australian Post's excellent facilities and a good variety of sturdy boxes for shipping things. I'd never forget the problems I had, trying to mail souvenirs from Italy and Spain. Beyond uncooperative, even thinking how rude to assume they'd have boxes for sale to mail stuff. For avid travelers, who tended to gather items, or collect printed material, as I did, not having to tote it from one place to another was a blessing, which also encouraged more of the same. When I considered the voluminous loads they moved around the world daily, it truly amazed me and the majority did get to it's destination.

After I'd sorted and protectively wrapped, I gathered up the various packages to myself, David and several other friends I'd be sending souvenirs to. I'd take them into town early, to mail before heading out to the airport for my flight to Cairns. The packing went a bit faster, not only because I'd done it so often before, but because I knew what I'd wear and needed for my few days in the sunshine city. After all these varying shades of ochre, I truly looked forward to the wet, cooler blues and greens. Just seeing how much Cairns had changed in four, hectic tourist-laden years, would be interesting.

I'd read and heard how Cairns and other places had become quite Japanese, after the disastrous, domestic airline pilot's strike. Allowed to go on almost a year, and not settled until untold numbers of businesses in tourist spots had folded. No one - foreigners or nationals - could get there to spend their money. The savvy Japanese, flush with cash, came in and scooped many businesses up for pennies. The old owners became the employees, and if they stayed on, had to quickly learn how to do business the 'Japanese way.'

I'd agreed with my Italian Townsville friend, "It's no way to run a damn country, when the unions are telling everyone, including the government, what to do." And now, many Aussies, especially in the unions, blamed the

Japanese for the loss of the businesses and their jobs. This sounded like the Americans. Historical amnesia was rampant everywhere in the world!

Overly organized as usual, I had some time on my hands before the flight, so I decided to take the shuttle bus to the airport to save a few dollars. Always fun to see the mixed-batch of people, these little vans picked up. We zipped here and there picking up an older British couple, then three Italian men, probably in their early thirties. I could not figure out their story, as they did not look like they'd been here on business, so they must have been just tourists.

They seemed quite wound-up, though with Italians it's hard to tell, as they do seem to be that way with most things. I'd have liked to ask them where they were from, but they kept almost two conversations going, among the three of them, until we stopped to pick up a young, quite pretty, shapely blond, wearing short-shorts. Their talk ceased, and I saw them primping to make space for her, jostling each other in the process, to vie for the best seating arrangement.

When she saw the lion's den, she was about to ascend into, she turned to the driver, an older, smiling chap, who had been whistling. "Would you mind if I sat in the front with you?" It was a very, clipped- British accent, and the request rolled ever so pleasantly off her lips. "I'm, …afraid I'll get carsick … crowded in the back."

"No problem." The driver quickly cleared his roster board and paperwork off the front seat, then shuffled her in without a word to any of us. He slid the door shut and kept smiling, as his tune picked up a quicker beat. I could not help, but snicker to myself. She obviously knew how to deal with these Casanovas, and proud of her. I thought women today knew how to handle men better than I had at her age.

I probably would have put up with it all, then been angry with myself I had. 'How far we've come,' as the commercial says. Only the year previously, I vividly remembered the dozen or so gigolos who pestered even me, in France and Italy. A woman traveling by herself was an easy target. And us older ones, they thought, were more desperate for company, and had more money. I smiled so devilishly, at myself and the irony. When younger, and had many choices, I rarely said 'no,' now older and had so few choices, I rarely said 'yes.' I no longer wanted to service, nor needed to be serviced.

Dashing back through the gap, my mind rolled over the days, and what all I had covered in the accelerated week. Many of the perspicacious encounters were still left dawdling, in the different spaces of my mind, as I'd be processing them for months to come. I could not say this landscape all looked differently to me, yet it did not have the barrenness, which had shocked me so, at first sight. We all piled out at our drop-off between Australian and Ansett Airlines - not exactly an airport one could get lost in. With the bag checked, I was free to wander the few shops in the time before the flight.

The people were friendly and anxious to sell, but I was solely passing the time and nothing really grabbed me. Not that I thought I had seen it all, it simply started to look the same, even when it was different. I'd experienced many times before - Mexico, China, Japan, Thailand or anywhere really, it first seemed to be so unique. It didn't make sense, but it's the novelty of it all being mushed together, which made it seem identical. Alice Springs and the Red Centre was a finished scenario, as for the physical souvenirs.

Tucked away in my aisle seat, out of habit, I pulled out the airline magazine to fill the time. I never was very good at doing nothing. I flipped through several pages, while everyone else got settled in, and the pilots got their bird aimed in the right direction. Another, almost four-hour flight, so I could trip to the light fantastic and have my own flight of fancies in my mind. It usually did not take much to carry me away, once we were airborne. And, glad to have the middle seat empty.

The young man sitting in the window seat, still had on his cowboy hat. After knocking it into the little window the third time, trying to look out, he finally removed it. His intense interest in what they were doing with the airplane, told me this was presumably a new experience for him. I loved observing the 'fish-out-of-water' syndrome, so I could not help myself from prying.

"Have you been to Cairns before?" I guessed it was much more pleasant and less embarrassing, than basically asking if this was his first flight.

HIs head snapped toward me, like rather surprised there were even other people near him. "No, ... actually, this is my first plane trip." The rust colored hair was a bit matted from the hat and sweat, more from nerves than heat. The indented hair had a ragged little edge all around it, and was several shades lighter from being exposed to the sun. Neat and clean, but the clothes had seen their use, as they were a bit faded, worn, too. The hat had kept him from being too darkly tanned, yet there was no question he spent his days outdoors. His bright green, wide-open eyes were taking everything in, with all of the wonderful awe and anticipation of a child.

"You going to visit friends, or is it just a vacation?" I felt like the doting mother or more accurately, the teacher trying to make the new student comfortable with the surroundings. Yet, another young man about my son David's age, with contagious enthusiasm for it all.

"Me girlfriend works at a resort hotel. I 'aven't seen her for four months. It's not so busy now, so we've got time to be together" Marvelous little dimples appeared, with his beaming smile and the term 'darling' sprung to mind. The girl might have moved on from him, but perhaps the good looks would keep it going for them, for a while, any way.

"Oh, I'm sure you'll like it very much. There's a lot to do up there, and the weather is great this time of year. How long are you going to stay?" He was watching me with a politeness, I could only describe as 'country-bred respect' for women and elders. Nice and endearing to a certain extent, but also made me want to ask for a sweater or tea or something.

"I've got ten days. I 'ave to be back Monday week. You don't sound like an Aussie, how come you know so much about Cairns?" His face showed he was ready to apologize, the minute I denied it. I knew I picked up accents quickly, and I'd even heard myself drawling somewhat in a modified Aussie way.

I lightly chuckled, "No, I'm American, but I've been to Cairns twice before, during my four trips to Australia." We had started taxing down the runway, and the distraction was too much, putting him almost into a frenzy. When the plane stopped and turned, setting-up for the takeoff, he glanced at me quickly to see if I was worried, and if he should be. "They just need the clearance, which I'm sure they'll get right away, because it can't be very busy." I used my most reassuring voice, which must have worked, as he smiled and peered back out the window. The takeoff tried to push him back in the seat, but he pulled hard to watch every meter of it. I glanced out as the MacDonnell Range dropped away, and the edge of Alice Springs was visible for a few seconds. My mind-computer blipped: *"Not one of us ever fulfills all of our own expectations. At some point we have to stop making demands."* I hoped this was a lesson I well learned.

* * * * * *

I drifted back to the last conversation I'd had with Lorraine, in the lovely, quiet, little restaurant surrounded by the Brisbane Botanical Gardens. How could anyone be lost or groping when surrounded by such myriads of colorful nature? Yet, I was. Lorraine, tried in her compassion, to give me feedback as to Travis' actions, the few times she'd spoken to him, the six months he'd stayed in Australia.

I clarified to her and myself, for my curiosity, not feelings. Just merely what had gone wrong with our marriage, and conceivably what I could do to prevent 'it' from being repeated. Having second marriage go down the tubes 'shouted' failure at me, even if not worth keeping! *"Try, try, again."* or better, *"Square peg in a round hole."* or best, *"Do Your best and even an angel can't do better."* These worn-out homilies screamed in my ear.

"Not one of us ever grows up to be what we intended, or what was expected of us. I think we become different people in response to different times, and places … and responsibilities." I took a swallow of my ice tea, looking rather sullenly into the glass. "I know I've changed … so many times in my life, sometimes I feel, 'Will the real Annie please stand up?' And, that's good, at least for me, because I'm never bored. I'm always searching for the next challenge." The sandwiches came and they were so big and generous, I knew I'd take half home for dinner. It always took a few days to get use to 'Real People' portions.

Lorraine held a piece of her sandwich with some hesitation and concern on her soft, thoughtful face. "I think you're interesting, because you have so many different sides to you. I haven't traveled much and I really like talking to you, hearing about your experiences." Chewing away, I stopped when she had, to see where she was going with it. "I think that was part of the problem for Travis, Annie … You're too much."

I put my sandwich down, wiped my mouth and washed the remainder in my mouth down my throat with tea. It was a personal- gully I avoided and denied. "How do you mean?" I had to ask the question, though there was no way I wanted to hear a truthful answer. I could only hope she either did not know, or would not say it.

She'd taken a bite of her own sandwich, and also used the time to formulate the right choice of words. She knew I cared, and not just because of Travis, but for my own self-discovery. "We all know he had emotional problems, but also I think he couldn't handle not living up to your expectations of him." She'd replaced her sandwich, and leaned back a little in the wicker chair to almost brace herself for the next statement. "I think it had all become too difficult to keep trying, … to be what you thought he should become. He wasn't at all multi-dimensional, just very one dimensional."

Defensive at first, as there was no way to hold back reaction to the verbiage. "I never pushed him, Lorraine. I only wanted him to be whatever he wanted to be. I supported whatever he wanted to do or try, and God knows, he certainly tried enough different things, unsuccessfully, and at great expense. But did I ever say 'no,' to him? NO, I didn't. Life sometimes moves us all around to become different people, and we have to go with the flow or be swept away by it." I tried not to pout, or feel she was defending his actions, when she knew, 'he'd done me wrong.'

"Annie, I don't think you realize the affect you have on people." She paused again to look me directly in the eyes, hers emitting benevolent understanding. "You tend to demand, no, not demand. I guess just *expect* some kind of excellence from everyone around you. You demand so much from yourself, and the pressure of your expectations are passed onto others, even without your saying it directly." She was on a roll, and home run was hitting me in my deepest, most hidden spaces. "Sally said, all the encouragement and support you gave them, made most of your teachers feel they *had to* perform better to live up to your expectations. No one wanted to be looked down on. But the measuring stick was yourself, which was a little out of reach for most of them."

There was a very definite part of me which was stunned, not so much by what she said, but she had recognized it, and actually said it. I sat back with my hands in my lap, clutching the napkin, and not knowing exactly what to say, as there was no denying any of it. I knew I'd done a lot of the same things to David, when he was growing up, without ever knowing I had. "I know I'm a perfectionist, especially with my work. ... I always wanted more for the others than they seemed to want for themselves, as I saw their potential ... just because I hate to see good talent wasted.

I guess I'm into more and better, especially when I think people are capable of doing it." I picked up my fork to stab a french fry. "I feel otherwise, ... it's like a retreat from excellence, which everyone should strive for ... and feel great once they've accomplished it. I only want people - whoever they are, to be the best they can be ... is that so bad?"

She smiled calmly. "It sounds great, but not very realistic. Even *mediocrity* is sufficient sometimes, in the real world. We all have our own goals and how we deal with them is our choice. Working toward a goal someone else sets for us is not the same. You need to learn to accept things and people as they are - including yourself. It'd make you a much happier person."

Lorraine had stopped, and was examining her napkin, as if it held the answers written somewhere on it. "I know I could have more, do more and be more. But, I made the decision a long time ago, when I almost died from cancer, to simply enjoy life … one day at a time and let a lot of it take care of itself. I was just happy to have my life. Some times, it takes a crisis for us to realize what is really important in life."

There was no denying, she'd taken a laid back attitude toward life, in so many ways and without my ever saying anything she knew, I'd been critical of it. No one had to tell me stress was eating me up, and a lot of my weight concerns came from it. My grand expectations, or unspoken criticism had been the basis of many quarrels, between not only Travis and I, but many other people I dealt with. "I do understand what you are saying, Lorraine. … I sometimes feel I'm so buried in this old psyche, I don't know how I'm going to break out. I want so much and yet at the same time, I want to run away." I took another sip of the tea and looked out into the peaceful trees and bright, blooming bushes. She'd picked up her sandwich and started eating again. It was said, but it was not settled. Would it ever be?

"You can't miss what you've never known, can we?" I was talking more to myself than to Lorraine. "I remember a friend in Chicago telling me, she coped because she expected nothing, then she'd never be disappointed." I stared back at her eating slowly. "Yet, most of us get funny streaks of sadness from time to time, because we know we are missing something. We don't know what it is, … whether it will ever be revealed, and if it is, or will we ever find it, or can even have it. And, then the kicker is, … will we still want it?" Lorraine stopped chewing.

It had basically been aired and we were both once again comfortable with one another. She continued on then about how lost Travis was. "He called me at school, just before he left, and insisted they get me to the phone. He seemed to be apologizing for everything. I don't know exactly what - maybe just for leaving - not doing what he'd said he'd do." She smiled again so knowingly. "I guess he knew you gave his life good direction, even though he couldn't handle not being in charge. Men like to think they are in control, even though we all know most of them aren't, but we still let them think they are in some way, to feed their egos."

"I know what you mean Lorraine, but I can't be somebody's remedy to their problems any more. I tried if for years with Travis, rescuing him from himself. No one should be some kind of medicine for someone else's soul. Some things we have to take responsibility for ourselves. Of course, then we have no one else to blame for our faults or failures."

I started to laugh, and we both noted how the conversation was exposing some deep- seated emotions. "I think now of how many things make me happy, I didn't notice, or wasn't aware of when he was there. God, I feel I've changed in so many little ways. I keep discovering things I like to do, I hadn't done in years because he didn't like to do them. I've developed mental lists of happiness, different lists for different times and places, you know. They are like barometers, recording and telling me how my internal climate is doing and you know what? Most of the time it say, 'You're OK! and I am having fun! or This is Great!' And, it's true, I am OK … and having fun … and things are great."

She was smiling back at me with pure satisfaction at my accomplishments, and knew exactly what I was saying. The spontaneity of the feelings made me bubble. "It brings to mind something my mother said right after my father died. I'd gone shopping and had bought a fresh loaf of rye bread. I took it out of the grocery bag and practically presented it to her, saying we could have some bread and butter, or I'd make sandwiches for lunch." I paused shaking my head.

"She looked at me with kind of a shy-smirk and said, 'Annie, I really don't like rye bread.' Well, I had to sit down, you could have knocked me over with a feather. I argued with her all those years I'd been raised, being told about good rye bread and buying it fresh, or the best brand. She just kind of tilted her head and said, 'You father was the one who liked it, … and it was easier to eat it, than to argue.'"

I leaned toward her, still amazed at this revelation I'd shared. "Lorraine, all those years she played martyr, … and stoically ate the damn rye bead - why? What was the point? What did it prove? Not one of us knew, and I doubt any of us would have *cared* what bread she ate. We always had several different kinds of bread in the house. My God, she could have eaten any of them. But inch by inch, little by little, we let ourselves get chipped away and for what? Why? I can't even imagine my father would have cared, as long as he got what kind he liked." Lorraine was laughing, covering her mouth not to draw too much attention, and nodding her head at the same time, as I added. "I think we women do a lot of this shit to ourselves, … you know what I mean? And, I, for one, … am going to try not to do it any more."

* * * * * *

"Excuse me, would you like some lunch?" My eyes opened easily and I turned to the young flight attendant holding the tray. She was neat and efficient, with the smile not too plastic.

"Yes, thank you. I'm sorry. I'll have some tomato juice or diet coke, if you have it?"

"The beverage cart will be along in a minute, and I'm sure they have both. Enjoy your lunch." I glanced at my seat partner, as he gobbled the food like it was manna from heaven.

I checked out the tray and began prepping the food with salt and pepper, removing the silverware, then to pour the dressing on the little salad. I glanced over at the cowboy, chomping away. "Do a lot of Japanese stay at your girlfriend's resort in Cairns?"

He'd not quite finished swallowing, but answered anyway. "Oh, yeah. I think a Japanese company owns a part of it or something. She had to learn some Japanese, but they have Japanese people working there, too. She says it's harder, but she likes the job." He went back to his tray, which was almost finished. "This is great, isn't it?"

I smiled and nodded, as not about to complain, since I'd certainly had worse food. Off the top of my head, I'd say worst was CAAC, the domestic airline of China - warm Coke and a bag of peanuts, with very bad English instructions on how to open the bag and to *eat* them. When we did get food on later flights, I removed some particles from it, which I had no idea what they were, but I knew they were not edible. It all kind of went along with the in-flight mosquitos, and the 'extensive' safety demonstration - of the flight attendant using sign language for connecting the seat belts. Grateful they had them, until I realized the seats were not fully-attached to the metal floor. It could always be worse, as David said, so I happily ate my lunch.

Cowboy was back peering out the window and I finished my coffee, while flipping back through the magazine. I glanced back out the window again, then put a broad smile on my face, thinking succinctly to myself. *"I could say, 'Life's a Bitch, then you die,' but I'm not a pessimist. I'm a true-blue, Pollyanna, who not only wants everybody to be very happy, but to be the best they can with it! I guess I'll keep looking for the missing link to happiness."*

I read a few short articles, then an advertisement for planning for the future with the right investments caught my eye. My inquisitiveness about the future had gone a long way back, probably high school. I'd dabbled in astrology with a professional friend, hypnosis and upon occasion, the palm readers or psychics. Often a few had told me some accurate things, but the last one in Brisbane had truly knocked my socks off, with some of the things she told me. I often thought it was interesting, how things worked out when we least expected them to - Fate or Divine coincidences, as a dear friend used to say. And, it was exactly it, which finally brought me back to Brisbane and my visit to the wonderful clairvoyant.

* * * * * *

Out of the city, on the Sunshine Coast Highway, heading north with the little rental purring along nicely at one hundred kilometers. I thought back to the psychic, I'd met at the River Market. She'd given me a warning and told me to make an appointment to see her, with no consideration I said I was going out of town. I guess she knew I'd find a way, and now sifting through the brain matter on how. Part of the inspiration for this trip was Barb's fiftieth birthday party, which I'd missed - because of work, at the beginning of August. On the telephone, before leaving Japan, I'd proposed to Barbara and Paul for them to join me on the trip to Alice Springs or several other ideas we might do something exciting together. But, I also wanted it to be a memorable birthday experience for Barb. They declined, so what to do with them?

Not only because of Barb's birthday, I had the guilts about how Travis had dumped on them for almost a month, before going on to Townsville. He had given her money, but I never asked how much. I wanted something special for Barb and something the three of us could share. Bingo! Barb loved going into Brisbane to shop, especially at the Duty Free shop - and maybe, she might even have an interest in going to the psychic. If she did not, well, perhaps she'd not mind waiting while I went.

Back to the three of us, what could we all do? Aha! Another light bulb flashed. The television news program the night before, had shown some highlights about whale watching in Hervey Bay. Travis and I had tried to go out to see them, the year we'd driven down the coast, but the waves were too rough for the boats to go out. Since Barb and Paul both liked the water, I was sure they'd be quite interested, unless they'd already seen them. Well, took care of at least two days of activities and unloaded a lot of guilt. I'd been to most of the sight- seeing places with them, and there was only so much shopping one could do.

There I went again, planning my holiday like my work, busy, busy, busy. Would I never learn to just sit, relax and do nothing? *"I could,"* I said to myself, *"if I were on a beach ... for a few days, especially if there was some snorkeling and not much of anything else I could do. I'd done it, so I knew I could."*

The pretty part of the drive was coming up with the Glass House Mountains in the distance. To the other side of the road, were miles and miles of the eerie ghost gum trees, many of them falling down or dying. There was something rather sad about their weary disintegration. I could not help but wonder why they were not cut, or thinned, or something. They were like pitiful, old men standing around, not really contributing to society, but congenially waiting to make a final collapse. I'd driven pass them, perhaps four or five times, and they still affected me the same way, yet I'd never felt any strong passion for trees, in the protective sense. *Fast forward this memory tape, it was too sad and without a solution.*

Unpacking some things in my room in the main house - Travis had stayed in the apartment above the large, double car garage. I pulled out the brochure from the psychic and went to see if I could find Barb alone. I was afraid Paul would consider it all frivolous, or some thing. She was in her well-appointed kitchen, putting the finishing touches on lunch for us, while Paul was in the adjacent den with his video collection. She beamed brightly, as I walked in.

"The rice is almost cooked, and I made the curry earlier to go with the leftover lamb." She was carefully preparing the condiments to compliment the lamb, which she knew I loved. She looked up at me again. "It's so good to have you here, and to see you are holding up so well through it all." I knew she naively deemed my divorce in a much more traumatic light than I did. Of course, she'd never had one.

She concentrated again on the details at hand, then added, "Paul is searching for the video tape from my birthday party, ... it was great." In a lower voice and leaning slightly toward me, "He better not have copied over it, or I'll just kill him."

I chuckled at her release of frustration and shook my head at the situation at hand. Then I wondered how two people could be together so much, AND still get along on a daily basis.

With both of them retired, all they had to do was wait for friends or family to drop in, visit or, as was the usual case, stay for a few days, since most were in Sydney. In between, they made their regular pilgrimages to Hawaii for Paul to fish and Barb to shop. Then visited Paul's grown children and grandchildren in Sydney, or took a trip to somewhere close by, like Fiji.

Occasionally, they got invited on yacht cruises, with Paul's 'mates,' as his was just a smaller fishing boat, or up to friends' holiday retreats. A pretty nice go all the way around, one would think from listening to it, yet 'even the sameness of perfect-Paradise can get boring,' as one island resort guide lamented to me. Personally, I felt any boredom was a lack of imagination, as they had both been workaholics in their respective successful professions. Lorraine's words came back, crashing the front of my brain. I definitely had to remember to especially not measure *my friends* by my yardstick.

"Barb, I wanted to mention something to you and see if you might be interested." I then condensed my story as best I could, without lacking too much to intrigue her enough to want to go. " ... and it's only fifty dollars, which I'd pay as sort of a special birthday present to you. What do you say? You want to try to give a call after lunch, and see if she has some time which would work for us?"

Her eyes had brightened up, as I'd explained, decorated with my own enthusiasm and drama, of course. "I've always wanted to go to a fortune-teller! Yes, let's call after lunch. Don't say anything to Paul, though, OK?"

I loved her need for the clandestine. I never quite figured out, if it was her way of having privacy, or she liked to see what she could get away with doing and him not know about. Kind of like collecting coups, just to prove to herself she could do it. I knew there was very little Paul denied her. We all have our little games we play, and some of the best games were played among and between married people. I knew, I used to be one and did it, too.

I leaned down playing into the scenario, "Oh, of course not, Barb. It's just for us." I smirked and even gave her a wink. "Now," I spoke up clearly, "which table should I set, the dining room or the patio? It seems warm enough to sit by the pool, if you want?"

"Well, let's check if Paul has found the damn tape, then we can eat in the den and watch it. Paul? ..."

He had barely saved his neck, and quickly snapped the tab on the tape, so he'd not by shear-mistake grab it to copy over. We all settled in, and Barb gushed a bit with pride as to how many of her friends and relatives came from far and wide to help her celebrate. Paul did a swell job taping, as I could tell he'd developed a deft hand in maneuvering the camera to catch some funny sequences.

I took some special interest, as Travis and I had helped them get the camera the last time there, at the duty free store. Fun too, to put a face on some of the names they had both mentioned, when we'd talked during the past few visits. Interesting, how you get to know people from the way they described their friends and activities they had shared together.

After the party tape, I mentioned about the whaling trip and they both jumped on it. Paul was quick to dig up the morning's paper, as he'd noticed there was an article and advertisement about tours. Barb picked it up from there. "Annie and I are going shopping for dinner, so we can stop at the tourist information center to see what they've got. What day's best?" We talked it back and forth, then settled on Wednesday.

That taken care of, Barb came up with the excuse to show me all of her gifts, which were still in the living room, at the far end of the house. This was convenient for us to be alone to talk. Paul was back into his paper, to see if anything was worthwhile enough to tape on television. We gathered up the dishes and put them in the sink. Barb motioned to me to follow her through the dining room, where there was another telephone.

"Let's call now, get the number ..." She whispered to me, "afterwards, I'll show you all my wonderful gifts." I went to retrieve the brochure, which I'd tucked back away in my room. I got excited too, at the thought of sneaking a peek into my future.

"Barb, I was thinking we could maybe combine it with a trip to the duty free shop, lunch, shopping or maybe a movie. But, I'm not sure of the restrictions with my ticket. I think they've changed it, so on some things you have to get within a certain number of days, before you leave." Her eyes had lit up again at the idea, and she pulled out the Yellow Pages.

"I'll just call them and check out the restrictions, then we'll see what we can do." While she checked the number and called on the foyer phone, I sat on the floor with my back against the wall. I enjoyed the gentle breeze coming in the screened front door. She repeated the date on my exit flight, to confirm Friday would be within the allowed time period. "OK, all set. You call the psychic and check if you can get appointments for Friday."

Two appointments back to back weren't available until late in the day, six and six-thirty. I checked with Barb if it would make us too late coming back home. "No, I'll call Paul to explain, when we're ready to leave." Glad she really wanted this, so I went ahead to book them. The anticipation of Friday a glowing-magnetism for us both, with the magical adventure of whale watching added, not exactly an ordinary week. I still had no idea, how precipitous this lark-like psychic escapade would be, nor how it would give me the strength to change my life.

* * * * * *

"Excuse me, could you put up the tray and fasten your seat belt. We'll be landing in Cairns shortly." She'd gently touched my forearm, as my eyes popped open, rested and relaxed. I glanced toward the window. Around the cowboy, I saw the luscious Reef, its wet-blues and greens.

Memories of Australia
Kuranda

Rainforest country - the Daintree
Where rainforest meets the reef.

Where hippies had been evicted by the police,
And the land made safe for American tourists.

Where the train station was full of flowers.
Where butterflies had their own sanctuary.

Where tourism was the only industry.
Where Nature became Real Estate.

And people talked, Of making a killing.

Thom o Oz

Chapter 9 ~ Cairns & Kuranda ~ Memories

The new airport looked great, and much better organized, as well larger. Once I hit the covered, open walkway, wonderful warm air hit me. In every direction the bursts of colors reminded me of a flower show, one which never ended. I decided to use the airport bus, as now into saving money, and luckily, one was about to leave. My hotel was on the Esplanade, almost next to the condo where Travis and I'd stayed before. The tourist center had been able to get me one of the older, cheaper rooms at the rear of the hotel. Happily, right down from the new Pier marketplace, and adjacent to the wharf, where the boats left for the tours - perfectly located for a bargain.

The room was simple, basic and more than sufficient, for Cairns was not a city one spent much time in a hotel room - except during the wet, and why would you be there?!? I unpacked the few essentials, then hit the street to check out The Pier. I really wanted to compare what was different after four years. Though late afternoon, the brilliant sun still bright and the five hundred meter walk across the Esplanade warmed me, while the breeze off the water kept me from perspiring. The pelicans and other water birds were having their heyday, as the tide was out and the mud-flats offered up such tasty morsels for them.

I remembered how disappointed we first were, when we arrived to find there was no beach in Cairns. Then, from the twelfth floor condo, we had both spent hours watching the tide coming in and out, while the birds fed. I smiled with pleasure, as the peace and quiet of the birds certainly beat the noise and distraction a beach would bring. I'd heard the town council was thinking of dredging it all, and filling it in with sand, because some tourists had complained. I truly hoped they'd reconsider the untold problems, a beach could bring with thoughtless people partying late into the night.

There were many fine beaches a short drive south and north into Port Douglas, for those who wanted them. As I walked on, easy to see not much else had changed. Of course, the building of The Pier had transformed this sleepy little town in more ways than just shopping. I thought again of how shocked we were back then, when we discovered the stores all closed promptly at five or five-thirty. If this was a tourist town, you certainly could not tell by the locals wanting to make things easy or convenient for shopping. We arrived Christmas week, and I'd done our grocery shopping on Christmas Eve, so I could cook in the giant kitchen the condo had. We barely made it out in time, as the store was closing at noon. Still, not being familiar with Aussie customs and holidays, we had no idea the shocks the next four days would bring.

Christmas, on a Sunday that year, which meant Monday was a holiday, not unusual for the States either, but the Aussies had taken the British Boxing Day holiday, too, which followed on Tuesday. This meant then NOTHING was opened from noon on Saturday until eight o'clock Wednesday morning! It might all be well and good for the locals, but if Cairns was supposed to be a tourist town, they not only liked to shop, but also eat, go on tours, visit museums, etc. For us in the condo, plenty of food, also gave us - me a chance to learn Cairns so well, as I walked everywhere to occupy the time.

Around town, I window shopped, the Esplanade, the city park, the wharf, for three days. Only during the high heat of the afternoon did I stay in. Evenings or mornings, Travis sometimes walked with me, but he usually preferred to watch the ships at sea with his binoculars, or sit in the air conditioning watching television. By the time we left on our tour Wednesday morning, I knew the street names, had visited every open news agency, and had been in every hotel, checking out what they had open and available - not much.

I still recalled the numerous backpackers, almost starving, as only the more expensive hotel restaurants were open. The ones which did not have restrictions on dress codes, had signs stating 'reservations only.' About five o'clock on Boxing Day, one of the numerous fast food shops opened, and instantly fifty people in line getting something to eat and drink. I'll never forget the sight of so many of them, standing around and quickly stuffing food into their mouths.

How things had changed, and it could be summed up in two words - the Japanese. Four years ago, the only two stores I'd found open on Boxing Day had been a Japanese-run duty free store and an import-export store whose owner was Chinese. Once the Japanese had bought the Hilton, things began to change, as they put pressure on the shops to stay open, or they ran their own shops in competition. Yep, Cairns was no longer a sleepy little, backwater town - now open for business every day from morning to night. I glanced over at the new, four star Radisson, adjacent to The Pier. Money, especially tourist money, changed the culture.

When I walked up closer to the gigantic building, I was totally amazed. There were several pedal carts, like modern-day rickshaws with bicycles at the front. another major difference was the peddlers were Aussies, and almost all of the customers Japanese! Positioned also in front of The Pier, were several food carts - popcorn, hot dogs, ice cream. I'd certainly not seen these before. Though capitalism had caught on to them, and sure the deep, long recession had been a strong impetus. Inside, the story not only continued, but got more detailed.

I'd checked with the hotel clerk on how long The Pier was open till, and she'd told me it also had a market on weekends. There were all kinds of handicrafts, homemade food and other gifts or souvenirs, at very reasonable prices. The variety, quantity and bargains were so much more than what I'd have ever expected. I knew the locals complained these prices outrageous, but I'd just come from Alice Springs and nothing beat Japan for high prices. Too bad, I really did not need anything and did not have anyone left to get omiage for. Yet, as I wondered around from one little stall to the next, I finally succumbed and purchased several things I'd not seen before. So, a most enjoyable way for me to spend several hours.

Then a bit startled, when I walked out and saw the purple haze, from the setting sun coloring the mountains to the west, as well the clouds above. A twinkle of lights along the Esplanade, were reflecting in the returned water, while the brighter lights of the hotels and shops decorated the streets. I sauntered lazily back to the hotel, soaking up the sights and sounds of the tropical night. How truly different they were from the dry, crisp sounds of the desert.

The raucously, loud cacophony of the lorikeets could be heard hundreds of meters away. I cracked up at their antics, of settling into their 'spot' before dark. The problem was, thousands of them and only a few of the trees, which met their grouping requirements. Too funny, they had no idea how 'human' they were acting!

I stayed to watch and listen for several minutes, then continued on to the hotel. I'd remembered there was a movie theater in town, and thought I might take in a movie. I knew my tour for Kuranda was at about eight-thirty, so I did not have to get up too early. The same lady was at the desk when I returned. "Excuse me, could you help me again, please? Is there still movie a theater here in town?"

She smiled widely at my packages, "I see you found the market. Yes, we actually now have two theaters. I have a paper, do you want to know what's on?"

"Oh, thank you, I'd appreciate it. There was a movie I wanted to see in Brisbane, and maybe it's here now." So helpful, and what a positive attitude change from what I'd remembered from four years before. She read off several movies and finally hit the one I wanted. "Ah, Yes! That's the one, 'Strictly Ballroom.' Could you tell me where and what times?" She jotted them down and began to give me the directions. "Yes, Shields ... and yes, Grafton ... Oh, I shouldn't have any problem, I know just about where it is. And, thank you, again."

I turned to go then asked, "Do I need to make a reservation for the dining room, and is there a dress code?" With a 'No' to both answers, I headed past the pool and up to my little room. I'd have a shower, a nice quiet dinner, then walk over to the movie theater. So far, so good - Cairns seemed to be giving me good memories, both new and old.

The gracious, but comfortably-aged dining room was on the second floor, with numerous large-potted, tropical plants scattered around the tables and huge windows. This not only gave some privacy, but also an alfresco-feeling without the noise and humidity. Not sure if I was early for dinner, or if they simply were not crowded, as the waitress showed me to a window table. After ordering some wine and dinner, I stared at the colorful lights surrounding The Pier area. The intensity of the black-velvet backdrop, gave them a Christmas-time tinge which made me smile. Further around to the left was a string of bobbing-twinkles from the masts of large and small sailboats, cruisers and yachts. In the far distance, I could barely see a few slowly passing lights of ships, or approaching boats returning to the safety of the harbor for the night.

Looking straight down, my eyes followed the brightly lit length of the street, as it curved along the Esplanade. Each restaurant, hotel and shop was vying for the attention of locals and tourists alike. There was not much traffic, which was good, since many people were busy crossing the street at various points. The wide sidewalks were filled with a stream of people, mostly tourists, surely, walking through and around others, lounging at the outside tables and chairs. Fascinating, a mingling of both a medley of backpacker-types at the take-aways and well-dressed clientele at the upscale cafes. There was little visible separation between, except for perhaps dress and what they were paying for their meal.

To me, a very positive reflection of the Oz acceptance and congeniality.

More than satiated with the delicious dinner, and even a little tipsy from the half-carafe of wine, I trotted down the street toward the movie theater. As usual, the mix of people and shops along the way, gave the short journey an air of venturing, other than just a walk to a destination. From the previews I'd seen, my anticipation of the Aussie comedy was heightened by the fact a farce and their dry sense of humor, was what they liked and did best.

Being early, I settled into a good, centered seat and took the extra time to check out the atmosphere, which had been done very well. I could relax too, and thoroughly look forward to the enjoyment of letting myself easily laugh out loud. Something I disliked about going to the movies in Japan. Even the Japanese who did understand with the translation, the cultural humor in English language movies wasn't easy, and laughing out loud was considered rude, so they did not. It could also be annoying to me and Kazuyo, when they really turned down the audio, as it distracted the Japanese, but we of course, preferred the English spoken. It never ceased to amaze me sometimes, how little kanji was printed on the screen after long conversations. So, much of the culture in English was lost to the Japanese, as not translatable, or not qualified translators.

Still chuckling to myself about one scene or another, I slowly returned to the hotel. Upon arriving, I decided to walk on to the Esplanade, and sit on a bench. I felt totally absorbed by the moment. Once in a while, a small wave might come in or a couple walk by. The silence was barely broken, by the muted tones of the occasional car or din of talk and laughter from the still- lingering sidewalk people. Into the secret obscurity of the night, I connected to some responses within myself. There were no ghosts from past trips to Oz, to haunt me any longer. At last myself and I enjoyed it so very much. Any mental reference to *him* was superficial and for clarity.

What I did now, was mine to do and remember as I desired. Visiting Kuranda again would thus be an immense thrill. The small village, on top of a big mountain, North and West of Cairns. Tour books would refer to it as 'charming,' 'historic' and 'unique.' Which, I must admit, was true on all accounts. One of the fun things about Kuranda was getting there, especially if the hour and half, scenic, thirty-four kilometer railway was taken. If the trip sounded slow, the building of it was incredibly slower, and a 'one of a kind' Oz story.

Cries for the railway began in 1862, with miners and settlers cut-off from supplies for weeks, and even months, at a time - because of the extensive rainy season. The railway had to climb 327 meters through rainforests, across ravines and over waterfalls. Not only were there miles of track, with ninety-three curves, hand-laid and dug, but so were the fifteen tunnels. In between all those 'minor' problems, were the Aborigines defending the invasion of their territory. By the time it was finished in 1891, almost six years of actual construction, the mines had played out. But, the Atherton Tablelands had bloomed into an extra-ordinarily rich agricultural and grazing land. Diesel had replaced the once steam engine yet the train was now almost exclusively used for tourists, as the paved road was much quicker.

Sunday was one of the Market days in Kuranda. The bus I took was more of a convenient delivery service than a tour. We were driven up early - beating the crowds coming by train - dropped off at the market, given a ticket to return by train, then picked up from the Cairns station, with a choice of three different return times. I'd not been able to see the Market before and I wanted a leisurely day to enjoy it all once again. Besides the street by the Market, there was only one main street in Kuranda, then the short walk down the hill, to the botanical garden atmosphere of the train station. So, not as if I could get lost or hungry, as a wide variety of food abounded both in the Market and on the street.

There had been two young Japanese women on the small bus, and I offered to the driver to explain about the train tickets and time schedule to them. Though they said they understood my basic explanations, I wrote down the train times to make sure they did not miss the last one.

With the basics out of the way, the guide drove easily along the winding roads, as it headed upward, while we gasped as each curve revealed a breath-taking drop to the crashing surf and empty beaches below. He congenially asked who of us had been out to the Reef, then gave several suggestions as to other islands to visit and things to do. I vaguely listened, as the music on his radio had begun to attract my attention more. The distinctive bellow of a didgeridoo, uncharacteristically set to rock music, and the few words I could catch were saying something about 'tribe' or 'treaty' and definitely 'land.'

Once our guide had answered questions on the water tours, I popped in quickly to ask, "Excuse me, do you know what that song is on the radio?" He turned up the volume before answering.

"Sure do." He had glanced back over his should, since more comfortable with maneuvering on this road than we were. "It's '*Yothu Yindi,*' the Aboriginal rock group. Quite popular and rightly so. Good sound and right-on words." His fingers tapped the steering wheel.

"Yeah, really sounds great." Needless to say, I'd been rather taken aback. How far they'd come, but a logical combination to move their cause into the future, which brought the young people into some understanding. I wished I could comprehend the words better.

Barely a cloud in the sky, as I stepped out into the shiny- warmth to head for the main entrance to the Market. Many of the stall keepers were still putting out, or hanging up their wares, while enjoying their own coffee and breakfast. I sauntered by each one with a smile on my face, as I loved markets wherever they were. I loved seeing people doing their own thing, with products they'd made or were just selling. Equally curious about the food, but one of the disadvantages of being a tourist on a short visit. I could treat my taste buds to a few things, though I longed to buy whole loaves of the great looking bread, filled with natural ingredients.

Wandering along, barely there fifteen minutes, when I head a great roar of applause then a loud speaker announcing the 'bravery of another lost soul.' Bungee-jumping, the boom of the clever promoters, and the bane of the challenged-victims. How many were actual dare-devils and how many were pushed into proving their machismo - and whatever the female equal would be considered, one would never know? I walked over to get a closer look, and the incongruity of the setup could only make me smirk and shake my head. A giant crane had been erected next to a small pond, with marvelously-lush, giant trees and ferns encircling it.

A small boat had rowed over to reel-in the young man, who had received the christening and applause. I listened to the amusing comments about him, coming from the various clusters of people, everything from the 'probable condition of his underwear' to the 'possible whereabouts of his stomach and heart.' I watched only long enough to take a few photos, of yet another causality of the gambit. The kind of 'rush,' I no longer was in pursuit of. Though, admittedly, in my younger, foolish days, especially with alcohol added to my braggadocio, on many occasions, I'd done some exceedingly stupid and dangerous things.

I continued on, relishing the ever changing sights of the enthusiastic entrepreneurs and soon found something I wanted. A talented young man had carved a vast variety of realistic animals out of wood. He had a few whales and porpoises, but they were rather large and bulky. Now with a goal in mind, I searched and quickly found the perfect sized whale, and this one carved from a gnarl, which made it even more interesting.

With my treasured purchase tucked into my tote bag, I went on my way, following the many paths which the booths had created, as they had obviously expanded the Market size over the years. I eventually came to an open-ended point, which suddenly revealed perhaps a dozen or more huge, tour buses, parking every which way on the street and a gavel area. The biggest shock was the one almost right in front of me, emptying out it charge of Japanese tourists. I'd not really seen many Japanese so far, as my hotel was not their typical choice. I'd thought the Market had become much more crowded, then realized among the maze of little cubicles, there were hundreds of people, with more pouring in every minute. I felt I'd seen enough and headed out.

I'd be dealing with the crowded masses soon enough, when I returned to Japan. I certainly didn't want them now. Maybe I could stay ahead of them, by moving on up to the the main street.

I wound up the hill, stopping in an occasional shop or gallery, especially those displaying some unusual Aboriginal artwork and design. I studied a few pieces, to see if I could differentiate them from those around Alice Springs. The main variances, my uninitiated eye could see, was many of these objects had fish and other water animals depicted. So, even with the great number and variety of the tribes, their obvious relationship to their area could easily be seen in their art work. I remembered then reading, there was an Aboriginal dance group which now performed in Kuranda, so I thought I'd see if I could get a ticket.

About in the middle of main street, at the top of the hill was the small Tjapukai Dance Theater. Even without the large sign, it would have been easy to find, as there were several performers outside, talking to both friends and attendants of the show, which had just finished. The men, probably in their twenties and thirties, were all wearing red diaper-like coverings, with their bodies highly decorated with designs in white, brown, ochre and yellow paint. Thrilled to see them, as most of the other Aborigines I'd seen perform before had been much older. So, good to know they were really into actively preserving their cultural heritage and future generations also, as several of them were holding children.

Tjapukai, was the Aboriginal word for 'people of the rainforest,' and also represented the name for the tribe and their language. The original dance troupe had started in 1986, with support from the white community and approval of the Aboriginal elders. Of course, based on the idea of sharing their culture through dance and music. While giving the tourist a small glimpse into their complicated traditions, it rebuilt it too, and the pride in all of the Aborigines in the area, not just those performing. The stories came from the Dreamtime, but all of the lyrics, music and words were written by the Aboriginal performers themselves. Many of the participants had previous experience, either in music or dance, while others were college educated. They were all from the surrounding area, thus members of the Tjapukai tribe.

I went into the box office and got a ticket for the next show. With some time to kill, after looking through all of the souvenirs and buying a few things along with a program, I went to find some lunch. Interestingly, I found a nice quiet, little French-style cafe set back from the hustle and bustle of the tourist traffic. I sat eating my quiche, salad and croissant on the back verandah, with a view of more foliage than I could imagine, outside of a jungle. But then, that's how things grew so quickly and easily in the north, just south of the equator with its various rain forests. One definitely did not need fertilizer, since upwards of a hundred feet of topsoil, which could grow anything almost overnight. While reading the program, still not oblivious to it all, for frequently a strange bug would pop by, or even a brightly, colored lorikeet or butterfly would stop or pause, as if inspecting me, before flying on.

Since the ticket was for open seating, I returned in plenty of time to be one of the first in line, so I'd have a good seat. The set was extremely colorful, the basic rainforest as would be expected, with a few huge, prop-rocks to give dimension. The troupe of eight came out, introduced themselves, then explained their tools, instruments and weapons. Important to them, we understood this was not going to be a sacred ceremony or something. Although, they sought to portray their culture with dignity, this show was written to be a fun celebration of their life.

Their sense of humor came out many times and had us all laughing. In their one scene where they were suppose to produce a fire from the fire sticks, they teased each other about their lack of success, then took great pride in being able to produce it. This celebration with, and of themselves, was contagious and kept us all in jubilant spirits throughout the show. All of the music was lively and the lyrics making a statement, but without any strong animosity. The didgeridoo player was excellent with his haunting tones, while the clapping sticks kept a steady beat reverberating through us. I wondered if any Aussies approached American Indians in the same manner of curiosity and appreciation of culture, as some of us foreigners did to Aborigines.

With the finishing chorus, they once again sang their theme song of 'Proud to Be,' telling about their Aboriginal heritage and dreams of the future for all Australians united. Not patriotic, but more humanistic and gave a strong stirring in most people. They stayed on stage, answered questions, then posed for group photos. Not surprised, at the large number of people who flocked down to them. I sat there for several minutes, as this upbeat scene was one I'd not often witnessed in person. It truly made me feel good all over.

I checked the time, and I'd just enough to lazily-amble along, inspecting the last of the shops and take a few photos I may want. I knew especially, my Japanese professor group, would be thrilled to see them all. Everywhere I looked, along the street, or the sidewalk descending to the station, were clusters of brightly colored flowers - pick a color, any color, even subtle shades or variegated. It reminded me of television test patterns with shapes. Once I reached the station, simply more of the same, but better organized and displayed. I'd forgotten how lovely it all was, though they'd modernized a bit with a kiosk added to the back. It did not really distract from its quaintness and beauty. It sure must be some job, controlling the vegetation and keeping it all from turning back into jungle.

I found my car assignment and took a seat by the left hand window, as I knew it offered the most of the views on the way down. The train moved slowly enough, so I might get some good shots, not that I needed them, as I had some from before. Within a few minutes the seats began to fill up. Delighted when I noticed the family I'd seen at breakfast in the hotel.

The man, possibly in his early fifties, with his light, chocolate- brown face, actually appeared to be more American Indian in his features. He had wonderful, long silver-gray hair, past his shoulders and tied back in a ponytail. But, his face was what I stared at unabashedly. Quite large, with a very prominent, aquiline-nose, with the equally big eyes, definitely a silver gray. Then, hooded by massive, black and white eyebrows. Each furrow, crease and wrinkle seemed to be chiseled deeply, into almost every inch of his face. Obviously, an outdoors man, weathered, dried from the wind and the sun.

Certainly, the kind of face you would see in a portrait of Indians, but would never believe such a face existed. So drawn to it, I wanted so badly to photograph him and it. For a while, I kept trying to figure out how I might snap it, making it look as if I were shooting something beyond him or adjacent to him. Only with my personal sense of propriety, of not invading his privacy stopped me. Many times I'd been photographed by

Japanese, who were total strangers. It had not angered me, but made me feel violated, in some personal way.

I could not quite figure out their relationship, as the woman appeared to be Hispanic and in her thirties, while the child, around seven or eight. And though dark haired, was very fair-skinned. I doubted he was the husband, or father, but perhaps the grandfather. The man, had a resonant voice, which carried and almost bellowed when he laughed. I could not remember being so drawn to a man, on simply his unusual physical characteristics in a long time. I'd have loved to have spoken to him and gotten to know his story. Not sure what held me back, though again related to it having been in Japan so long. As curious as I was, I contained it to frequent and fervent glances of him, and their interactions.

We soon chugged along with the dramatic and breathtaking scenery of Barron Falls and Gorge keeping my attention. In between the highlights, my body became accustomed to the gentle rocking of the car, and I'd doze. The heat and activity of the day had taken its toll on me. We had two photo stops, and one where we could actually clamor out of the carriage for five minutes to stretch our legs. Later, after some dizzying waterfalls, I got a few nice shots of the small town below, balanced with Cairns in the distance against Trinity Bay and the mountains. It put our height in perspective, as they were all very far away and down.

There was only one other couple from my tour, on the last train with me and we soon located our little bus. The driver waited several minutes until most of the people cleared, then he went on. Apparently, the Japanese girls never made it back. 'Shogan nai,' as they say, 'it can not be helped.' I had tried and all one can do sometimes.

With the late afternoon quickly descending, I decided to walk over to the Esplanade and watch the birds for a while. The noisy, lorikeets were once again getting ready to fight it out, and I could see how the tops of the two trees were almost bare of leaves from their landings, wing-flops and squabbles. Like a cartoon picture, the crazy birds reminded me of rainbow-fans madly opening and closing at lighting speed. They were so beautiful to watch, especially inflight, but so annoying in large numbers. I made a wide path around them, to make sure they did not decorate me for my critical thoughts.

Once I reached the sidewalk, the view out onto the bay was postcard perfect, with a sea plane just landing, amongst an assemblage of colorful sails-blazing on last streaks of the sun's light. I paused, reflected, took a deep breath and continued down the way, to the closest spot where the seabirds were. I sat on the bench, to be simultaneously entertained by both the birds and a young man joyfully playing his guitar.

A couple of pelicans must have had a good ear for music, for they slowly waddled over and stood only a few meters away listening. It did not take long for a small crowd to gather, watching the pelicans listening to him so intently. They regularly moved their heads back and forth, as if they knew the song. The scene was almost frozen for several songs, without them making any noise, then either the birds became bored or tired of being stared at, so they flew away. Definitely one of those moments I'd file away for future enjoyment.

Once the sky had run the gamut of today's choice of sunset colors, it ended with a nice pale-silver amethyst. I walked on back to the hotel, to take a nice long, cool shower and rest before dinner. Laughter in the courtyard woke me, as I lazily rolled over to check the clock in the dark. The illuminated numbers glowed back 7:45, and it took a second for them to register, before I pulled myself up to get dressed. The bright overhead light, hurt my eyes and it took another moment to adjust, then check out the wardrobe situation of what I wanted to wear. I had no plans for after dinner, as it would then be rather late to go trotting around town anyway.

My mind still a bit slow, but feeling no need to push it, I just grabbed the next outfit sitting on the top of the open suitcase. I put on my underwear then slipped into the navy blue and white, tie-died looking top and culotte. With the red belt and new red shoes, I should look rather spiffy, without putting much energy into it. I glanced at the clock, which now said 7:53. I moved pretty good for still half asleep. The glaring lights of the bathroom made me wince, and I noticed I'd picked up some sun on my nose. I dabbed on some foundation and lightly did a little more make-up, combed through my curls, then finished with some lipstick. I picked up the room key, the city tourist newspaper and opened the outside door. I caught my reflection in the closet mirror and said out loud, "Not bad, for an old broad!" I chuckled to myself. The outfit hid a multitude of sins and accented the few assets, while the softer patio light took years away.

There were perhaps a dozen people in the dining room, but there was a small table by the other window, which my same waitress gladly showed me to. I pondered to myself, *"Whoever said good tipping didn't influence the Aussies were crazy."* I had a slightly different view to look at and noticed the golden moon had risen like a fire-bird, as if it had survived some maelstrom, as a result of its struggle away from the setting sun. I had appraised about every nuance, by the time the half carafe of red wine arrived.

I'd decided to go of the half-rack of lamb tonight, as tomorrow would be the last night not only in Cairns, but in Oz. I figured I'd be too wasted then, from the heat and exercise, after the whole day on the Reef, to dress for dinner. I planned on selecting some of the choice, scrumptious looking deli food, on the way back from the wharf. I'd also planned to drop off my film, to get it developed before flying out, as it as so much cheaper than in Japan.

"Organization, Annie! You're too organized! You've got to do more things spontaneously!" Still mumbling to myself, when the waitress came with my salad.

"The rolls were just coming out, I wanted to bring you the hot, fresh ones. Be right back." She'd glanced at me for approval, which I returned with a big smile. *Yes, good tipping.*

I picked up and unfolded the large tourist paper, turning a little in my chair to open it up, without getting it into my salad. Out of the corner of my eye, almost diagonally across from me, at the same table I'd sat at last night, I noticed a man watching me. I'd not meant to catch his eye, but I also had not expected to catch someone staring at me. He quickly smiled and lifted his wine glass to toast me. I certainly did not want to encourage him, yet I did not want to be rude, so I simply smiled, then spread the paper in front of me. There was no use now to pretend to read and I knew, I'd feel self-conscious until he left.

Why is it, no matter how old we are, for most of us, the adolescent socialization patterns kick in and take over our actions and reactions. I'd only been out with a few men, and to my own shocking surprise, I'd turned into a shrinking violet, as soon as any intimacy was even insinuated. These personally-felt disasters made me refrain from any further excursions into the competitive single world. I had several older, male gaijin friends I spent time with, but it was more a companionship for us, than anything really sexual.

Considering how sexually active I'd been, in the nine years between the two marriages, I'd not been able to put a finger on my hesitation. Or, maybe I just needed more time, so maybe now I'd begun to feel I'd let go of it all from the divorce, I'd be ready soon. Truly, I didn't have any real hang-ups about my age or my shape, considering I'd prefer someone to be around the same as me. And, considering all I'd recently accomplished physically, there should be no hesitation. On the other hand, I'd be leaving for Japan in two days, so unless he lived there also, kind of no point. The dichotomy of being so strong and outspoken in so many ways, yet still vulnerable in others. OK, I couldn't believe I, Ms. Gregarious would be hiding

269

behind a newspaper, because some strange man had toasted me from across the room!

"Here are your rolls, and they're hot, too!" A bigger smile had come back on her face, as I smiled and thanked her. She then turned to check other tables. No plans to look back over to him, I concentrated on buttering my roll then took a bite. I picked up the paper again and folded it partially, to hold in my left hand, while I tried very nonchalantly to eat the salad with my right. I found the story on whale- watching, but not too much was being ingested mentally. I seemed to be working on remote control, as I'd take a few bites of salad then one of the roll. Sure it tasted good, but the signals from mouth to brain to stomach were somehow detoured and intercepted. I was getting very annoyed with myself, in letting this situation get to me.

Suddenly, my mind transported me back to the visit with the psychic: "A Teddy bear, yes, I see you with a man with a bit of a *tum*. You need someone with a similar childhood and back- ground, so he can understand, … your values, morals. He needs to have the same educational level, so you can relate to him - a friend, lover, companion. He likes women, was very close to his mum, so he may be a bit shy. You may have to make the first move, … the right approach, like lunch or a movie … I'm sure you know how to do that." I'd laughed at the same time, because of course, I knew how, I just did not who or when I'd be ready to make such a move. Then, she added, "But get all this divorce, left-over stuff first. It's unfinished business, poisoning to your system. You're not ready yet for the Teddy bear, but you'll know when you are."

I suddenly felt relieved. As if I did not have to worry about the situation because, THIS was not going to be IT. He was not the Teddy Bear. Back in control of myself and the whole scenario. About to congratulate myself, when I realized I'd almost finished eating my lamb chops and I'd not even remembered the waitress serving them to me. At least they were delicious, so I knew my taste buds were back.

Without much thought, I glanced over at the man, and saw he'd finished eating also, so was staring out the window. I figured he must be European, as I really could not imagine an Aussie or a Kiwi, or even an American being so gallant as to toast me. Besides, the Europeans, God Bless them, enjoyed older, fully-shaped women. He caught my glance and I smiled quickly, more a reaction than a response. I looked back at my plate then took another sip of wine. I picked a little more meat off the bones, then finished up the vegetables which were nicely done al-dente.

I'd just reached my napkin up to my lips, when out of the corner of my eye, I'd seen him come walking over toward me with a fresh, half-carafe of red wine. I turned to watch him kind of lumber, the twenty feet or so with his napkin and glass in his other hand, as well a big smile on his face. *"Oh, shit!"* My mind shouted, *"Now, what do I do?"* I'd hoped he was only lonely and not playing out some fantasy, of thinking he was rescuing some desperate, old board. *"Don't get hyper now, Annie. It's a nice restaurant with lights and attentive waitresses. I'm sure they'd not allow sex on the tables or floor."*

I watched his face, though I wished I had my glasses on, because it looked like a rather interesting face. Nicely tanned, and handsomely framed by an unreal shock of salt and pepper gray, wavy hair. Not exactly handsome, but more rugged like a Richard Burton type, and similarly stocky, solidly built. He appeared to be in his early fifties and definitely an outdoor type. I could not help smiling at him, when he stopped at the corner of my table and held up his hands, as if to show his offering. "I hope you don't mind … I join you, since we both alone and drink red wine. The accent was strong, but the English was clear, if not perfect, as it rolled out of his mouth in a lightly resonant, melodious tone. My guard was back up, as I was sometimes a sucker for his kind of accented voice.

"No, not at all." I had no idea if it was the truth or not, as the intrigue, quickly out-weighed the caution. "Please, sit down." I waited until he'd settled somewhat. "Where are you from?" I'd learned not to guess outright, as many Europeans considered the wrong country associations to be insulting. Though there was still some wine left in my carafe, he filled my glass, before pouring some into his. The waitress had appeared and quickly removed my plates. We both waited then I said to her, "Thank you. It was all, very delicious." She smiled once again and was gone. I was kind of surprised at her deftness with handling it all so smoothly.

"Munchen, … Munich, but I have not lived there for a while. I have got tour cruising business out of Bali. That's why I down here. I get another, bigger catamaran built at marinas." He started to take a sip of wine, then brought his glass over to mine. "Prost!"

I touched my glass back to his, "Danke! Campai!" He stopped his hand in mid-air. Not sure if it was my saying 'thank you' in German or my 'cheers' in Japanese. "I have friends in Munich and 'Campai' is Japanese. I live in Japan." I sipped quickly, then decided to plunge ahead on him, rather than answer the twenty questions on myself. "I've heard the marina here is excellent, and turns out some pretty, sharply-designed boats. I'm sure they're backed up in business here, for the same reason you are - the Japanese tourists." I paused momentarily. "Are you out of Denpasar?"

The look on his face, after he swallowed, one of stupefaction. He had totally unforeseen I'd know anything about his business. He took another swallow of wine, and the attitude change of his face was now more of tolerance and some resignation. "Are you in travel business, … you know so much?" A logical question or conclusion, so I laughed at his directness, which I knew was very German.

"No. It's just I know the Japanese, … and my ex-husband thoroughly checked out the boat-building business, the last time we were here, and … I've been to Bali." I took another sip of wine and was please with myself, at keeping him off balance. I loved parrying, even when it was not necessary. A little bell went off in my head — *"There's no need to test him or yourself. You don't need to prove anything to him or have his acceptance or recognition. Just treat him like another human being, out there struggling and trying to understand it all."* The voice definitely sounded like the psychic's and I could only think, *"How handy, now I'll have someone to reign me in, when I let my ego go wild. Simply trying to cover up my own insecurities here, I thought."*

" … in Denpasar?"

My eyes were blank, as I realized he'd asked me a question - maybe more than one. *"This is cute Annie!"* I focused my brain. *"You going to be zeroing-out from time to time?"* "I'm sorry, what was it you asked about Denpasar?" I was not even going to try to make an excuse and perhaps he'd think it was his accent.

"I said … Where did you stay in Denpasar and when were you there?" He was speaking slowly, and more like an elocution teacher. I'd frustrated him and felt embarrassed. Still, explaining to him I'd heard a voice in my head not to tease him, would be more confusing.

"OK, I apologize. I didn't mean I didn't understand you." I smiled as sincerely as possible. "I didn't stay in Denpasar, I stayed in Ubud, you know the artist-colony area. And, about a year and a half ago. And," I leaned forward coyly, "I might add, I'd like to go back again and see more." Now, as if the Scorpio in me could not contain my flirting nature.

"So, why don't you … or when will you?" He was back smiling again, and I just noticed he had either a small cleft in his chin, or a large scar. Slipping a bit, as he was attracting me in an unexpected way. I needed to keep this under control, but why I was not sure.

"I really don't know. I also don't like to go when it's so busy, like Christmas. The Japanese go during Golden Week, too, which is the first week of May. It's very expensive then, just to get out of Japan, no matter where you're going. I'd love to go in the fall, I've heard the weather is great then and it's not crowded. But it's not a time when I'm usually free." I took another sip of wine and put my glass down. He refilled it immediately.

"That's the problem with living in Japan, the usual three vacation times are the same for the whole country. Now, is Obon, which is actually the middle of August. But, I'm sure you know from the influx into Bali." He'd taken a big swallow of wine himself, and was refilling his glass again. "Of course, you get a lot of the honeymooners, who can sometimes go at different times of the year on package tours. I do business management training intensives and cross-cultural discussion classes, so I'm tied into the corporate system and the college schedule both."

I had the feeling he wanted to switch the conversation from business, but I preferred to keep it away from the personal. "So, how do you like doing business with the Japanese?" Trying not to tease him, although I knew he'd been watching me intensely.

His eyebrows tightened, as I'd thrown another curve, and made him put off whatever it was he was about to say. Fascinating, too, to watch those massive eyebrow hairs move at side angles on his face. "Well, it's usually tour guide I deal with or hotel, … you know they usually stay at big resorts. I get a few who speak some English, and they ask more questions than needed, but always pay in cash … then sometimes don't show up." He was getting more into it, as he thought about some specifics.

"They never know to dress - either swimsuits and burn during the day and complain it's cold at night or too much … the clothes. I had men in suits and women in high heels. I make them take them off on the boat, … it's dangerous. You have feeling they never go to an island before, and they live on one, … for god's sake!"

He was funny venting his frustrations with the broken English and I laughed loudly. "I know exactly what you mean. They don't dress for the situation, but for the occasion. They're on their honeymoon, or for the older ones, they have a chance to show off their clothes and jewelry. The cruise ships in Japan are like sailing restaurants - big, air conditioned and they sit at tables or on couches. They don't expect to feel a breeze, much less get wet! I've been on some Japanese yachts, which have never been out of the harbor they're moored in. They just have them for show, to have friends in for a party." Now he was laughing and shaking his head. "So, how long have you been in Cairns waiting for your boat, … sorry your 'cat' to be built?"

"Oh, this my third trip down. I stay few day, push them, complain a lot then go back for a few weeks. They almost finished, so I not sure … I want to wait, sail her back with helper from here or get one of my helpers to go with me. It good training to learn the cat, before we have passengers on her." He lifted his glass, but did not drink and a slight smirk came across his lips. "So, why about you? Why are you back in Cairns, … Alone?"

He was about as subtle as a tsunami, but I did admire his typical, German business acumen in dealing with the Aussie. Much better than how the Japanese did it, which would have been to leave a Japanese in charge, who'd probably report daily to Japan. I smirked right back at him, as he drank and I never let on as to his insinuations. "I visited friends in Brisbane, then went over to Alice Springs for a week. I thought a few cool, wet green days would be nice after all the hot, dry red ones there. I'm going out to the Reef and Green Island tomorrow, to do some quiet snorkeling. It's my third time to the Reef - each time a different spot. I really enjoy it."

"You go with friends?" There was definite heightened curiosity in his voice.

"No, it's just a regular all day tour and I'll probably be swamped with Japanese tourists. But, I don't mind, I'm used to them. I'll find a corner to squirrel away by myself. They usually leave me alone when I'm in a foreign country. Once I hit the water, it's all serenity for me and I'm in another world. It's my last day here, so I'm just looking to escape into the underworld of color." I sipped some more wine and smiled almost serenely.

"I got a boat available for me, ... you want some privacy?" His voice was now a little anxious, as he added, "I know Japanese people are patient and polite - which not to be confused with friendly ... ah, but you not need to spend more time with them than you have to." The grin which now crossed his face, could only be called salacious. Sure he was considering this a prize chance to kill time, and perhaps even stroke his ego with counting coup, too.

A temptation in the form of a pandora's box, like I'd not had in a long time. This man had the time, money and resources! And, ... I'd probably regret it for even a longer time. "Thank You, that is very kind of you, but no. I kind of want this time to myself. I'm sort of working through some things, and sometimes the best place to be alone is surrounded by a lot of strangers." He seemed a bit crushed. "I know this sounds weird, but I'd almost like to ask for a rain-check. Like if you gave me your business card, I'd try to look you up in Bali. I do love boats and I think you'd be a lot of fun."

He stared very hard into my eyes, trying to decide if I was sincere or not. He took a long swallow of wine, then reached his hand toward his back pants pocket. He pulled out the gently worn wallet, thick with different colored bills, and began to dig for a card. He stopped and slightly leered at me, as if he did not want to waste his time or even a card, if I was bullshitting him. "You are not, ah … the women that think, ah, what is it, 'women need man like fish want bicycles,' ah … something?"

Cracking up at his wonderful misquote, I said, "No, I'm definitely not. Though the key operative word there is 'need.' I think mutual-want and desire is much nicer and preferable, don't you?" He put the card down almost defiantly, then gently pushed it over toward me. I picked it up and read out loud. "Gunther Schmidt - Paradise Cruises - Day and Evening Sailing - Denpasar, Bali." There was a little blue catamaran against an orange sun about to set, and the Paradise Cruises done in bamboo-style letters. "Very nice and impressive design. I'll fax you before I come, so you can chase all the beautiful, young Balinese women off, before I get there."

He feigned surprise and I laughed. "I don't have any of my cards with me, but if you don't remember my name - Annie Lane, I'll remind you of the offer you made me in Cairns, … one starry night, when we both had a little too much wine." I picked up my glass and drained the last sip of it. "Now, I should get my check, because I do have to get up early." Before he could say anything more I waved at our waitress, who had been patiently standing off to the side. The last other couple was also just getting ready to leave.

She quickly came to the table. "Yes, ma'am. Would you like another half-carafe of wine?" My eyes followed her glance and hand, as Gunther was giving her the empty carafe. He'd refilled the glasses, so was smiling devilishly from ear to ear. I wanted to ask him if it was a cleft or scar in his chin. Oops! I was slipping again.

"No! Annie, you are not going to be involved with this man, ... at this time! Now, get control of yourself." On the other hand, perhaps I needed to uncover the false rules by which I'd emotionally imprisoned myself. *"No, this was not the time for philosophical examination. I am getting drunk and I'll shortly get horny."* Truthfully, there was no shortly about it. I was.

"Uh, no, thank you. Would you just bring me my check, so I can sign it." I smiled at Gunther and very politely said, "If you want more wine, please go ahead. But, I've had enough and I do have an early tour tomorrow." With a fake sigh of defeat, he shook his head. I looked back at the girl, "Thank you." She left and returned as quickly again with the check in hand. Gunther sat quietly while I signed and included another big tip.

"Thank you and I hope you both have a nice evening." She smiled and was gone. I wanted to giggle at what she was thinking. I also wanted to tell her it was not what she thought, but then I really did not know. I had a lovely, little wine buzz.

I looked up at Gunther and he was getting maudlin from all the wine he had. "I want to tell you all evening, ... but you kept interrupt with your talk about Japanese."

How quickly "What?" came out of my mouth surprised me.

His perturbed face softened into a mellow glow. "You have most beautiful eyes, ... I have ever seen. They are so light, ... almost green and ... blue and so, so ... romantic."

"Thank you very much." I always appreciated them being noticed, and his words were endearing. "And, I think you have a wonderful, melodious, accented voice. I enjoy hearing you speak, and I hope we can talk again ... soon." I reached for my room key, as I added. "Thank you for sharing your wine with me, too. Such a gentleman."

"Can we look this like destiny? You know, two ships passing the night, … we should signal, … acknowledge one another or be in touch, …" With this he slid his hand over and laid it on top of mine, first looking me in the eyes, then glancing down at our hands, then back into my eyes. Though he meant to be sentimental, I felt like we were reenacting-out some old black and white, 1940's era movie. I did not want to laugh at him, not because I did not know what kind of sense of humor he had, but I was enjoying the hell out of it myself.

Perhaps he picked up the vibes this was not working, so he strove-ahead with a more dramatic tactic. "Better … we are strangers in strange land, we have … responsibility to know each other, … more or ah … better." Movie scenes kept flipping through my head, like it was trying to find the one right movie dialogue we should follow. As *Casablanca* came into view, the whole picture scenario became too much, and I could not contain myself any longer. My snicker slid louder into a giggle. I truly wondered what he'd do, if I suddenly got up and jumped in his lap or said, 'Let's hit it!'?

I'd heard a lot of good lines in my younger, single days, but this was a pip. He'd no idea how corny or cliched he sounded. On the other hand, I may have underestimated him, he may have been quite a silver-tongued dude. Coming from a foreigner, in his non-native language and with all the tourists in Bali, he probably did not do too badly with these old, worn-out lines.

I moved in for the Scorpio sting. Without removing his hand, I looked back into his eyes, with all the sincerity I could muster, and without giggling again - although he had either not noticed or cared. I whispered a little breathlessly, "What a beautiful analogy, Gunter. Yes, two ships passing in the night … Only, this one is 'listing' and needs her sleep."

He had perked up with anticipation, then slumped with the rejection. Still smiling a little slyly, when he moved his other hand to clap mine between them both and drew it up to his lips, as he bent his head down. He tenderly kissed my lightly-tanned hand. Since he continued to stare at it after the long kiss, I wondered if he'd forgotten what he'd just done or where he wanted to go next. "Is there *anything*

… anything I can say or … do …you change your mind?" He'd not really propositioned me yet, but we both knew the ultimate question and he'd assumed it was 'no.' His face now across from me was one I could only describe as a puppy dog wanting affection. Amazing, the changes alcohol could make in a man, as the night draws late.

"Anything, huh?" I queried to myself. *"Is this a test or a fantasy?"* I reached across picked up my refilled glass with the other hand, and took a swallow of wine. I wanted to shout out loud. *"Yes, Yes, Yes!! Tell me you're a multi-millionaire, and you're hung like a bull moose and stretch-marks turn you on!"* No, I'd not had *that much* to drink. Too, I'd learned from past, flippant remarks of challenges, when you least expected them to be taken up, were. Then either you follow through to save face, or slither away like a snake. I'd done both in my wild, fun days.

I put my mind to rest, as I spoke straight and honest to him,. "No, Gunther. Thank you. I didn't make this trip looking for a sexual escapade, or a holiday affair." Sincerely smiling at him, I sipped from the glass still in my hand. "Perhaps, I'll regret this in the morning, but I'm at a point in my life, where I want to have time to leisurely enjoy the sex, not some quickie or alcohol induced attraction. And, there is an honest attraction, but no real leisure time to enjoy it."

He brightened back up, but still obviously looking for a night's company, while I'd have enjoyed a long distance relationship with him in Bali. I mean, come on, Bali! I looked at him for another moment, then gently pulled my hand out of its sandwich and switched the wine glass over to it. "It's been delightful and stimulating. I wish you the best of luck with your boat. Now, I must say good night."

He slowly pulled his hands back and lifted up his glass of wine. There was a moment's hesitation before he spoke. "To a most lovely and … interesting woman, she almost gave me … perfect night." A little over done from the alcohol induction, but I'd take my kudos where I could get them. We clinked glasses for the last time, drank and smiled at each other. He sighed in resignation again. I laughed lightly, got up, leaned over to kiss him on the cheek and left.

I did not hurry to my room, as I knew he would not follow me, though he was well aware of the room number, if he wanted to. I decided to take the stairs down to the ground floor instead of the elevator, and soon I could smell the fresh, cool night air. The mixed florals wafted to my nose and smelled rather sweet after all the wine. There was still a soft din of talk and laughter occasionally coming over the courtyard walls, but only a rare sound of a vehicle.

The placid pool sparkled brightly with the spotlights, while other various decorative and security lamps cast shadows around the massive jungle plants. The clouds floated quickly over the moon and only a few stars peeked through the passage. I walked quietly up the stairs and opened my door. I'd checked my bag for the snorkeling- Reef trip and totally prepared myself for bed, before I let my mind drift back to Gunther. *"Timing!"* I thought, as I stretched out in the sheets. *"It's purely a matter of wrong timing."* This time I spoke out loud, as if it would help me convince myself what I'd done by walking out on Gunther, was the right thing to do. *"There is no coincidence, yet we have to make our own life happen sometimes."*

I needed to let go of my decision, and accept it as being the best for me right now. *"Why did I have to meet someone like him now, when I am not fully trusting my own feelings? Especially, with all the wine, I can't trust myself. Why all this testing - first physical and now emotional? Do*

I really need to realize how insignificant I am when up against nature, and how insecure when tempted by a man's attention for sex? Oh, how much easier it all was, when I was twenty-six, divorced and free for the first time to do whatever I wanted, with whomever I wanted. None of it was questioned, much less debated within myself, I just had fun exploring it all.

I listened to the silence, hoping it would signal back some answers. *"Age ... Have I matured or fossilized?"* I laughed out loud and rolled over to sleep.

Female Knowledge

Inner strength grown, a female knowledge of surrender's
value. Move easily with the wind, it can't
blow you around or down. Dominate her own will with
choices, not a whim come and gone. A gift of mutual
enjoyment, he'd never realize she'd given.

The initial time a woman truly sees her power, …
it's bloomed. It's a different point for each, and
regrettably never to a few. A transient moment
looked back on, not noticed at instance, But things
changed, and would be remembered succinctly.

A learning curve, how - when to use it for maximum
success. Not treated as another variation of women,
her age or place. He hadn't known her long, but knew
not a facsimile. Not fads, passing styles, whims or
flavors of the month.

More a woman of substance, she used what she knew.
Unlimited enthusiasm, to fearlessly approach the
unknown. Rarely the same twice, she took on new
ideas feverishly. Belief: another book to write, bridge
to cross or dance to do.

Her life, … she loved it passionately, without
compromise. Took a while to get there, so not
changing her stance. Acquaintances came and went,
but friends stood the test, accepting her as she
changed, and felt better for them all.

Alice Parker

Chapter 10 ~ Self~discovery on The Reef

I could not have asked for an nicer day, with the morning sun skipping across the water, keeping time with the gentle breeze. I walked along the Esplanade, always busy with birds, past The Pier mall, which had not stirred awake yet for business, and over toward the Trinity Wharf. I decided to cut through the back of the Hilton Hotel gardens, rather than go all the way around by the street. I did not allude myself, to thinking this was clandestine, but it was kind of fun to feel, perhaps getting away with something.

There were only a few men, trying to launch a boat, who even glanced my way with curiosity. By the time I reached Marlin Jetty, probably a half dozen tour buses were unloading with mostly Japanese. I figured they must have come down from Port Douglas, where the Japanese owned Sheraton Mirage, and other expensive resorts were located. They were a curious mix of older, middle-aged couples and those obviously, newlyweds.

I traded in my voucher, got my ticket and joined the familiar masses, to locate the right catamaran for my Reef and Island cruise. I padded up the ramp, in my colorful, rubber-soled shoes, and greeted by the bright-white uniformed, smiling staff. Some of them were so anxious about practicing their basic Japanese, it took them aback to speak English to me. After taking my ticket and checking my destination, they assured me I could wander to plant myself anywhere on the cat's four levels. I headed for the top, since I wanted to have the wide-open spaces for whatever panoramic shots available.

The smaller upper deck, was obviously only for sunbathing or standing to take pictures, or lookout, as there were no chairs or benches. Then I noticed the large, square lifejacket-storage area, and I headed for it, tossing my bag up on it. Once I checked it seemed solid enough, I perched myself up on it, too. I slid back, and leaned against the support railing from the stairs. I thus, not only had an outward view, but could also see what was going on two decks below.

I took out my sun block, and began to plaster my exposed areas. I'd learned, I thought, long ago to keep myself covered from head to toe. I usually burned like a crisp-critter, especially here in the tropics. My thick, pink-flowered T-shirt sleeves, which I wore over my suit, came almost to my elbows and had a high neck. I wore also, my purple, spandex exercise-capri leggings, which came to about mid- calf. I felt they were sufficient protection, since my diving booties came way above the ankles. My curls were banded up and tucked into my hat, which shaded most of my face. I dabbed the creme on my protruding nose and chin thickly, while covering the rest lightly.

Numerous Japanese had trotted up, looked around, spoke quickly to one another, then descended back down the stairs. Some stayed to take photos of each other before the railing, with Cairns in the background. Most of the young couples would do the 'V' sign with their fingers, as they thought it to be very *Western*, and even some of the older ones would participate in the juvenile gesture. Once I'd finished greasing myself, I offered to several of them to take their photo together, and they were thrilled. Interesting, they'd not think it strange in Cairns a foreigner would speak Japanese to them, yet in Alice Springs, most were astonished.

I'd just resettled myself, when a young Aussie couple came to the top of the stairs. They surveyed the situation and stepped over to me. "May we join you, or is someone else with you?" They were in a bit of a state of shock, of being the definite minority on an Oz cruise.

"Oh, sure. Come on. There's room for the three of us, I think." I'd known, of course, no Japanese would have been brave enough, to even ask to share my space. I moved my bag to the floor, and my body closer to the edge to accommodate them both. Figuring we'd probably be spending most of the day together, I went ahead and kicked off the basic introductions, then answered the usual Japan questions. By this time, the catamaran had pulled out, and the first stop would be Norman Reef, a lovely, little coral-key on the outer Reef.

Jonathan and Lynn were from a town outside of Brisbane, and could not believe I knew right where it was. Probably in their late twenties, Lynn was as substitute, high school teacher waiting for a full time position anywhere around their area, and Jon a department manager for a large store. They'd certainly felt the restraint of the recession, but had decided to take a ten-day vacation up to Cairns, since they'd not been there before. Though they'd occasionally seen some Japanese tourists in Brisbane, this was their first experience to be surrounded by so many. I gave them a little run-down on the basics, and they were rather surprised when I'd describe a scenario, then it would unfold before their eyes. Such as with the picture taking process, though to me it was such a given, as to how they'd act.

The parade continued up and down the stairs, as I slid back again against the support, to watch with slight amusement and sporadic fascination. Hidden behind my dark sunglasses, I felt oblivious to the Japanese, who I shamelessly stared at. There was no guilt, as part for me was feeling justified in this mild retribution, for all the un-edified ones, who'd done the same to me for the years I'd lived in Japan. Taking a long assessment of myself, I thought I must appear as rather a caricature, with the white creme and strange clothes, as well my wading shoes.

Lynn and Jon were practically mesmerized with this open public, close-up viewing of the Japanese cultural habits. And, particularly of the rituals of interaction, displayed by the young honeymooners, who were now deciding to stay and sunbathe. Typically, the Japanese man simply stood there, as his wife stretched out the blanket or towel, pick-up his clothes, as he took them off, then proceed to put suntan creme on him. Rarely, did we see the man help, or even put the creme on his wife, unless she asked. With each little scene, Jon or Lynn turned to question me, as to why or how or if it was an usual action for honeymooners.

I began to relate to them, the unique phenomena of, the so- called 'Narita-Divorce.' Most marriages were not *'sealed'* until registered in their Prefecture - State area, and most did not do so until they returned home. So, as many of these young women had arranged- marriages, upon return to the international airport outside of Tokyo - Narita, they'd inform their new husband they wanted a divorce. "Thanks for the trip, but you showed yourself to be boorish and ignorant of how to act in international surroundings, and/or you were not romantic enough to me." The amazed look on the Aussie faces, encouraged me to explain further. "The women are more into learning English, and most of them have done home-stays or even spent some time going to school aboard a semester or two. They've learned how much more *attentive* foreign men are, and of course, knowledgeable in a restaurant situation or other interactions, sexual or otherwise.

These somewhat Westernized-women, then expect the man to take the lead." I gestured more with a movement of my nose and chin, not wanting to be too obvious of talking about them. "Most of these Japanese men don't have the language ability, or the socialization skills or processed knowledge to do any of it. From junior high school on, they've directed all of their energy into getting into the *right* schools, colleges and universities, so they get into the *right* jobs, in the best companies.

They then become the 'salaryman' or 'corporate warriors' of Japan's white collar slaves - everything for the company and noting for the self or family." I shook my head slowly, showing my true pity for the naive-ones stretched out in front of us. Truly, most of them trying to have a good time. And most also, very conspicuously uncomfortable, because free time was such a rarity, they did not know how to handle it. I could say I'd been learning myself.

Jon said he'd participated often in corporate game-playing, being in the retail business, and he knew long hours periodically. Now with the dire recession, he had more responsibility to be creative in managing his staff and employees to keep their enthusiasm up. He strongly added, "We all have to give up some things for our job and our career. I have." He glanced at Lynn. "I've had to cancel things with Lynn, or turn up late many times to family functions or other things." There was a natural defensiveness I'd seen and heard in other gaijin, wanting to prove they worked hard also, in their jobs.

"I understand what you're saying Jon. God knows, I've done the same thing myself for years, even before Japan, in the States. But, you didn't give up your youth going to a juku - cram school, just to pass ridiculous exams. And, I'm sure you have taken your vacation time when it was allotted." I gestured with my head again. "Most of these guys are in their late twenties or early thirties, and this is probably their first *real* vacation-holiday, since their university days. One reason they look forward to getting married, not only because it is expected and they get a bonus from the company, but they also want the accepted, sanctioned vacation. For them, to take off otherwise, could jeopardize a bonus or promotion."

Lynn had been studying several couples closely. "What about the women? Do they say anything to the men to let them know how they feel, or just shock them by asking for the divorce when they get back?" Though Jon still had a lot of disbelief, as to all I'd said, Lynn was moved by this lonely plight of miscommunication.

"I don't know all the details, but what I've been told, some of the women argue with the men, and tell them what an embarrassment they've been. Others, who may really love their husbands, may want to train him in

288

etiquette, behavior and how to say or do something. Whether or not these men are accepting of this, would be rare. You know, the macho-syndrome is not unique to any country, no matter what name they call it." Amused, as I remembered how many times, I'd tried to delicately explain something to Travis, when he created a faux pas. "No, a lot of them, I think, simply get hit with the shock once they are back in Japan. The woman knows, she can get the needed support from her family there, in case he gets real angry or even violent."

An older couple had come up the stairs, and they'd excused themselves to a young couple so they could pose by the railing. We silently watched this now common scenario - first the stiff unsmiling picture of him, then her with almost a grin, but more concerned about her blowing hair and squinting into the sun, as she held her hat. Finally, they asked the young couple to take their picture together. "Why don't they smile for their pictures?" Jon asked.

This was one of those constant questions, which never really gets answered clearly, because it just does not make sense to Western- culture people. "Smiling is basically considered frivolous and not being serious, which would then make one look foolish." I chortled, responding to the bizarre look on their faces. "Hey, don't ask me for clarification on that one, because I've never been able to understand it either. Just like so many other weird, or counter things in Japan, it's changing with more and more Western influence. They see all of us smiling all the time, and we all can't be stupid. I've actually had students, confidentially tell me I smile too much, and I should not do it, because the people who don't know me, would think I'm stupid. And they knew, I was not." I had to laugh out loud on this one. "I told one of my adult students, it was required in our constitution that we had be happy, so we showed it by smiling." They both laughed.

We watched the older couple bowing and thanking the young woman, as she returned the camera to the older man. They headed back for the steps, the older woman still trying to keep her hat on in the wind. She'd started down the steps, then the man stopped at the top, turned and quickly took a photo of all the young-lovelies in their bathing suits. It cracked me up, but I covered my big mouth, so he'd not hear me laugh at him. It'd be one photo he'd not show man-san, but he'd definitely show the other men at the office. Harmless enough, compared to what plenty of the other lecherous, old men in Japan did, since harassment was standard behavior.

"It will be interesting to see how the recession, which has finally hit Nagoya, where I live, affects both the older ones and the younger ones. I know the new generation, just graduating and the ones still in the universities, certainly don't want to follow in their father's footsteps … And, the companies are beginning to see the drawbacks in the life-time employment." I paused to contemplate it all, as Jon and Lynn turned to look at me.

"Some hard times will be coming to both the older and younger ones, but change is always good, and it might even break the slaving of the job into *karoshi* - dying at your desk - as well ignoring the family syndromes. The women are speaking-out more and if they have a good chance at a career, they're either not marrying, or not wanting to have children when they do marry, because of the lack of day-care. It sometimes depends how much control the mother-in-law has over her son, and his position in the family. With the slow down, there won't be a need to have all the useless overtime anyway."

I glanced back down again, toward the old couples below, who had given so much to their companies. "I just wonder how many of them are going to get dumped-out in the cold, if the recession gets bad. I young ones are cheaper and better trained for leaner-competing internationally." I glanced back up to Jon. "I wonder too, how many of the manufacturing plants and joint ventures in Australia will be dropped, since so many of the companies have lost their patience with the Aussies and their unions. I have a feeling, they may just want to turn Oz into their playground, rather than a working-partnership."

Before Jon could respond or question, over the loud speaker came an announcement for morning tea and biscuits. As I was about to suggest we go down for some, the announcement was repeated in the much longer Japanese version. Jon and Lynn both looked at me questionably. "What was that?" Jon asked.

I laughed again. "That was 'morning tea and biscuits' with all the politeness and honorifics used in the Japanese language." We each slid off our makeshift seat, as I left my bag behind, and indicated to Lynn it was OK for her to do the same.

As we started down the stairs, ahead of most of the Japanese, since they'd stop to at least put on a shirt, she asked me, "Can you really understand all that?"

"Hell No!" I almost snorted, as I laughed. "I've rarely used honorifics. I only know a little, because it's like a whole other language. I only use the basic politeness, as it takes so much longer to say what you want to say. As a gaijin, it's acceptable to make mistakes, as long as you try, they're happy. As a matter of fact, some older Japanese especially, resent gaijin who are fluent." Lynn looked at me in wonderment, as we proceeded to the enclosed section, where the tea or Japanese green tea, and coffee were laid out with cookies or small slices of different fruit breads, all on paper plates.

Jon, who had let me go ahead behind Lynn, leaned toward me and almost whispered, "Annie, you say what you think about the Japanese, even with them around you." I looked at him smirking, as I knew what was coming next. "Do any of them ever understand, or say anything back to you or get angry?" I comprehended fully his curiosity and criticism, which to me was so ironical, with his inexperience of living in a foreign-speaking country.

Some of the most curtly, public cries about the Japanese were the Aussies and Kiwis. Who did not acknowledge their own racism or discrimination of the Aboriginals or Māori. As well, I'd grown up through the long, most deadly, embarrassing Civil Rights experiences, in what was supposed to be a heterogeneous America, land of the supposedly, Free environment.

"Personally, to me only two times, though more may have understood, I'm sure. I don't feel I am being so derogatory and rude, as merely talking about their *real* habits or actions. I have been with some very critical gaijin, who've said some nasty things. And, a couple of times I saw them get called on it by Japanese, and they deserved it. I can honestly say, everything we've talked about, and I've said about them, I've also discussed with my Japanese friends, who are international, and totally agree. I discuss Australia's problems with my Aussie friends, too, but I must add, most of my American friends are tired of hearing me criticize the U.S., because I've done it so long. The nice thing about travel, you have a variety of countries and people to talk about and harangue." I laughed heartily, at my compunction to constantly verbalize.

As I fixed my tea, I gave a bit more thought about my response. "Like most observant people, who travel and live outside their native country, I've gotten a more objective-acceptance or understanding. Even as being critical to the U.S, as of course, so many more countries with worse governments. I might even say, awareness and realization of the 'Big Picture' of the world situation. Things are never as they seem, and rarely as we see them." He continued to stare, as I returned to our seat.

The pace of the conversation slowed down considerably, and I soon took out my book on the Aborigines, which I'd been reading. They asked me a few questions, as we talked back and forth about my various experiences with the Aborigines, then a short comparison to the Native American Indian. Not surprised, Jon and

Lynn had not been involved in any real experiences with Aborigines or their culture, except what they had learned in their high school text books. Most big-city Aussies, only knew of the local Aborigines who were either craft-artist people, or hanging outside the pubs, as few were in the mainstream jobs.

We were still out about fifteen minutes from stopping, when the coral key came into view. One of the crew had come around with a sheet of paper for us all to sign, since they wanted to make sure, all of us would be collected back up on board, once we'd checked our names when we got off. There must have been several hundred of us on the catamaran. I dug out my boots and slipped them on, as I wanted to be ready to go straight into the water, at the earliest possible moment.

Once that finished, I took out my camera, then waited to get some shots of the key. Over the loud speaker, they gave instructions for perimeters and safety precautions in the water. We had a choice of snorkeling, going in the mini-submarine, diving, or even diving instructions, or staying on the boat. The buffet lunch would be served until one-thirty on the floating dock, we were about to reach. After each set of instruction and information, the Japanese translation was given. Jon and Lynn were still fascinated by how much longer it took.

After my photo shots, I returned my camera, removed my ring and earrings to tuck them into my change purse. I then rummaged in my bag to make sure I had my gloves, ear plugs and bathing cap. Satisfied all set, I anxiously slid off the seat. "Well, if I don't see you in the water, I'll probably see you for lunch. Have a good time." Down the stairs in a flash, while most others were gathering themselves together. By the time the boat had docked, I was in the front, waiting to board the floating dock. I could see the various crew people launching the row boats into the water, preparing the snorkeling equipment and checking the tanks and suits for the divers. Once the ramp was in place, us early birds marched across.

There were several dozen circular tables, with attached benches and rows of chairs facing out in the three directions, all under the giant canopy. The unusable-end held all the storage and kitchen facilities, where the trays were being set up for the food. There were three boats in the water and we could alight from the three sides, via a platform. I walked to one of the first tables, plunked my bag down, then took out my ear plugs and cap. Once they were in place, I took out my snorkel and mask, then slipped on my cotton gloves. I knew the dangers of the coral and wanted to be prepared, in case I inadvertently had to touch it. Once I zipped up my bag, I padded down the dock for the platform on my right. I knew I looked a sight, from the way everyone stared at me, but I loved snorkeling, so was willing to do whatever I had to, to enjoy the sport but be protected from the sun and sea.

I stopped at the edge of the dock, looked over the view, which I'd not taken time to appreciate, since photographing it from a distance. The various coral was easily visible through the glimmering turquoise water, and even a glint of fish could be spotted. I felt a rush down my spine, then stepped carefully onto the platform, grabbed hold of the railing, turned and began to descend down the metal steps. The first surge of cool water, hit my sun-hot skin and I tingled from my toenails to my hair follicles.

I took a deep breath, stepped on-off, yet hung onto the railing, so I could prepare my mask and slip it over my head. Finally, ready to psych-myself-up, to do what I loved. Even snorkeling was a challenge for my claustrophobia mind, I had to prepare for. I dunked myself a few times, and noticed the young man in the closest boat watching me very carefully. Sure he was not looking forward to diving in after me, so early in the day. I got my panic-breathing under control by talking to myself, so finally ready to swim away to my adventure.

The two-thousand kilometer coral chain, I considered a blessing tossed to Oz: the hottest, driest, flattest continent in the world. The wonders created by the billions of tiny, marine animals - polyps, had been accumulating for over fifteen-thousand years. I cannot imagine anyone who had seen coral like this, would not want to see it again and again. The variety, the magnificent color, the great and small may be enjoyed on a TV screen, but truly best as a personal experience. Added to all this glory, was the spectacular fun of the fish - name a color, design, shape or size and the Great Barrier could probably produce a fish to fit your desire. Maybe not all at one time, or place, but the more you see, the more you want to see.

Into this water-wilderness, I eagerly swam and floated, enjoying everything from the delicate purple and greens of the fan coral, to their massive companions, the round mushroom shaped and dotted brain coral. Scattered here, there and around were large collections of the horn coral. I paused to study the sea anemone, with their bright-colored clusters, resembling a bucket of flowers. I flustered the giant clams, with fuzzy-looking electric-blue rims, making them close up as quickly as possible, when I approached, too close. Among all these sea decorations and laurels, darted and dashed the fish - spotted, stripped, or mottled with hues of blue, purple, yellow, black, red. etc. I was in heaven under the sea.

When one little coral oasis was thoroughly explored, I'd swim onto the next and next, until I reached a most exciting canyon maze. I'd only seen one once before and though a bit frightening, because currents could come through rather strongly, to drag me where I did not want to go. Still, I could not resist entering, but I watched carefully for the deadly stone fish. Whether this was their happy hunting ground or not, I always was aware of their danger. Some really big and colorful fish popped up before me, as surprised to see me as I them.

Around and around I went, investigating the odd shapes and combinations, until I could feel the strong pulling, then pushing of the under-tow current. I knew it was time to exit, at the next opening, but it did not come soon enough, as I was pushed into a massive coral heap.

My gloved hands and booted feet, saved me from tearing scraps, but I could feel the salt water tingling my right elbow, letting me know the skin had been broken. I surveyed the situation, and saw with a pull upwards, I could probably hoist myself up on the coral. Perhaps, on the other side it would be more open. I checked the coral hunk out closely, to make sure there were no visitors attached. I then waited for the wave to totally dissipate, as they'd been coming periodically.

I leap-frogged up, keeping myself in a squatting position, using my hands to balance myself against the waves on top. It took me a second to focus on where the boat was, and how far out I was. I'd made a very wide and deep loop, perhaps a kilometer of swimming. I knew the boatman would not be happy, having me so far out of sight. As I spotted him rowing in my direction, he saw me and waved vigorously for me to return. I waved back, then studied my situation. The canyon on my left, looked like a very complicated jigsaw puzzle, but it also had a lot of sameness, so I'd had enough. To my right were more lovely clusters, so I thought I'd explore my way to the boat. I jumped in gleefully. Cognizance of time had totally escaped me.

There was some new variety, but it was not until the third or fourth grouping, I noticed some really different looking coral. Maybe getting tired or I'd lost some of my awareness from being in the water for so long. As I swam closer to the large, very smooth and round- shaped object, I questioned myself as to what could have made this coral so smooth and soft looking. The mixed grouping of coral around looked quite ordinary, so I figured it could not have been wave action. Less than a meter away, a large, black eye snapped open and stared directly at me.

My heart in my throat, as several of the tentacles began to move up and toward me. I propelled myself backward, and managed to inhale a gulp of water, even though my snorkel had a protective guard-valve on it. I spun in the water, going as fast as I could in the opposite direction. I never looked back to see if it followed me, yet my legs became super-sensitized to react the moment I felt anything touch or brush across them.

I could only remember feeling that kind of fear, when learning to snorkel and trying to overcome my claustrophobia. The pressure on my lungs, and the pounding of my heart, did not stop until several minutes after, I finished my mad swim. I honestly felt like I was sweating, and I probably was in some strange, adrenaline way. I pulled myself-up, out of the water to look for the boat and get my bearings once again. I quickly saw the boatman, who'd obviously been looking for me, as he started to wave again. I waved back, then began my laborious return swim. Obviously, ravenously hungry, and glad they'd probably not be serving octopus for lunch.

By the time within fifty meters of the boat, I could see most of the people were on the dock, but a few still in the water. Less than ten meters away from the platform, they were playing around more than snorkeling. The boatman had rowed over toward me and now gotten within speaking range. "I thought I was going to have to come all the way after you. You were much too far out. We'll be leaving shortly, so you might want to get some lunch." I'd been out more than an hour and could feel it all over, the exercise, the excitement and the sun.

I finally reached the steps and tried not to get aggravated at the young Japanese women fooling around blocking my way. I told myself they had no idea what I'd been through, yet on the other hand, their awareness of others around them was about zero. I stood on the bottom step and took off my mask and snorkel. *"Seemasen!"* I rudely called-up, in a very colloquial Japanese, asking them to excuse me. To this they, of course, jumped in surprise and began giving me their profuse, *"Gomenasai"* taken to extreme politeness. I smiled a very plastic smile, as not in a mood for niceties.

My boots squished and sloshed, as I tromped across the platform, my T-shirt dripping as I pulled off my swim cap. I'd removed my ear plugs and was carefully rolling them into my cap, by the time I reached the table. My bag had been moved to the floor, and I ignored the people there, as I looked around to at last see Jon and Lynn sitting several tables away. I picked up the bag and plodded over to them. I plunked myself down and began taking off my boots, which was always a bigger chore wet than dry. "So, did you see some great fish and coral?"

"Yeah, I did, but Lynn didn't like it, so she came back in, then she went out in the submarine. You were gone a long time. How far out did you go?" He watched me, with both curiosity and amazement.

I'd gotten off the first boot, but struggled with the second. "Well,… I made a kind of big loop, following one cluster of coral after another, … until I found a kind of … underwater canyon." The other boot finally released its suction with a whoosh. "Oh, what time is it, I better get some lunch." An announcement came as I'd finished speaking, advising lunch would be tossed to the fish in about fifteen minutes. "Let me grab a plate, and I'll tell you about it."

There was not much left of the numerous salads, but more than enough to pick and choose from. A young man at the grill offered-up hamburgers, hot dogs and sausages. I only took the sausage, as the others looked like they'd been tastier a hour before. Digging in the moment I sat down, and in between began to tell them of my adventure with the octopus. I assumed, as Jon questioned me, if it could have been a squid. "Boy, you got me on that one. You know I didn't stay around to count, if it had eight or ten tentacles. I wouldn't

know the stomping grounds of either. All I know is, this huge eye opened-up, from a big round mass and part of it, like tentacles started moving for me. With the fear, I had at the moment, exact description was lost. Let me get a few more shrimp." Lynn's eyes had been as big as saucers, while I'd been talking, and again with Jon's questioning.

I'd not even sat back down, when I asked Lynn, "So, what didn't you like? Was it too crowded here, near the boat, or not enough coral and fish?" I continued to watch her, as I peeled the succulent shrimp, and popped them gingerly into my mouth.

Rather hesitating, then I realized a little embarrassed. "Well, I guess I'm a little afraid in such deep water, and with the mask and snorkel-hose-thing." She waited, trying to get the words, as if talking about it also bothered her. "I couldn't breathe properly, ... and I kept swallowing in water, so it wasn't much fun." She'd been speaking, looking down and now regained a bit of composure. "I just thought it would be better for me to go in the glass bottom boat, so Jon could have some fun and not have to worry about me. It really was nice in the little submarine and we could see all the fish and coral. The man described the fish and coral, too." On this last part, she perked up and smiled, so she felt it had not all been for naught.

I swallowed down another shrimp and took a sip of tea before I responded "It sounds like you're claustrophobic like I am. I wish I'd known, because I could have helped you. It takes time and patience to work through it the first few times. I still have to psych-myself-up each time before I start, especially if it's been a long time since I went snorkeling. I guess some of mine comes from almost drowning twice when I was a kid, but I love the water so much, I feel it's worth it."

I pulled out my towel, wiped at my face and hair, then patted at my wet clothes. I could see most everyone was going back aboard. "Well, if we want to get our spot again, I guess we better get on." Jon and Lynn agreed, and we gathered-up our stuff, when the announcer came back on to suggest we do just that. I dumped my trash, wiped off my snorkel gear, then stuffed it back into my bag, with my damp towel. I left the bag open, so I could take it all out later to dry in the sun and breeze. I carried the still-dripping boots separately back-up with me. I was surprised to see a couple of Japanese leaning against 'our' little seat. When I explained to them we'd been sitting there before, they quickly apologized and moved.

"I know that was a bit manipulative, but they weren't sitting on it, and I was sure, soon as the boat started to move, they wouldn't want to be up here, in the strong wind." I went about setting out my things to dry, and wiped off my sunglasses again. I settled back to read and doze on the ride over to Green Island. I felt Jon had been scrutinizing me, but I chose to ignore him, as I did not really want to go into another, long dissertation on the Japanese. If he actually asked a question, I would answer it.

I'd adjusted to living with the Japanese, and had learned how to easily get what I wanted, without causing any great offense. Some of this perhaps came from my belief, if they were not going to get the enjoyment out of something that I would, I spoke up for it. How many times I'd seen Japanese sleep through tours next to the windows, or have the most expensive seats, at any kind of performance, then snore through it, or order the largest, most expensive meal and eat maybe one-third of it. I could honestly say, I may not have the total appreciation of some things very Japanese, that they did, and likewise, they were far from enjoying some things too, Western. To this, I brought my own sense of justification of speaking up, or maybe just all those years of being raised with the Protestant-work ethic, and of not to be wasteful.

Jon finally leaned back to doze, as Lynn had also brought a book. We spoke only rarely now, as the curiosity and even awareness of the Japanese had about worn off, like anything new and different. By the time the announcer said Green Island was in view, we'd all napped a bit and all of my things were dry. I took out my camera and waited for a few good shots, then prepared to start all over again for my next water folly. When I sat up and moved around, I could feel a little warmth on my back, which surprised me, since my T-shirt was rather thick. I dug my sun block back out of my bag and put a little on my face, legs and arms. I pulled my leggings back down, as they'd ridden up with all the swimming. I started to ask Lynn to put some creme on my back, but decided not to bother her, as it was much later in the afternoon.

The announcer explained all the things we could do on Green Island, and we'd be given vouchers for the aquarium and other things. As we got closer, I could see it was much more built- up than I'd expected. Consequently, there was not a lot of coral near by, but the water looked wonderfully clear. There would also be a choice of two boats going back, so they were not so concerned about us signing in and out. "It looks like a really nice beach Lynn, I'd be happy to work with you here, if you want to try snorkeling again. The water doesn't look too deep close in and yet there seems to be a lot of fish." We were about to dock, so amazed by all the shadows and movement I could see in the water. Likely to be real fun, without any great challenges, which considering how stiff I felt, could be a good thing.

"No, that's OK, Annie. I'm just going to sunbathe … and play in the water and sand." We had gathered-up our stuff and our little road show was on the go again. We traipsed down the steps, out the gangplank, and along the long, wooden pier, pass the underwater observatory, where so many people were already lining-up to go in. Once we got to the island, we split up with them heading to get a drink, and me going to check out the beach - snorkeling area. I paused at a gigantic sign, in both English and Japanese. It explained how Green Island was now owned basically by several Japanese companies. And, in the process of totally rebuilding, modernizing and upgrading all of the facilities, it would then contain condo-style rentals. "Well, another one bites the dust of the average person!" I said it out loud, with much disgust as a few people stared.

I scanned around for a moment, at the typical commercial facilities and the people using them. The Aussies were both young and old, with most of them looking like very, middle-class folks. There were already several islands, which had become practically private and four star. The government justified the sell-out, in that *a small corner* had to be held for national park status and campers. This was all well and good on paper, but without facilities, who would want to go there, unless the most rustic lot, who could bring everything in themselves.

Green Island already had bungalows and cabins, though the majority of people were day-trippers, out for a day in the surf and sun. For them, this would all end, as the Japanese project was very clearl making it an exclusive island, with prices to reflect the clientele, which they wanted to attract. And, most definitely it would be almost all Japanese. They never questioned a price, because no matter how expensive, it was cheaper and less crowded than Japan. I was sure most of them on our day trip, had paid anywhere from fifty to one hundred percent more for their ticket through the Japanese tour agency, than Lynn, Jon and I. I'd seen it numerous times, and my students had also told me, what they paid for things while in Australia.

I huffed and puffed for a few minutes, venting my anger once again, at how the Japanese companies aways ripped off their own people. And, how the Australian government went along with it all, simply because they wanted the money, and did not want to anger the Japanese. Not the Aussies getting ripped off, so why should they care. Yet, the Japanese tourists considered it the Aussies who'd cheated them. *"Enough of politics!"* I found a spot to sit and put on my boots.

I followed the little path, through the rocks, and stashed my bag where I thought it would be out of the way. I marched into the water and began to assemble myself once again, before plunging in. The water was very pleasant, warmer than out at the Reef, though the space was more confining. There were a dozen or so young people, learning to snorkel or dive. After wandering around, I finally found an area I wanted to go into.

I'd enjoyed several, different small areas and lazily swimming around the deeper water searching out another coral or fish spot, when a humongous fish, much larger than myself, came right up to my face. As I panicked once again, and began furiously to try to move backwards and away, it seemed to keep coming after me. I recognized it was more in curiosity, than probably danger to me. But today, not up to another *close-encounter* of the personal kind, with any fish more than half my size, and this one was closer to double my size. For the second time that day, I was swallowing water and choking on it, with my heart in my throat, at the same time. I did not look back because of fear, but I'd also had enough of the dangerous games in the water.

BINGO!! 'You are in some kind of danger, which has to do with water.' I practically slugged my way out of the water, and onto the beach, quite disgusted with being frightened, when what the clairvoyant had originally said all came back to me. When I needed to remember it most, I'd forgotten the warning. Not that I'd have *not* gone on my snorkeling trip, as I'd considered it to be a real highlight, of this continuously momentous trip.

To do everything in a state of high awareness would not have been much fun either, for I was sure to have become a nervous wreck, expecting danger to lurk around every corner. Here the 'testing' popped its ugly head up again. I plodded across the beach, stripping- off mask, cap etc. to where my bag was and dug out the towel to wipe my face and gear. Well, I'd gotten another thirty minutes or so in the water, which added to the hour-plus before, gave me around two hours. It's pretty good, I thought since now feeling almost exhausted from the second bout of being scared-silly.

Not in a space for deep thought, so I decided to not put any more energy into my realization for now. I walked on up the path to find a small table in the shade. I left my bag, taking my change purse, as I looked for something to drink and maybe snack on. I'd figured the coupons did not go far and I'd go get more coupons, if they didn't take cash for anything. I finally returned with an ice cream cone, melting like it was on fire, and a fruit squash drink, I knew to be refreshing and delicious. I sat with my feet up and enjoyed the lovely, warm breeze, as I looked out on the variegated-blue water, between the swaying palm trees. It may not be a perfect paradise, but really satisfying to me. I sat there enjoying the simple, rare pleasure of licking the dribbles of ice cream off my hand. Once I'd finished, I dug into my bag for some wet wipes, to take the stickiness away. I watched some of the people drinking beer and carrying on in a very typical Aussie way. Then, at the next table were several Japanese also drinking beer, but doing their thing, the very typical Japanese way. I could only think of how alike, yet how very different at the same time. The Japanese were close into each other, though there was plenty of room, while the Aussies were leaning back, spread-out and occupying as much space

as possible, as if to air out.

I almost giggled, as I thought it'd make a wonderful cross- cultural study - "The Comparative Habits of the Residents and Tourist of Australia." That's one I could certainly do, as I'd observed and

participated with a variety of them. Just as many people can spot an American when traveling, I can usually pick out an Aussie, especially if it was in Southeast Asia. The hearty laugh and the 'bloody' language, were dead give-aways every time, as well as their propensity for beaches and bars.

Unconsciously, I placed the cold can of soda against my warm skin, and the reaction so strong, it quickly got my attention. I lifted up my sunglasses and took a closer look at my body. *"By God,"* I thought, *"I'm sunburned!"* I began to finger, pressure-test on my skin, to see how long it took for the white to show and the pink to return. *"Shit!"* I thought, *"So much for the sun block's effectiveness in the water."* I leaned forward and moved my swimsuit strap. A bright pink was already appearing on the skin. I moved my back around to feel the reaction, and defiantly getting taut from the sunburn. I could not believe under my thick T-shirt, I'd burned so much. I decided to finish up my drink and change into some dry clothes. If I was that burned, I needed to got some Vitamin-E on, as soon as possible.

I went to the outside shower to get the saltwater off, then preceded for the toilets to change. Yes, difficult to spread the magic lotion around my back, so I just dribbled it down and smeared it as much as I could. By the time I finished with all my fiddling around, they were making an announcement for the boarding of the cat back to Cairns. I'd decided to sit down below on the way back, as I did not need even the late afternoon sun or the chilling wind on my toasted body. I did not see Jon or Lynn, and probably better, as we were about talked-out. And, for myself, feeling very drained from the over activity and the searing I'd gotten. At the back of the first group, I decided to wait on the second boat, so I could get a nice seat off to myself.

In my little corner, I managed to get enough space to put my legs up on my bag, and even doze for some of the ninety minutes or so back. One of the nice things about the Japanese - they could sleep anywhere, anytime on a moving vehicle. My body was burning, like a blow-torch followed me, as I made my way off the boat. With every pull or movement, the tight skin felt like it would pop any moment, with all of my melted cells pouring out onto the floor. When the light evening breeze hit me, I could feel the chill go down my back. I grabbed hold of the docking rail to keep my balance. A bad burn, no doubt about it, I'd have to deal with, as best I could.

Once off and away from the crowds, I felt as if I were a walking-puppet or robot, trying not to touch or pull my skin in any way. I figured I should stop at the chemist to get some aloe, and even something else to keep from getting an infection. The girl in the shop was very helpful, as she'd seen idiots like me many times before. The aloe had Vitamin-E in it and a bright green gel. I tucked it in my bag, then trotted to the deli around the corner, where I'd planned on picking up dinner. I chose several nice looking salads, as I surely did not want anything heavy on my stomach, which was starting to do flip-flops. I kept telling myself, it was only another couple hundred feet to the hotel and a cool shower.

The short walk up the steps to the second floor was one of the longest and most painful I could imagine. My body, on its own, was visualizing climbing a thousand, steep-steps, through a blazing, fire- storm. I dropped my bag on the floor, pulled the window curtain closed, to carefully begin to strip away the clothes, tossing them wherever. I got to the shower and balanced myself with a hand on the wall, as I turned the cool water on. I adjusted it to a gentle flow, as the first bit had felt like needles. I wished I could stay submerged forever. Not until I had a thick layer of the aloe with 'E' covered over my skin, did I begin to feel in control again. I carefully sat down and when I looked at my stupid legs, there was a band of red skin, where it had been exposed. So, between the leggings and the boots, then another bright pink band, from when I wore the wading shoes. Above and below that, a rather a stark white in comparison.

I opened up the can of soda, took a deep swallow, then the containers of salad, picking and nibbling at it all with my plastic fork. *"Quite a difference from dinner last night,"* I thought. *"If Gunther could only see me now. I'm sure he'd not be so enthralled with this bright red, cooked-lobster body."* I finally let my mind drift back to what the clairvoyant had said about danger. I realized this bad sunburn was the real result, not the fish or octopus scaring me.

"Maybe part of my compulsive craziness - which I loosely refer to as workaholism, though it seemed to be still in effect, even when on vacation - and not recognizing my limitations." A definite need for a change in lifestyle

was being whispered into my subconscious. I needed to have a warning signal, like an idiot-light on the control panel of the car, saying it was time for an oil change. Or, an inspection light flashing. Something to slow me down, from the constantly pushing to do more, because I usually did too much.

I continued to talk rather rationally to myself. *Not time for 'the men in the white coats to carry me away' - for now at least. "I somehow have designed these ground rules, of not wanting to be thought of as inadequate, or basically boring by anyone, but especially by myself. I need to learn to give myself some space, and not criticize myself for not being able to keep going, when the circumstances were running against me."*

"Well," I said loudly, "Here's another challenge, which you are learning to evolve from!" I glanced down at my hot, colorful body. "Interesting challenges, I choose for myself." I shook my head in wonderment of my own complexities. "I've had this argument with myself a hundred times before - One side says, 'Nothing you do will ever be enough to make you feel totally satisfied or accomplished, if you don't accept yourself right now, as complete within yourself.'

The Other side says, 'I'd rather take these risks and challenges, which give me great memories, than play it safe, … than be ordinary like everyone else.'"

I gingerly leaned down on my knees with my elbows, while I held the carton of salad in my left hand, and slowly ate with my right. *"OK, let's get a little esoteric here, as to why we did this whole trip with the challenges, shit call it what it was - testing, pushing yourself to see if you could handle it all, do it all on your own."* I swallowed some generic salad, … its individuality had lost its importance, then took a sip of the fruit-flavored club soda.

Then out loud again. "But, you know Annie, you are quite capable of handling things on your own. You did before your married Travis, and you did almost everything, after you married him. That *was* part of the problem, remember? You did too much, you rescued or tried to fix every situation." I stretched up to see my strange reflection in the blank, old fashioned TV screen and I talked to that other person.

"Yes, I know, yet somehow with his manipulative, criticisms and basic rejection, Annie came to question her worth and ability." I suddenly remembered scrubbing the shower after he left, as if chemically- removing any remnant of him, any where in the apartment.

I countered back to keep from feeling sorry for myself. "You knew for a long time, he didn't know how love was suppose to feel, or manifest between two people without resentment or rage, for it was all he'd ever seen as a child. He had a bewildered, damaged self-image."

"That doesn't make-up for how he continued to treat me, in the name of love." I took a deep breath and repeated to myself, *"No one is ever, truly 100% victim."* I started to sound like a self-esteem seminar, which felt 'band-aid' or superficial.

"Yes, I know, and I acknowledged it. Now, let's get back to the main point. Why did we participate in this situation happening? This damn sunburn hurts and what has it proved?"

I stared at the TV, framing my remote, mirrored-image, and thought what an alien or sci-fi picture it made. Through this blur, some clarity was coming, so I spoke back to it. "When we look for emotional satisfaction, only through another person, we will never be satisfied within ourselves." *How long had I known the marriage was bad, yet had done nothing to get out?*

"It's not stoicism, but shallowness, laziness, which keeps a person in a non-productive relationship." I crinkled my eyebrows and nose. Where did that come from? I'd said it before, but not directly to my *self.* I paused to consider what corrective steps I'd taken.

"Never forget the most important point, *'Something good, alway comes out of something bad, even when we can't see it, or it takes a long time to fruition. '"* Who was behind this voice?

"Now, you've lectured yourself and women everywhere, who may have had the same feelings at one time or another - let's get your ass covered and take your film down to the developer, so it will be ready tomorrow!" Talking to myself was sometimes so entertaining, and also rather educational. I'd obviously reached a point, where only so much was going to sink in at a time, or maybe I could deal with more of it later.

I finished off the soda and stuffed the empty cartons into the deli bag. Raising myself slowly, I took it over to the trash can and dropped it in. I dug through my suitcase for the loosest clothing and decided to put back on the damp swimsuit under the clothes - no bra now. I gathered up the twelve rolls or so of film, and trudged ever so slowly down the stairs, to the store about one block away. On my return, I managed to pause in front of the hotel, and enjoy once again the serenity of the setting sun. Like a song, cast-back across the scattered clouds, and lyrical on the last shreds of twilight, as they left a silvery glow, accented by lights popping on here and there. Burn or no burn, Cairns was a delightful place to unwind and enjoy the surrounding nature.

Back in the room, after removing my clothes, I did not want to pack or do anything else, which required any more movement than necessary. I checked the TV guide and there was a movie I'd seen being shown in Brisbane - *"Truly, Madly, Deeply."* One of those British films which required a second viewing, to totally comprehend and make the emotional story almost indelible on the brain. I needed both the escape and relationship lesson, so

I stretched the towels across the bed and positioned my re-coated self on my knees and elbows to watch. I balanced my toes on the bed headboard, and placed the pillows under my elbows. As long as I did not have to get up too often to go to the toilet, I'd be fine. Eventually, after the movie, even sleep would be possible. So obviously, I still was not ready for the next episode of my personal-life analysis.

Though quite stiff in the morning, I managed to pack, get breakfast, pick up the photos, check out and sit out front waiting for the airport shuttle by eleven o'clock. I'd again decided to wear my swimsuit under my loose clothes, as still no way I could have endured a bra for the severn hour flight. I'd taken my Advil after breakfast, but there would be no relief from the pain and pressure of my red swollen skin for several days. I knew from previous bad experiences what was in store for me and, … I'd have to just handle it, as best I could with my Aloe-E gel.

I knew the plane would be mostly Japanese and luckily, keeping with their policy of keeping the tour groups together, as a single Qantas bumped me up to business class. Wandering around the gate area, trying to find a comfortable spot, I decided before boarding time, I'd go into the toilet and put on some more cool gel. To my advantage, there was even a handicapped toilet available, which would give me so much more space to move around. I prepped myself with several wet and dry paper towels, not only to wipe my swimsuit after I peed - there was no way I was going to try to pull it down to go, - but also wipe my hands after using the gel. I felt like a doctor preparing for surgery or something. I actually had to keep from laughing out- loud about the ludicrous performance I was about to do in privacy. While the rest of the area was filled with young Japanese women, checking their make-up and so forth.

Once again, struggling to get the gel cross my back, I decided to ask a Japanese to do it for me. If I chose an older one, and said the very, polite request,

"Onaigaishimus," there was no way she would refuse, as it would be considered rude. *"Smart girl, Annie! Use the system to work for you."*

I carefully opened the door to survey the audience I had available. I'd pulled my blouse over my front, and the swimsuit clearly visible around my blistered, red back. Not that I was nude or would put her in any kind of a compromising position. Once she saw my condition, I was sure she'd accommodate me, and I'd offer her a wet and dry paper towel for her services. Yes, it'd be embarrassing, more for me than her, but relief from the pain was my priority.

It only took a moment or two to locate my candidate. I whispered 'excuse me' in my best Japanese to get her attention, made my polite Japanese request, showed her the gel, then turned my back to show her where I wanted it. Naturally, she was taken-aback by a gaijin approaching her so, but she quickly responded, stepping over to me. I stood just inside the door, so she'd not feel strange, and people could easily see what she was doing for me. She gently and aptly, began spreading the gel around my back. I could almost feel it sizzle, as it hit the heat.

She responded herself, feeling the rising temperature through her fingers - *'Atsui, atsui, desu!* ' Yes, it was very hot. Once she'd finished, I thanked her profusely, in my best, honorific-Japanese, and gave her the wet and dry paper towels. I even bowed four or five times, which of course, she responded to likewise. As I breathed deep to exit, it suddenly hit me, the lesson I'd learned. Knowing Japanese women, as I did, I could depend on them for help. I'm sure I'd be a topic of her discussion, regarding helping a gaijin, and it would give her some recognition of her 'Internationalization.' Something, which had become rather a status symbol. We both then benefitted from her acceptance and generosity in helping me.

Once in my comfortable, business class seat, I gently leaned back after take-off. I then pulled the packages of photos from my tote bag, and peeked to put them in order, for reminiscing. There were a few left over shots from the whale-watching and I gloried once again in the truly marvelous experience, of seeing the graceful, humongous creatures almost soar in the air. I closed my eyes to review what the camera could not capture - how the whales had passed and played like argentine-eclipses, beneath the sun-struck water. The sunlight caught their fins, making them appear like rotating chevrons, as they turned and rolled. The silky, luxurious appearance dazzled, flashes in the sunlight, as meter after meter rounded up to our applause.

It had to be awe, which made the largess reflect such a response of ambient beauty. Yet, the apex was truly their contained power, which was first suspect, then implied, until finally came the breach, which released it in such full bloom. The prodigious wave rocked every inch of the large boat thoroughly. God, what a rush! I opened my eyes to the recreated tingle, my memory had brought back. Then, there were the more sedate and happy photos taken of

Barb and Paul, in their lovely gardens. Their dedicated, kind friendship had been a springboard for this whole trip. I could not thank Paul enough for his patience and understanding, as well his support. His smiling, plucky face, with his round, chubbiness and jolly, congenial attitude. I chuckled, as I could almost hear his melodious- voice praising, any lovely-displayed food put before him, "Beautiful, Beautiful!" I closed my eyes to bring back those smiling faces, to the forefront of my vision.

* * * * * *

There we were, me and Barb, running around Mooloolaba, doing errands, shopping and commiserating about men in general, as well those we'd known. "Annie, I can't tell you how I hesitated to ask, … about you and Travis separating. I mean I couldn't believe it, then he just landed on our doorstep and stayed … and stayed." She kept her eye on the street in between the burst of conversations. "Turn right at the next corner. Paul and I discussed it a lot, then when Travis just kind of took over … I had to ask him to contribute money for food and everything. I knew it wasn't the way you were at all. I mean, … you've always been more than generous when you were with him." She pointed again, "Here we are. This is the new garden shop, … everyone says is so cheap." Few things delighted her more, than finding a good bargain on lovely things.

I chuckled to myself, when I thought of how protective they'd become about me, just like I did for some of my friends, I thought could not handle a difficulty. My memory bank seemed to fast-forward then, to the drive into Brisbane to see the clairvoyant. As if, I didn't need more reminders of the reassurance of their support.

Barb was as nervous and exited as I was. "Maybe she'll tell if you're going to get married again." A definite sarcastic laugh came out of me, as she giggled like a schoolgirl.

Secure in the long stretch of road, I turned my head from the highway driving and gave her a long look. "That's a stitch, Barb! After this mess taking so long, and me loosing so much money on him, … it will be a long time. I never say never, but …" I turned back to the road, serious and quiet a moment. "I'd like to think Barb, … I'm not bitter about men in general, … but a reality about relationships."

Silent again, forming together the right words to express the deep thoughts. "There's an emotional price, which we usually have to pay, when we have given it our all." I snickered a bit to lighten up the heaviness. "As my friend Maureen used to say, 'Warts and all - when you bare your soul, as well as your ass.'" Barb laughed along with me. I did not know if she'd ever given, and/or trusted that way. And, I truly wondered if I ever would again.

"So, when it ends, whether out of mutual choice or not, …we must separate ourselves from the other person, while recognizing what all the relationship was … what was good about it." I paused again to see if she was following. "Obviously, we participated in the relationship …even somewhat willingly, so we don't want to say it was all bad, because it then reflects on us, … Kind of like the Japanese not wanting to fire someone who does a bad job, because it shows *they made a bad decision* in hiring them in the first place." I glanced at her and the puzzled look told me my analogy was lost on her. "Never mind, … What I'm trying to say is, I still believe in love and relationships, … I'm just going to try to go about them in a very different way."

A funny thought came to my mind. "You know, it would be nice, if men were like the cans or packages on the grocery store shelf, where you could just turn them around and read the label on the back.

… You know, sort of like their personality or psychological ingredients list: Kind, trustworthy - definitely the true 'Boy Scout' type; Always kept his room clean; Gave nice cards and gifts to his mother; … Good, manly-relationship with his father, but not too macho. Ambitious, but still likes to have a good time; … A great sense of humor." Barb laughed almost hysterically, as she began to get into the methodology.

I continued trying to keep myself from laughing too much, at the idea. "That would be the one for me … And likewise, I'd know from experience to avoid the ones which said: Umbilical cord never fully detached from mother; Can't make a decision on his own about anything; … Goes into fits of depression over age or gray hair, or loss of erection; Addicted to drugs, or alcohol, or sports or vestal virgins or any combination thereof." By this time, we were roaring and I had tears in may eyes, which I had to wipe at, to see the road ahead. "I can just visualize these shrunken versions of the men on the shelves, 'Just add water for instant mate.'"

Barb had somewhat gotten control of her laughter and chimed in, "Two more things you might want to request, would be an expiration date - either the kind which would let you know when he'll kick the bucket, … or when his practicing of all the good things would fall by the wayside." She was trying to sound straight in her expounding, and I went back into wild laughter. "I mean, why put all your energy and hope into someone, if they're going to expire next year, or all these good practices were only for show, … until you are hooked on them."

Gasping from almost convulsions, I broke in with, "You mean kind of a … 'truth in advertising.'" I turned to her and practically shrieked, "I wonder if they have a … 'Good Housekeeping Seal of Approval' for men, or if the FCC ever checks out how illegally they often advertised themselves." It took minutes, before either of us had any control whatsoever, then I added another sobering thought.

"You know, it's alway been the responsibility of the woman to adapt or accept. It's getting better with the younger generation like my son, but at my rate of failure, I figure I'll be about 295 years old, before I get it right, or get the right man. … They say there are no guarantees in life, but … a few one-year warranties for faulty packaging, mislabeling or simply a lemon, would be a nice touch." Our jaws hurt from the happy strain, but our hearts bubbled over from the sharing of the frustration.

The long drive back, cloaked in darkness never slowed down our excitement, or talk about our great experiences with the clairvoyant. We reiterated to each other all she'd said to us individually. "Well, Annie, then you have something to look forward to with changing jobs, maybe moving and most of all, your Teddy Bear man!"

Barb could not see my reaction, of my own contained excitement, nor did I want to deflate her balloon.

But, my current directions were more toward my career goals, rather than romance. "Barb," I started slowly, not sure of how I'd say it. ... "I pay rent on my 'Castle in the Air,' just like most other women. I even remodel it, furnish it and move it from country to country, trying to decide where I eventually want to live." I hesitated then went on. "I see a man, but he's no longer dominant in the picture, ... nor a Prince Charming rescuing me. ... I see me and me doing the things which make me free

... and happy." I turned quickly to speak to her, although I could not see her face. "And, Barb, its OK. I'm happy. Right now, ... I just want to get my act together enough, to not be desperate in feeling, ... I need a man to make me happy."

At this point, I knew Barb and I varied the most, as she felt part of her true fulfillment was centered on Paul. "Annie, that would be great ... and I think you're determined enough to do it." She was quietly thinking then, expanded into those most profound of words echoed by so many women. "I do like to be needed, but sometimes not *quite so much*." Perhaps it was the bane of all women, we'd been raised to be the caretakers, but some people *took too much*.

* * * * * *

I opened my eyes to the clinking of glasses, and looked around at the soft understatement, of the elegant amenities being provided on my Qantas flight. The lovely, blonde fight attendant had soon served my complimentary drink, and I went back to perusing the photos. Each one brought back the people, great times and great accomplishments - Ayers Rock, Kings Canyon and all the others. I spread out some of the contrasting colors between the Red Centre and green tropical North. Amazing what a palette lay before me. I became mesmerized, as I focused and unfocused my eyes, blending them all together.

The metaphors which had sustained me, had lost their freshness and potency. How could I be both disenchanted with my life and yet so happy with myself? Change. That was it! I knew I was changing, and everything in my life would change with it. The clairvoyant had predicted it and I certainly was now ready for it. The amusement of it all tickled me. I mumbled to myself, "Enjoy every moment of it kid, because you're going back into the black and white world of reality, called Japan. And, IT has not changed enough yet, to fulfill your needs! They haven't started shooting the foreigners yet, but I'm sure some gaijin would take it, as an easy way out." "Excuse me?" The flight attendant leaned back from the next row to question politely. "Did you ask me for something?"

I looked up at her, and gave her my broadest grin. "No, you already gave it to me. I had a great trip to Oz." I might be sunburned and hurting in several parts of my body, but I was happy.

She smiled that great Aussie smile. "Oh, good. Well, I hope you come again."

"I'm sure I will. I'm even definite I will." I beamed and looked back at my great photos. I passed the 'test,' all the tests, so of course, I get to come again. Every good, little girl gets her reward … and every woman does, too.

THE END

Zen & Now
During me -
Long time Dreamtime
Before me - laughter, ritual warfare, tribal
gatherings Bora rings, corroboree, didgeridoo earthbeat
dronings
Just before me -
Fringe camps, reserves, kanakas, stolen children.
Occasionally, a drover in the streets, brown-faced,
male With the wisps of his eyes far away.
Poverty, racism, hatred of indigenous cultures,
land stolen Glaucoma, drunkenness, infant mortality,
One or two singled out for ambivalent fame -
Yvonne Goolagong, Kath Walker
Yet the rest, dying out in concrete houses.

Languages and traditions lost Until Aboriginal
culture sold to tourists -
Now, bark painting galleries, dot paintings awards
Didgeridoos (white boys) busking on city streets Yotho
Yindi on MTV
Poor fella, my country

After me-Olympic Games
Protests for Land Rights No apologies for stolen
cultures
The great white-out This land holds their bones
Like the air sings them to sleep O kadaitcha man
Where be the Dreamtime keep?

Thom o Oz

Appendix:
Aboriginal Myths of the Red Centre
Dreamtime Tales

I felt adding a selection of the Aboriginal myths would be entertaining, and also enlightening to the average person, who knows very little about the wonderful, imaginative tales from the Dreamtime. I have concentrated on those from the Red Centre, because a focal point of my memoir, and also a source-power believed to be emitted from the area. I've presented a variety of the legends, with the bibliography, as well a recommended list of books which can give greater detail, on the enduring and fascinating Aboriginal Cultural. Please step into this very allegorical world, with the same open mind you had as a child. Go back to when you were first listening intently to fair tales, recounts from the Bible, or even your initiation into science fiction - fantasy. Think of them, too perhaps, as another *Trip to Oz*.

Traditional archaeological evidence holds the Aboriginal culture existed, in what now is called Australia, sixty-thousand years ago. But, more recent evidence indicates the period was more likely one hundred twenty to one hundred fifty thousand years. Considering, the most ancient rocks were found in Western Australia - sixty-million years old, and they're still trying to date some of their drawings. So this means, these myths, their rituals, beliefs and cosmology represents the deepest, collective memories of our species. As I pointed out in my memoir, though the Aborigines were spread across a vast, almost empty land space, there was a basic connection or thread, which related or connected most of the myths to many of the tribes.

Since the myths were always verbal, there was what is currently referred to as 'song lines,' which crisscrossed Oz in those ancient ties. This 'cross-communication' was what had given the power and belief to the Dreamtime, their tribal stories. To these people of this island continent, it was and is, the same as the Bible, Torah, Koran, Book of Buddha, Confucius Sayings, or any other written word, which guided followers through their daily lives. Some, including myself, would say the Dreamtime was even more so applied. Aboriginal belief and roots were based also on the interconnected system, or vast network of relationships between human, mammal, bird or fish, which were traced to the Great Spirit, and the ancestors of the Dreamtime, *Alcheringa* or *Tjukurpa*. These great Spirits, as they traveled across the land, created all the forms and designs upon the barren landscape - from mountains, gorges and rivers to the smaller rocks, trees and plants. They named and chose certain species to be their descendants - totemic beings - and these Spirits would often live upon the land in the form of a human or animal. They controlled and influenced the seasons, which in the Aboriginal calendar there were six and in turn, the cycle of life for all beings. Thus, the Dreamtime was the whole cultural pattern of the Aboriginal people, their Spiritual lives and those ceremonies to reenact them.

NOTE: These myths are copied as written, no editing was done.

Rain On The Rock

She lives! Her form organic as changes!
She gives wisdom in caves of initiation men with their
rituals - women with their skills each as separate as sky
to
Earth-both connected in lines as flowing as this rain
making
new waterfalls from old paths that walked stories into
Dreamtime knew 3 languages and spoke 10 dialects.
Earth speaks in rock and tree and wallaby emu, snake
goanna - and Malachanges colours as the clouds
that kiss her brow.
You stitched pins into her skin
for conquerers to have heart attacks upon.
She waits - most below your feet while rain drips into
pools and lagoons
watering holes fill with her sky blessings. Uluru - older
than time - fluid as truth -
a story shared with pilgrims who walk upon her, yet do
not know her ways. She stays.
They leave for others to return - a point of learning
referencing all others. Her songlines sing
in clapsticks and boomerang.
She may seem made of rock - her heart is the Earth.
She goes deeper than we will ever see.
We walk around her mystery - listen to her silences hear
tree creak and water splash.
Watch her Change - even as we watch again.
Most come only once. She waits for us to see her like
this blessed rain that makes an olde world newer.
We are revived by her - stories last forever and she has
names we may never learn.
It took thousands more than time to teach her.
Stories in raindrops and red dust seasons.
We will go with the wind.
She will be witness and watch us watch over us - like
this rain on the Rock splashing changes…

Thom O Oz

On a more Universal-Feminine observation, the Aboriginal women were not simply the food gatherers and producers of children. In addition to their exclusive ceremonies, they were often the storytellers, molding the enduring values and dynamics of the tribe. And many times, women were also the object of these stories. These 'Wise Women,' as they were called, were both feared and respected for their deep, magical, feminine power. Their unwavering respect for the Earth, gave them the affinity and relationship to it, which also developed their protective stance of it.

It was spoken, these Wise Women had visionary capabilities and through the use of chants, could bring Spirits to dwell within their bodies. These Spirits then, at their command, could perform tasks of productive or destructive energy, extending to life or death. Based on the idea of their 'Wisdom,' their responsibility to give balance to all things in existence. Thus, as well interestingly, today's women are becoming a stronger focal point in our ecological and environmental quest. This gives a new balance to this Earth of ours, which some of us have begun to respect. The future can learn from the past, and for women, nice to know there were 'Mothers of Us All.' They are the great teachers for us all, if willing to learn and practice.

Ayers Rock - Not only because of its massive size and mysterious color changes, but Ayers Rock commanded attention from the Aborigines. It's rugged surface also contained many life-giving waterholes, some of which were permanent, and its numerous caves offered shelter. The run-off rain from the Rock, created a narrow fertile area at its base, where many plants grew and animals frequently visited to drink and feed, so available as a food source, too.

The Kuniya and Liru - 1

Long ago in the Tjukurpa, the Kuniya or *non-venomous* carpet snakes, journeyed from Paku-Paku, a waterhole near Mount Conner, west of Ayers Rock, until they came to a large flat sandhill, in the centre of which was a waterhole. Each day the Kuniya women were able to find plenty of food, which they carried home to camp in their carved wooden carrying dishes. They prepared their bread from seeds gathered from grasses on the plain, and cooked it in the ashes of their fires. The Kuniya men, after hunting kangaroos, emus and wallabies, liked to lie resting at the edge of the sandhill, as the sun set. The sandhill at the close of the Creation era turned to rock. The Kuniya people themselves were changed into various features, of what is now called Ayers Rock. The women seated in their camp, became large boulders in Tjukiki Gorge, while their *'piti,'* wooden carrying dish, became a tall slab of rock at the head of the gorge. A rock hole represents their campfire, and small grasses and bushes which grew in tufts, in the gorge were their hairs. The sleeping Kuniya men turned into boulders, which now lie motionless in the sun on the plain beneath.

While the Kuniya people were staying at Ayers Rock, however, life did not remain peaceful. A party of *venomous* snake-men, the Liru, were traveling around in the Pitjantjatjara country causing a lot of trouble. The Liru camped at the Katajuta - Mount Olga, then decided to approach Ayers Rock to attack the Kuniya. They were led by the great warrior Kulikudgeri, and traveling in a a large group they crossed the sandhill and arrived at the camp of a powerful Kuniya woman named Pulari. Pulari had separated herself from the rest of her people, as she had just given birth to a child. Enraged and desperate to protect her child, she sprang at the Liru with her child in her arms, spitting out the essence of disease and death, or arukwita. Many of the Liru were killed, but they continued to attack. A young Kuniya warrior challenged Kulikudgeri to a fight to the death and the Liru man, after an arduous battle, fatally wounded the Kuniya man, who crawled away over the sandhill.

Kuniya Inkridi, the mother of the slain youth, rose in a fury and struck Kulikudgeri a great blow on the nose with her digging stick. He died in agony, his blood streaming over the surface of the land, leaving stains on the rock, which remained today. Kuniya Inkridi mourned for her lost son. She covered her body in red ochre and sang and wailed into the night. She spat out *arukwita*, the essence of death and disease, so any man approaching the site today would be stricken.

Meanwhile, a huge battle took place between the Liru and the Kuniya at the waterhole, on the top of the sandhill. The Liru speared a great many Kuniya and victorious, left the area and went back to Katajuta. Kuniya Inkridi, the great mother, carpet snake despaired; hearing of the death of her people, she sang the arukwita song to kill herself and the remaining Kuniya.

At the close of the Tjukurpa period, when the giant sandhill turned to stone, these epic events were enshrined in stone, also. The route of the Liru men from Katajuta to Ayers Rock was marked by rows of desert oaks, the metamorphosed bodies of the invaders, while the tracks of the Liru men were turned into deep fissures of the south-western face of the Rock. The spears the Liru men threw made indentions in the sand, which were seen as potholes on the vertical cliff face. A large boulder was once the body of the Kuniya woman Pulari, who gave birth at this place, within the boulder was a small cave in which her child was born. Near the Pulari stone was a shallow cave with stones in front, which were once Pulari and her child. Until recently, pregnant women gave birth in this cave, believing Pulari would make it an easier delivery.

When the young wounded Kuniya warrior crawled away, the track he left became a watercourse. He died at a place where today there are three waterholes, each of which contains the blood of the dying man transformed into water. His victor, the leader of the Liru, Kulikudgeri, became the large square boulder, while his nose, which was cut off by Kuniya Inkridi stands out, as a huge slab which has split off the main rock.

The bodies of Kuniya Inkridi and her husband remain today as large and small boulders and rocks, the fig trees which tenaciously grip the smooth rock surface and send roots burrowing into the crevices were believed to be their hair. These boulders remain very important sites for the descendants of the Kuniya, as increase or fertility genres for carpet snakes.

The Hare-Wallabies, Mala, and the Spirit Dingo, Kurpannga - 2

While the carpet snake people were camped at the waterhole, on the south-eastern part of Ayers Rock, a party of hare-wallabies, the Bala, left their camp in the country north-west of Mount Liebig and travelled to Ayers Rock, in order to put their young boys through ceremonies, which would make them men. The route the Mala took was now a line of bare rock on the north-western corner.

The Mala women and children set up their own camp each day, while the ceremonies were going on. They went out to search for edible seeds, berries and small game. They gathered plenty of fruit and cooked it for the evening meal. One old Mala man did not take part in the ritual. He was sent to watch the women, to make sure no-one came near the secret ceremonies. These matters were the sacred business of the men, and women were compelled to keep away or the power of the Ancestral Spirits would be broken.

The young boys were guarded by the old men, and the actual rituals were performed on a hard patch of ground, which was transformed into the back wall of a long cylindrical cave on the side of the Rock. This cave was absolutely forbidden to women, who were not even allowed to look in their direction when passing. While the Mala ceremony was proceeding, the Wintalyka or Mulga-seed men of Kikingkura in the Peterman Ranges, sent their messenger, the bellbird Panpanpanala, to Ayers Rock to invite the Mala people to a ceremony, and ask them to bring material for decorations with them, so they could use some for body designs. The Mala people were angry at this request, and sent back some white ash and a discourteous reply.

The Mulga-seed men were furious and urged their sorcerers, their knowledgeable medicine men, who knew the greatest secrets and had the power to communicate with the Spirits, to devise a revenge. The medicine men created a malevolent, giant Spirit dingo called Kurpannga, and sent him to Ayers Rock. Kurpannga had the appearance of a dingo with very little hair. His teeth were savagely sharp and the songs of the medicine men filled him with the urge to fight and kill strangers.

When Kurpannga reached the Mala camp, it was the hot midday. All the Mala people were asleep, except the old kingfisher woman, Lunba, who kept watch. She saw the movement of Kurpannga and gave the alarm. Kurpannga, however, crept up to the camp and with his ferocious teeth he killed two men. The rest of the Mala men escaped. The Mala men managed to save their sacred emblems, then the Mala fled eastward with the young men and with the kingfisher woman.

As with the story of the Kuniya and Liru, the camps of the mythical people, their battles and their deeds were transformed into boulders, clefts and natural features of Ayers Rock, at the close of the Tjukurpa. The main camp of the Mala women and children was now a large cave in the north-western corner of the Rock. The erosion patterns of the cliff face represents the transformed features of the women. The men carried out sacred ceremonies on the northern and north-western sides of the Rock. A long curved line of caves in a large eroded area were once the young men lying on the ground, being decorated by the old Mala men. A dark water stain on the rock face, was the bark brush used to paint ceremonial designs.

The Lizard Man, Kandju or Linga - 3

While the snakes and wallaby were camped at Ayers Rock, a little lizard man lived alone, somewhere to the west. One day, while he was trying out a boomerang, the weapon spun away and buried itself in the soft sand of the mound, which later turned to rock. Kandju, upset over his loss, dug everywhere in the sand until he found it. Many of the spectacular features in the Kandju Gorge were the result of his desperate search - the holes and gutters he dug in the sand were now the deep potholes and vertical chasms of the gorge.

The lizard stayed in this area for a while, then moved to another side of Ayers Rock near Taputji, the camp of the Mala women, and here the Yangkuntjatjara call him Linga. Linga lived mainly on honey ants, but the worker ants chased and bit him every time he stole the honey. As he was unable to find any other food, he became very hungry, and almost starved to death. One day he saw a young carpet snake girl asleep, in front of her wet-weather shelter and killed her to eat. The body of the Kuniya girl changed into a boulder, the wound in her neck into a rock fissure. Having eaten the girl, Linga left the area and travelled away into the distance toward the Musgrave Ranges.

The Sleep Lizard Man, Lunkana - 4

During Creation times, an unmarried sleepy lizard man called Lunkana, lived by himself at Ayers Rock. Despite Aboriginal law about sharing food, he was so mean he kept all the meat he caught for himself. When he caught emus, he would bring them secretly back to his camp and eat after dark. His cooking place became a small rock- hole. After a while, the carpet snake people became angry at such meanness and decide to kill Lunkana. While he was asleep, in his wet- weather shelter of boughs, the Kuniya men set fire to it and the lizard died in agony. The windbreak where he slept was turned into a cave, the smoke was now a large area of lichen and the dead body of Lunkana was a low boulder, at the base of the Rock. This low rock was the increase centre for sleepy lizards and was full of Kurunba, or the life essence of the lizards.

Willy Wagtail Woman - 5

Tjinderi-Tjinderiba was a willy, wagtail woman who set up camp with her children, at the northern end of Ayers Rock - now transformed into a rock-hole. Not far away was a long cylindrical boulder, which was the body of the wagtail woman, who was speared by a Liru man. Her numerous children were now large and small boulders. In a nearby shallow cave were four small rocks, once four infants. This cave was believed to contain an inexhaustible supply of Spirit children, who would become human babies if they find the right mother. The Pitjantjatjara have a deep fear of the willy wagtail, and believe it would do great harm if hurt in any way.

The Mythical Snake, Wanambi - 6

On the summit of Ayers Rock was a steep-sided rock-hole in which a mythical snake Wanambi lived. This snake, which was very dangerous and unfriendly, lived in huge caverns beneath the water. It was hundreds of yards long, and could assume the form of a rainbow when offended. The Wanambi would take the water from all the springs and rock-holes in the area, as another means of hurting his enemies. This Wanambi was not in the same category as the totemic beings of Creation times, as he had not created any of the topography of the rock, and remained the same today as he always was.

Katatjuta - The Olgas

Katatjuta, literally 'the place of many heads,' was a spectacular group of enormous rock domes, which rose precipitously from the level sandy desert. Apart from the group of domes to the south, where the poisonous Liru snakes camped, before setting out for Ayers Rock some distance away, the Olgas do not link to the Rock. They were created by many different mythical beings.

Wanambi, the Mythical Snake - 7

The largest monolith in the Olgas was the permanent home of an immense, highly-colored Wanambi, similar to the one which lived at Ayers Rock, with a flowing beard, a mane and long teeth. During the Wet Season, the Wanambi lived in one of the waterholes on the top of the mountain, but during the Dry Season, he made his home in a waterhole in one of the gorges. If these dried up, he retreated inside the rock itself. A wind blew constantly in the gorge, sometimes gently, sometimes like a hurricane. This was the breath of Wanambi when angered. It was forbidden to light a fire in this area, or to drink at his waterhole or, rising into the air in the form of a rainbow, he would kill the intruder by taking his Spirit from him.

* * * * * *

Most major boulders, domes of rock and caves, which occurred throughout the Olgas were associated with Totemic Ancestors. The caves in the southern side of Walpa Gorge, probably more than 490 meters (1500 feet) high, were once piles of cordwood tree blossoms, collected by the corkwood tree sisters in Tjukurpa times. From these they obtained a sweet drink, by soaking them in their wooden dishes. The stories of mice women and the curlew man were lost in time, as their descendants had long gone. Their camps, however, remained as the series of large monoliths on the eastern side of Katatjuta.

Katatjuta was still guarded by the traditional owners, however, who could relate stories of their creation and the Totemic Beings associated with them. One highly spectacular pillar of rock on the eastern side, with the smaller one leaning against its side, was the transformed body of Malu, the kangaroo man who was arrested in stone, as he died in the arms of his sister, Mulumura, a lizard woman. He was killed at this place by a pack of dingoes, after his long travels from the west. His wound was an erosion in the rock and his intestines, which spilled out appeared as a rock mound at the base. One of the most interesting stories, which told the history of Katajuta was of the Pungalunga men, giant cannibals who lived in distant times and preyed on men and who appeared as domes on the western side.

The Pungalunga Men of Katatjuta - 8

The Pungalunga were huge men who lived entirely on the flesh of Aboriginal men, women and children. Each day they killed people, tucked them into the hamstring belts around their waists, and carried them home to be cooked and eaten. Their jaws and teeth were extremely powerful and they ate the whole body, crushing the bones completely. They broke the backs of their victims into sections and swallowed these whole. They were particular about the way they cooked their victims. After the removal of the intestines, the body was buried in an earthen trench and the fire lit above it, similar to the method of cooking kangaroos today. The body was dismembered after cooking. It was first broken in half at the base of the spine then the heads, unless the Pungalunga were extremely hungry, were generally kept in the fork of a tree to be eaten the next day.

The Pungalunga men were a terrifying sight, as they strode across the countryside in search of victims, but gradually the Aboriginal people began to grow in numbers, as the Pungalunga disappeared one by one. Finally, only one Pungalunga remained.

One day, two men went out hunting Malu kangaroos and did not reach camp until it was getting dark. Their wives went to the waterhole to collect water, and as the day left and night came, the men became worried for their safety. They climbed a hill and seeing a huge campfire burning in the distance, they knew the

Pungalunga man had caught their wives and were eating them. That night the men decided to end the terror of the Pungalunga forever. They straightened their spears over the fire and made sure their spear throwers were strong. The next morning both men walked toward the waterhole. The Pungalunga watched from behind some trees. One man acted as a decoy and kept going to the waterhole, while the other crept around behind the monster and speared him in the back. Screaming with pain, the Pungalunga ran into the scrub to escape, but he was finally speared to death, and died in the Kuniula Cave, near Yulara Spring. The two hunters then lit a huge fire at the mouth of the cave and destroyed all traces of the last of these cannibals.

* * * * * *

Following are several more stories about Uluru - Ayers Rock, from another tribe source. Some of the same words are spelled differently, and how the Dreamtime tale unfolds, was also of an individual perspective.

The Wiyai Kutjara Story - The Two Boys - 9

Uluru - Ayers Rock itself - was built up during the creation period by the two boys who played in the mud after rain. When they had finished their game, they travelled south to Wiputa, on the northern side of the Musgrave Ranges, where they killed and cooked the euro. Then the boys turned north again toward Atila - Mount Conner. A few miles southwest of the Mount, at Anari, one boy threw his tjuni - wooden club at a hare wallaby, but the club struck the ground and made a fresh-water spring. This boy refused to reveal where he had found the water, and the other boy nearly died of thirst. Fighting together, the two boys made their way to the table-topped Mount Conner, on top of which their bodies were preserved as boulders.

The Kuniya Story - The Pythons - 10

The Kuniya converged on Uluru from three directions. One group came westward from Waltanta - the present site of Eridunda homestead; and Paku-Paku, another came south through Wilpiya - Wilbia Well; and the third, northwards, from the area of Yunanpa - Mitchell's Knob. One of the Kuniya women carried her eggs on her head, using a manguri - grass head-pad, to cushion them. She buried these eggs at the eastern end of Uluru. While they were camped at Uluru, the Kuniya were attacked by a party of Liru - poisonous snakes warriors. The Liru had journeyed along the souther flank of the Peterman Ranges, from beyond Wangkari - Gills Pinnacle.

At Alyurungu, on the south-west face of Uluru, were pock marks in the rock, the scars left by the warriors' spears, two black- stained watercourses were the transformed bodies of two Liru. The fight centered on Mutitjulu - Maggie's Spring. Here a Kuniya woman fought, using her wana, her features were preserved in the eastern face of the gorge. The features of the Liru warrior she attacked, can be seen in the western face, where his eye, head wound - transformed into vertical cracks, and severed nose formed part of the cliff.

Above Mutitjulu was Uluru rock hole. This was the home of a Kuniya, who released the water into Mutitjulu. If the flow stopped during drought, the snake could be dislodged by standing at Mutitjulu and calling 'Kuka! Kuka! Kuka!'- Meat! Meat! Meat!. The journey to Uluru and the Liru snakes' attack were described in the public song cycle recording the Kuniya story.

Mita and Lunkata Story - The Blue-Tongue Lizards - 11

At Wangka Arrkal, on the border of South Australia, beyond Mulga Park, two Bell-Bird brothers were stalking an emu. Disturbed, the animal ran northwards toward Uluru, where it was killed by Mita and Lungkata, Blue-Tongue Lizard men. The two Lizards cut-up the emu meat with a stone axe at Kurumpa. Large joints of meat survived, as fractured slabs of sandstone, on the west side of Mutitjulu, but the Lizards buried the thigh at Kalaya Tjunta - Emu Thigh, a spur on the south east face of the Rock. When the Bell-Bird brothers arrived, the Lizards handed them a skinny portion of their quarry, claiming there was nothing else. In revenge, the hunters set fire to the Lizards' shelter. The two men attempted to escape by climbing the rock face, but they fell back and were burned to death. Lichen on the rock face at Mita Kampantja was the smoke from the fire, and the Lizard men survived as to half-buried boulders.

The Tjati Story - The Red Lizard - 12

Tjati was a small, red lizard who lived on the mulga flats. In the creation period, he travelled to Uluru past Atila. When Tjati threw his kali, a curved throwing stick, it embedded itself in the north face of Uluru. Tjati scooped with his hands, into the rock face to retrieve the kali, leaving a series of bowl-shaped hollow at Walaritja. Unable to recover his weapon, Tjati finally died in a cave at Kantju, where his other implements and bodily remains survived, as large boulders on the cave floor. Tjati was the Yankuntjatjara name for the lizard, the Pitjantjatjara called lingka.

* * * * * *

Uluru was a point where the tracks of several ancestral groups crossed each other. These Dreaming tracks tied together the people of the living desert throughout central Australia. Under traditional Aboriginal law, each group was obliged to look after the Dreaming places or sacred sites, created by the ancestral heroes in its estate, and to hand on the traditional songs, stories and ceremonies which commemorated the ancestors' adventure in their territory. I hope these few myths help you to understand, then respect more of the Red Centre land and its historically protective people. In Australia, they are the Land, and the true wizards of Oz.

Passed Present Future

Australia is slipping away -
Like the view one gets, from a ship leaving harbor
-
When the shore gets smaller and further
That is what is happening to me As my childhood home,
Melts in to my adult years …

I never thought this would happen to me. I thought we
are sustained by memories.
Yet, even they become mysteries, Placed in the pile
called -'history.'
I spent 40 years – 4 decades growing up. In all parts of
that, most ancient continent.
Seeing suburbs and shopping malls, Turn

Gondawanaland into *little* America.
Now, I am in BIG America - the original Babylon.
And, I like it here!
What is worse, I live in Texas!
Where they pick Presidents, like Florida fruit.
And, it is good!

Perhaps, that is what makes the past the past And,
the
present a present.

Thom o Oz

Bibliography

Introduction:
Ellis, Robert. *Aboriginal Australia - Past & Present*. Gladesville, N.S.W.: Shakespeare Head Press - division Golden Press Pty. Ltd., 1982, pp. 10 -16

Isaacs, Jennifer, ed. *Australian Dreaming - 40,000 Years of Aboriginal History*. Sydney: Weldon Hardie - Lansdowne Press, 1980, pp. 33 - 35.

Myths:
1   Isaacs, pp. 35 - 38.
2   Isaacs, pp. 38 - 40.
3   Isaacs, p. 41.
4   Isaacs, p. 42.
5   Ibid.
6   Isaacs, p. 44.
7   Isaacs, pp. 44 - 45.
8   Isaacs, p. 45.
9   Layton, Robert. *Uluru - An Aboriginal History of Ayers Rock*. Canberra: Australian Institute of Aboriginal Studies, 1986, p. 5.
10   Layton, pp. 7 - 9.
11   Layton, pp. 9 - 10.
12   Layton, p. 10.
Conclusion: Layton, pp. 10 - 12.

Recommended Aboriginal Reading

Besides, of course, those books which I referenced, for those who would like some various sources about the Aborigines and their culture, myths and history, the following list is useful.

Australian Aboriginal Mythology - Editor L.R. Haitt. Excelsis Press Pty. Ltd. Carlton, N.S.W., 1975. Essays in honor of W.E.H. Stanner, a noted Aboriginal historian.

Australian Aboriginal Religions - Ernest Ailred Worms. Spectrum Publications Pty. Ltd. Richmond, Victoria, 1968. Translated from a German Missionary in the field.

Kakadu Man - Bill Neidjie, with Stephen Davis and Allan Fox. Mybrood P/L Inc. N.S.W., 1985.
This book includes stories, poems, and photos about the Aboriginal people in the Northern Territory area, where Kakadu National Park is located.

Legends of the Dreamtime - Charles P. Montford, Text: Ainslie Roberts, paintings. Weldon Hardie - Rigby Publishers, Dee Why West,
N.S.W. Shorter stories with paintings.

People of the Dreamtime - Alan Marshall; Illustrated by Miriam Rose Ungunmerr. Hyland House publishing Pty. Ltd., Melbourne, 1978.
Illustrated stories simplified from the Dreamtime.

The World of the First Australians - Aboriginal Traditional Life: Past & Present - R.M. & C.H. Berndt. Rigby Publishers, Sydney, 4th Reprint, 1985. Anthropologists with over 40 years of experience with Aborigines. A most comprehensive work.

Of special and separate note:

Crystal Woman - The Sisters of the Dreamtime - Lynn V. Andrews. Warner Books, Inc.; New York, 1987. This is one of a series of books about Medicine Women of the world. They are a great education to understand the power women once had, and all still capable of having.

Additional Poems by Thom o Oz (Pen name) - Biography

Brisbane, Queensland born, Michael Kelly, actually taught at Alice Springs High School, when they were just re-introducing Aborigines back to their own languages, then Melbourne bound. He created *Street Poetry* and *Dial-A- Poem* in the 1970s. Played and improvised poetry with bands - *Poor Tom's Poetry Band, Mother Gong, Kangaroo Moon,* etc. Touring America with *Mother Gong,* the eco-feminist band, when he met his future wife. He moved to Austin, the music capital of Texas in 1982. Thom hosted *Gong Unconventional Amsterdam* (2006). He has self-published 235 poetry chapbooks. And also, Co-Founder of *Austin International Poetry Festival*. He's hosted *Expressions, The Hideout,* etc. in Austin, Texas. Still improvising with jazz musicians in *Wordjazz LowStates,* etc. And, still performing nightly in Zoom/Skype, Open Mics - *Spoken N Heard, Poetry Aloud, Soapbox Poetry, Corroboree,* etc. He's available for poetic adventures.

His poems previously published in: *Poet Meets Magpie, Zen and Now, Australia 2006!*

Author's Biography:

Originally from Chicago, Alice Parker has degrees in psychology, marketing, and English ESL-bilingual–bi-cultural studies in graduate school. A Dale Carnegie Trainer for 3 years, leading classes, she's traveled to 36 countries and 40 states – lived in 6, and wrote for an international business-travel magazine, and others. A corporate business trainer in Japan for 7 years, then 8 years in San Francisco as HR Mgmt. to 1000 employees. She's passionate about her poems and empowering published memoir *Choices, Changes & Friends - 1970s After Divorce*, four friends got their divorces together in the crazy 1970s. As a Life Coach, she used her Self-Help book, *Move Past Your Past - A Process for Freeing Your Life*, to do numerous workshops/ classes. In Dallas since 2013, 10 years teaching memoir classes, she 's also finished 2 biographical books on the American Occupation of Japan, a memoir on Australia, and a romantic novel on Croatia.

Acknowledgements

To my Oz friend Patrica, now living in Tasmania, for her supportive friendship from Japan, and all these years after.

To my friend Pat Brown, for being my Beta-Reader and so supportive from Upper Peninsula, MI.

And, to Thom Woodruff, my enthusiastic poetry-friend-contributor in Austin, born and raised in Oz.

Thank you to John Alexander, my publishing-tech support - you are amazingly patient!

As well, great love to all my Oz friends, who supported this book and me.Lorraine & Graeme, Barb & Paul and all those I met along my journey.

Thank YOU, each and everyone!